Welcome Home

Christopher J. Alexander, Ph. D

Published by Mountain West Publishing
3615 New Mexico 528, NW Suite 200
Albuquerque, New Mexico 87114

Second edition: 2005

The Mountain West Publishing Web Site address is: alexanderphd.com

Library of Congress Cataloging-in-Publication Data

Alexander, Christopher
Welcome Home: A Guide for Adoptive, Foster, and Treatment Foster Parents.

ISBN: 0-9754144-0-2
1. Adoption   2. Foster Care   3. Parenting   4. Attachment

Printed in the United States of America

10 9 8 7 6 5 4 3 2 1

Disclaimer: This book is designed to provide accurate and authoritative information in regard to the subject matter covered. It is sold with the understanding that the publisher is not engaged in rendering professional services. This book is not intended as a substitute for psychotherapy with a qualified professional, nor can its content be used to render diagnoses or to develop treatment plans for children and families.

WELCOME HOME

A Guide for Adoptive, Foster and Treatment Foster Parents

By Christopher J. Alexander, Ph.D.

Mountain West Publishing

Contents

> *Some of us are born by the wayside, and some of us soar to the stars. Some of us sail through our troubles, and some have to live with the scars.*
>
> — Elton John,
> "Circle of Life"

My Journey as a Child Psychologist

I CLEARLY REMEMBER THE FIRST FOSTER child with whom I worked professionally. I had just completed my post-doctoral training at Children's Hospital in Oakland, California, and I immediately went into private practice. This was in 1992.

I had started out doing psychological evaluations for the local child protection agency, though frankly, I had little knowledge about the complexity of the child welfare system. Looking back on it, the evaluations I produced probably didn't tell the social workers or families much more than they already knew. I'm sure I wrote something to the effect of, "This is a troubled child," and then went on to recommend the child receive counseling. Information about what would actually help the child was likely missing, an omission that would persist until I fully understood that myself.

The boy I worked with, I'll call him Steven, was 10-years-old. His biological father abandoned him at birth and his mother was a chronic heroin user. His maternal grandmother was raising him, though it would have been best if he was with a foster parent or family who could better tolerate the range of his behaviors. At one moment, Steven would act as helpless and insecure as an infant, while at other times he was active, destructive, and nearly impossible to control.

Unaware of alternatives to this approach, I worked with Steven individually. I would bring him into the office for an hour and we would spend the time doing what he wanted. The depth of his helplessness and anger, as well as the extent to which he felt out of control was very clear to me. Steven would quit playing a board game if he was losing; he could not sustain his focus on one activity for very long; he was resistant to my directives; and he would try to wrestle with me in a violent and aggressive manner.

After meeting with Steven, I would then meet with his grandmother. Inevitably, she would spend the time crying, telling me that she didn't know how much longer she could handle Steven. She emphasized that managing his behavior was taking a toll on her health and she spent more time yelling at him than talking with him. As I listened to her talk, I ended up feeling almost as helpless as she did.

When I look back on this case, I realize that no harm came to Steven or his grandmother by meeting with me for six months. But sadly, I can't say that either of them derived much benefit. Steven probably liked the diversion of being able to come to my office and play, but I doubt this translated into any behavioral or emotional change in his life at the time.

Similarly, I'm sure Steven's grandmother appreciated being able to share her frustrations about raising him with someone who would listen. Yet, I made suggestions that were unrealistic for this family system and my limited knowledge of attachment and foster care issues limited what I had to offer.

I believe I am finally at a point in my career where I have a better grasp of what can and cannot help people like Steven and his grandmother. After working almost exclusively with this population for nearly 13 years, I now have an appreciation for the ways that biology, attachment, and the complexities of the child welfare system blend together to shape the behavior and identity of many foster and adopted children. My experience has shown that there are approaches to parenting and therapy that are highly effective, while other approaches virtually guarantee a poor outcome.

The goal of this book is to share the techniques and treatments I have learned from and taught parents and professionals, including some of the very latest developments. If you are a parent or professional who raises or works with foster or adopted children, I hope this book will give you the tools you need to approach this role from a position of strength and confidence.

Introduction

T HE SUCCESSFUL PLACEMENT OF A CHILD in an adoptive or foster home lies with the parents. The parents are the first line of defense to help children manage the confusing feelings and troublesome behaviors that can result from trauma, abuse, abandonment, and loss. While all parents require information and skills about raising children, this is especially true for foster and adoptive parents. Unfortunately, most parents who foster or adopt a child get training and guidance about the needs of this population of children long before a child is placed in their home. Foster and adoptive parents often report feeling overwhelmed and ill-prepared for the challenges of a parenting a child with a difficult past. Studies also point to the need for greater education and training for these parents.

Findings from the 2000 Census indicate 1.6 million adopted kids under 18 now live in U.S. households. Of these, 87 percent were born in the United States. The data suggest that adopted children make up about 2.5 percent of the country's 65 million children. More than one in 10 adoptees were born overseas with most coming from Korea, China, Russia, Mexico, and India. Girls were adopted more often than boys — 835,000 to 750,000.

In contrast, an estimated 542,000 children live in foster care in the United States. Upwards of 126,000 are awaiting adoption. The majority are male, with an ethnic profile of 56 percent black, 28 percent white, 9 percent Hispanic, and 1 percent Native American. On average, children wait at least 18 months following termination of parental rights to be adopted. The average age of a foster child is 10.

Greater numbers of single and older persons are now fostering or adopting children. In an effort to find homes for hard-to-place children, agencies have broadened their outreach to people and groups previously excluded from consideration. Captured within this phenomenon is the increasing rate of adoption by gays and lesbians, who are coded statistically as a single person even if they are in a committed relationship.

Not every foster or adopted child presents troubling emotions or behaviors. But, this population of children is over-represented in therapy offices and correctional facilities. While one of every 10 children is believed to have a serious emotional disturbance that severely disrupts daily functioning in the home, school, or community, foster and adopted children experience even higher rates. Emotional and behavior disturbances in this population range from 22 percent to 80 percent. The source of this disturbance varies: biological factors such as a genetic history of behavior and emotional problems; damage to the central nervous system from prenatal exposure to alcohol, drugs, or tobacco; or environmental problems, such as abuse, neglect, exposure to violence, or loss of an important person.

I am a child psychologist, working with children and their families. In my practice, I conduct psychological and neuropsychological evaluations of children and provide family therapy. I consult prospective foster and adoptive parents and their providers about placement issues and also provide clinical supervision to clinicians working in this field. My specialty area is bonding and attachment. I rely extensively upon attachment theory to guide my under-standing of children's mental health, as well as which interventions are most effective with these children. In essence, the theory holds that humans are innately social beings who derive security from early attachments to their caregivers. Because of my specialization, the children who are referred to me are often coping with tremendous sadness, anger, or confusion related to loss and multiple changes in their lives. They have a difficult time trusting all other adults, sometimes fearing for their personal and emotional safety. In extreme cases, the children appear to have wounded bodies, hearts, and souls.

It is important to keep in mind that many foster and adopted children do well in their placements without any significant emotional or behavioral problems. This book should not lead readers to believe that foster and adopted children are always disturbed and the parenting process will be excessively frustrating and demanding. While information in this book will prove useful to most parents, the content is mainly directed to parents who provide care or placement for children who could present conduct, emotional, or attachment disturbance. I wrote this book after repeated requests from parents to direct them to resources that offer practical strategies and advice.

In my role as a psychologist, I devote a good portion of my time translating children's feelings to themselves and to their parents. I consistently find there are often two distinct experiences occurring simultaneously. On the one hand, a parent or set of parents are excited about having the addition of a new child to their lives. From the parent's perspective, the future promises much joy, hope, and anticipation. But, for the child a new home can be a source of ambivalence. Although many of these children are excited about the prospect of living with a safe family, some are clouded by doubt, a history of grief, and limited ability or willingness to suddenly become an active member of an already intact system. In many instances, parents are looking forward with hope and excitement, while their child is looking back with grief and confusion.

Generalizations about any group of children are risky, especially so with foster and adopted children. Though factors exist that make many foster and adopted children vulnerable to medical, psychological, learning, or social problems, each child's collective history and experience must be carefully understood. Similarly, all parents have different attitudes, approaches, and experiences with regard to raising children. While some parents appear to have the ability and talent to effortlessly guide children through life, others feel like they are flying by the seat of their pants.

In biological families, invisible threads seem to connect the parent and child to one another. The parent and the child unconsciously have faith in these ties, knowing and believing they are unified through thick and thin. When the biological mother of a school-age child disciplines him, he doesn't automatically think or worry that he may be removed from the home. But, for some foster and adopted children, this is a common fear. Therefore, foster and adoptive parents should continually think of ways to develop their own invisible threads to their children. These threads cannot be developed with love alone. The parent must communicate to their child — through words and deeds — that these bonds can be just as strong as they are in biological families.

This book is broken down into three sections. The first section, "Welcome Home: Bringing a Child Into Your Life," provides an overview of steps parents can take to prepare their home for a foster or adopted child and ensure a good placement. The second section, "Settling In: Your New Family," discusses strategies for establishing rules, promoting bonding, talking with the child about adoption and foster care issues, and helping

Historical Note

The concept of adoption was not legally recognized in the United States until the 1850s, with the inception of the first adoption statutes. While transfers of children to substitute parents had occurred informally since American colonial times, adoption statutes legitimized the informal adoptive arrangements which previously existed. As the number of informal adoptions rose, a greater need for a formal process for adoptions arose. In 1851 Massachusetts enacted the first adoption statute. Adoption in Massachusetts required judicial approval, consent of the child's parent or guardian, and a finding that the prospective adoptive family was of sufficient ability to raise a child.

parents understand how to communicate with their child. The last section, "Emotional Issues: Providing Your Child with Opportunities for Growth and Healing," is the longest portion of this book. Practical advice and guidance is offered to help you understand diagnosis and treatment and other areas of children's mental health. An extensive section on attachment as well as a detailed discussion of counseling approaches to use with foster and adopted children. Finally, since this population of children must often leave parents and families, advice for saying goodbye to your child is offered.

P A R T   O N E

Bringing a Child into Your Life

Waiting for Your Child to Arrive

WHEN AN EXPECTANT MOTHER DISCOVERS she is pregnant, she knows she will give birth to her child in approximately 36 weeks. She can then schedule time to set up the child's room, pick out birth announcements, notify her employer, explore names for the child, and purchase diapers. Similarly, her partner, friends, and family share in collective anticipation, sometimes placing bets on the arrival date.

With few exceptions, foster and adoptive parents usually don't have the luxury of knowing when a child will be placed in their home. It is safe to say that foster parents are mostly prepared for the placement of a child in their home, since they know it can happen quite suddenly. Given the demand for foster placements, few of these parents go too long without having a child placed in the home. Adoptive parents, on the other hand, can wait anywhere from months to years before their child arrives. I would say that in the majority of cases on which I have worked, adopted children were never placed with a family on a schedule anyone could anticipate. Rather, the parents were more often given short notice, requiring them to quickly change schedules, prepare the home, fly to a distant city or country, notify friends and family, and suddenly make the mental shift to parenthood.

All of this is quite stressful for adoptive parents. Unfortunately, it is a natural part of the adoption process, and adults wishing to adopt a child should expect it might happen. Prospective adoptive parents should pay attention to the impact of the waiting process on one's identity. Whereas a pregnant woman can identify with the role of "mother" or "parent" months before her child arrives, adoptive parents are often required to assume this identity at a moment's notice. This is one aspect of the adoption process and experience that doesn't receive much validation by friends or family. We use terms such as "expectant mother" or "parent-to-be" with women who are pregnant. Adoptive parents don't usually receive this acknowledgement before their child arrives.

If you will be entering into an open adoption arrangement, this brings a new set of challenges and issues. In a standard adoption, the adoptive parents have little information about the birth parents. But in an open adoption, you and the birth mother will share some type of communication, both before and after the adoption. This brings new dynamics for the child, particularly as he ages.

RESOURCES

ON THE WEB

National Adoption Information Clearinghouse
www.acf.hhs.gov

Adoption Parenting Support
www.comeunity.com

Historical Note

Adoption was also a peacekeeping device in many early societies. It was used to build alliances between families and clans. In addition, by adopting the children of your enemy, you reduced the chances of invasion.

— Elizabeth Cole,
"History, Values, and Placement Policy Issues in Adoption"

Preparing Your Home for a Child

Most of the preparations to be made for the arrival of a baby are the same whether you are adopting, fostering, or giving birth to a child. In anticipation of a new child, consider the following:

Prepare the child's room. This may include getting a crib or small bed, putting a dresser or shelves in the room, and stocking the room with a few books and toys. Unless you are adopting an older child, consider putting a baby monitor in the room. Even with school-aged children, the use of a baby monitor will help alert you to sleep difficulties or nightmares the child may experience. Foster parents don't always know the age of the child who will be placed in their home. Therefore, anticipate having bedding, storage units, and play items suitable for children of different ages.

Get in physical shape. A pregnant woman gradually adjusts to increases in the amount of weight she carries before her baby is born. You too need to be in the best physical condition possible. A young baby who often cries or an older child who experiences severe adjustment reactions to being in your home may mean many sleepless nights for you. Also, you may be required to frequently hold or carry the child, which puts added strain on your arms, legs, and back.

Talk with the teacher. If you know which school your child will be attending, arrange to meet with the principal and teacher. Find out about their style and routines. Ask the teacher if your child should wait until a certain date before starting to attend, as she may prefer that he start class after the holiday break or after the class finishes the current project they are working on. If your child is taking medication that needs to be given while he is at school, obtain copies of the forms the school will require before they will agree to dispense the medication. If you are a foster parent, talk with school personnel about the children likely to live in your home. They need to know that the foster children you care for may have been in several schools or suffered educational neglect before coming to live with you. In turn, this could affect their mood, behavior, or ability to learn new information.

Pick your pediatrician. Since adopted children can present special health considerations — particularly if they came from abroad — it will be important for your child to see a pediatrician soon after their arrival in your home. If you adopt a child from abroad, obtain any medical or immunization records and give these to her new physician. Before your child arrives, meet with a pediatrician, in order to establish the relationship. Even if your child is in foster care, his doctor may not live near you. Also, the child may have been scheduled for a medical examination, but it was cancelled due to a change in placement. Therefore, always ask for and maintain documentation of medical and dental appointments, including: the appointment date, the provider's name and number, and any recommen-dations or prescriptions. Find out what vaccinations your child's school will require. If your child had a recent physical examination, try to obtain copies of any written results or recommendations. You may need this for daycare programs or schools or before your child can attend extracurricular group activities.

Take a parenting class. Most likely, you will have taken classes through the placement agency that focus on the emotional needs of foster and adopted children. Still, it can be helpful to take general a parenting class which is offered through community colleges or local mental health organizations. This is especially important if you haven't raised other children or if you don't have a support network of other parents. Many classes are geared toward certain ages or stages of development. I believe it is also useful for parents to identify the adoption and foster care professionals they can turn to with questions after the child arrives.

Meet other parents. It is important to know other parents who are fostering or adopting a child. Not only can they relate to your experiences and provide validation for the changes in your life, but they can also offer emotional support and help you learn about resources available in your community. The placement agency can help you find other parents. Word-of-mouth and the Internet can also prove useful.

RESOURCES

ON THE WEB

Picking a Pediatrician
www.thehealthpages.com

Parents Encouraging Parents
Website and Online Classes
www.parentingonline.com

Although many different perspectives have been offered on the adjustment problems of adopted children and their families, a common thread can be found running through most of them— namely, that adoption is experienced as stressful *by many children and parents and, consequently, results in a variety of coping efforts, some of which are successful in handling the stress and others which are not.*

— David Brodzinsky,
"The Psychology of Adoption"

When Your Child Arrives

PARENTING A FOSTER OR ADOPTED CHILD is a process of mutual exploration. Even though you may have received documents that provide background on the child, rarely do these capture full aspects of the child's personality, interests, behavior or temperament. A child may behave one way during a weekend visit with a prospective family but may act quite differently once he actually moves into the home. Children who have conscious memories of living with a birth or previous foster family will be comparing parental styles and expectations in their new home. Some may expect the placement in your home to be temporary. The finalization of an adoption can be very stressful for some kids. As a result, they may act out with anger or aggression, become more insecure and clingy, or experience more confusion.

If you are providing foster care, you may be asked to care for a child who has never had an out-of-home placement. The child may have lived with abuse, neglect, or chaos and have no idea about living in a family with rules and mutual respect. They will behave in ways that are familiar to them, even though you or the members of your family find the behaviors startling or confusing. You must be prepared to assume a proactive and hands-on role in order to keep everyone safe and to maintain control in the home.

When adopting a child, keep in mind that it is common for children to act defiant or oppositional prior to the adoption becoming final. This is particularly true with older children, kids who have had prior disrupted placements, or those who have a high need for control. Much of this can be viewed as testing behavior on the part of the child. They may give you what they consider to be their worse, with the conscious or unconscious motive of seeing if you can handle it. More often than not, the child genuinely wants to be adopted. Yet, he is terrified of being rejected or abandoned again. I had one client who said he tried to sabotage a placement on purpose. When I explored his reasons for this he expressed the opinion that he'd end up being hurt by these parents one way or the other. By forcing them to give up on him, he felt that he would be in better control of the hurt and pain.

If a child you expect to adopt acts out in the pre-finalization process, you should not take this personally or view it as some form of rejection. You will need to listen to your child's concerns, and yes, this may include the ways he doesn't see you as the ideal parent. Stay strong during this time and if necessary, seek advice for yourself or counseling for the family. Many times, in doing pre-placement counseling, children and adolescents tell me they just want assurance that their new parents are able and willing to listen to them, and that the new parents can handle their anger and fear.

In both foster and adoptive situations, parents and children should expect the arrival will be an awkward time. Parents are often shocked at the ways in which their normal routines are disrupted by having a child. Subtle things, like reading the newspaper in the morning, sleeping in on weekends, or getting by with little food in the refrigerator are suddenly re-examined.

ADOPTION NOT TIED TO INCREASE IN RISKY BEHAVIOR

Despite feeling more emotional distress and disconnection from their families, adolescents who are adopted don't appear to engage in more high-risk behaviors or have worse adult outcomes than nonadopted adolescents, Dr. Cheryl Kodjo reported in a poster presentation at the annual meeting of the Society for Adolescent Medicine ... Good parenting might be one reason Dr. Kodjo saw no increase in risk behaviors among the adopted adolescents. "Maybe we're just not giving adoptive parents enough credit," she said in an interview. "It could be that the jobs they are doing in setting limits and enforcing rules effectively keep risk behavior down." However, she noted, the survey did show that adopted adolescents reported more emotional distress and family disconnectedness than their nonadopted counterparts. "In talking with people who have adopted and who have been adopted, one thing has come through across the board: The kids never really get over that initial feeling of rejection. It's something they struggle with their entire lives," Dr. Kodjo said.

— Family Practice News, July 01, 2004

The new parent has to pay close attention to behaviors previously taken for granted, such as leaving scissors on the table, keeping the front door open when coming home, showering with the bathroom door open, or being able to lie down after work. Children don't always know — or think to ask — about all the rules of the house, and they proceed to behave in ways familiar to them. Parents may find this runs counter to their expectations, creating additional tension in the family.

Neighbors, who may not know that the family is adopting or fostering a child, become curious when they see a new child in the neighborhood. Some may approach the family and ask what is going on, while others will keep a curious eye trained on the home. Adoptive and foster parents suddenly start to realize that they have a life and world that is totally unfamiliar to their new child. The challenge is to bridge these two worlds by establishing relationships with schools, pediatricians, daycare providers, and others with whom their child will interact.

Based on his age, your child may require an orientation to the neighborhood. This will include introducing him to other children and adults who live nearby. He should be told early on which of these persons to turn to in an emergency situation. It can be helpful to give him a tour, showing him where you will shop for food, what restaurants you will frequent, where the park is, and the location of his school. In the event that you permit your child to walk or ride his bike through the neighborhood, talk with him about precautions he should take, what to do in an emergency, and how to get in touch with you if he is lost or late.

If you are adopting a child but will continue to work, I recommend that you take as much time as possible off when your child arrives. This allows time to build trust and safety, establish routines, review basic rules, and help your child acclimate to his new surroundings. Even if the child arrives during the school year, he doesn't necessarily have to begin school immediately. Instead, the child and his parents should place the initial emphasis on getting to know one another and toward establishing routines. You don't want to overwhelm the child early in the placement. Similarly, if you are a foster parent who works, be very clear about this fact with the placement agency, letting them know your schedule. Otherwise, they may put a high needs child in your home.

A DISRUPTED PLACEMENT

I just received a request from a social worker to do an evaluation of a five-year-old girl on her caseload. The worker tells me that the girl was adopted by a couple five months ago. Unfortunately, the level of stress in the family reached a point where the couple wants to relinquish the adoption. Fortunately, they are willing to let the girl stay with them until I can complete my evaluation and make recommendations regarding placement and treatment.

When taking the information for the referral, I asked the worker to provide me with some background information on why the adoptive placement didn't work. I said to her, "I don't want this to sound accusatory, but is this a situation where the family was not adequately prepared, the adoption was rushed, or it just turned out to be a mismatch?" She told me that the family believes they were not given the full story with regard to this child's behavior history and that they are extremely overwhelmed. She pointed out that the wife has most of the caregiving responsibilities, and she is feeling incredibly anxious.

She added, "In my opinion, the family did not take disciplinary actions early on in the placement. The child went with this and decided she would make and follow her own rules and not follow theirs. So they didn't know what to do when she started having temper tantrums. Instead, they gave into her. Now, the adoptive mom is worn out."

In my practice, this is a common referral. Usually, by the time a case like this is referred to me, most of the parties are angry with one another, often feeling betrayed and helpless. Could some of this have been prevented? Perhaps. I mention this case to stress the importance of gathering as much information as possible about a child before placement; taking steps to be adequately prepared in the event you are given a high-needs child; and making sure you have ample emotional and practical support from people in your life. In addition, parents need to be prepared to exercise full authority once a child arrives, just in case there are power or disciplinary struggles waiting to happen.

Many adult adoptees I've spoken with now realize that they were saying to themselves as children: "My birth mother gave me up because I was a bad baby, so I must do whatever I can to be good. If I don't my adoptive parents will reject me too.

— Sherrie Eldridge,
"Twenty Things Adopted Kids Wish Their Parents Knew"

Am I Bad Because I'm Adopted?

I N MY INTERVIEWS WITH ADOPTED children, the consistent theme they raise is that of parental relinquishment. Regardless of whether they knew their birth parents, adopted children report to me the belief that Moms give kids away. Certainly, this makes sense with regard to their birth mother. But, some adults fail to grasp the ways that children can broaden this categorization to all parents. Most adoptive parents are clear that their commitment to a child is a well-founded, permanent decision. They believe their child will perceive this commitment, deriving satisfaction in its sincerity. Unfortunately, many children cannot reciprocate this trust. Particularly if the child has already experienced a disrupted adoptive placement, they will have even less reason to trust that this one will be permanent.

For people who have not been adopted, it is difficult to relate to feelings and awareness of being given away at birth or at a young age. Our minds tell us that children should not grow up in homes that cannot facilitate their physical and emotional development, and we are thankful we have adoption and foster care as an option in our society. Unfortunately, this line of thinking appears so forthright for adults that we sometimes fail to look at the experience through the eyes of the child. My work with children shows that a great number of foster and adopted children live with feelings and beliefs that they are bad, damaged, and unworthy. These children proceed through life, looking for confirmation of these beliefs.

To manage feelings of shame related to adoption, some children will become overly compliant, while others may act rebellious. The overly compliant child believes, "If I act perfect, people will like me and not reject me." The rebellious child, on the other hand, believes, "If I reject people, they cannot hurt me." Whereas the compliant child may appear shy to others, the rebellious child communicates his shame through behaviors such as stealing, lying, acting tough, hurting others, or refusing to obey adults. One of your greatest challenges as the parent is to understand what messages are being communicated and to let him know you know it. This is what lets the child know that you genuinely understand who he is and how he feels.

Children respond to parental relinquishment in different ways. Some children won't focus on it or appear bothered by it, while others will think something is wrong with them. Unfortunately, it is not until a child is older that he can understand that his birth parents could not care for him and this is not his fault. In the meantime, we must remind adopted children they deserve a happy life, filled with love, happiness, and playfulness. We need to reinforce that being adopted does not equate to being inferior to others. The child needs to recognize that his circumstances are the result of how others treated him, not because of who he is. Listening to the wisdom offered to us by adult adoptees proves important. They consistently tell us they felt they were somehow less than others while growing up, that they were damaged, or that something was wrong with them. Therefore, remind your child often of his worth. Tell him how special he is to you and why.

Many children are not able to verbalize the reasons they feel bad about themselves. Instead, the feelings might manifest in ways that can be troubling for the child or others. This can include depression, school failure, social withdrawal, acting out, or indifference to the point of view of other people. Because these symptoms or behaviors command so much of our attention, it is easy to lose sight of what could be causing the reactions in the first place. We can't automatically assume that the child is acting in self-defeating ways because he is adopted. But, we still need to entertain that possibility. If a child feels defeated or hurt because he perceives others have given up on him, he may be apt to give up on himself. As we do the detective work exploring why the child feels or behaves as he does, we must be willing to ask him whether some of his reactions stem from emotions related to parental relinquishment or abandonment.

RESOURCES

ON THE WEB

Website for adoptees
www.webreflection.com/aiml/whatisaiml.html

Perhaps the most difficult aspect of the adjustment period for those adopting for the first time is not knowing when — or if — it will end. The adjustment of our second child was not necessarily easier than the adjustment of our first, but our experience told us it was temporary.

— Lois Ruskai Melina,
"Raising Adopted Children"

Will the Child Love Me?

ADOPTIVE PARENTS ARE TYPICALLY ready to greet their child with open and loving hearts. The process of getting ready for a child — that includes months, if not years of anticipation — is an exciting one for adoptive parents. Many tell me they have fantasies of what family life will be like once they have a child, and the majority expects to have a child who will be loving, grateful, and relieved at having a permanent home. Sadly, many children do not greet adoption with open hearts and feelings of gratitude.

Adoptive parents sometimes say they never felt such pronounced, unconditional feelings of love before their child came to live with them. In turn, they want their child to love them. A sad reality, though, is that some children either will not — or seemingly cannot — allow themselves to love their adoptive family. In some instances, they'll appear to love one parent but not the other. More often than not, at least from what parents share with me, adoptive moms receive more of the brunt of a child's ambivalence or rejection than do fathers. This is incredibly painful for parents. When this happens, many parents start to question their parenting style or how loveable they are. Old feelings of previous rejections start to surface, sometimes to the point where the parent feels bad about herself.

Reasons vary for why a child may have a difficult time feeling or showing love for an adoptive parent. For some children, it may represent a loyalty conflict. The child may believe that their love must remain with their birth parent, and that to love an adoptive parent is a betrayal. The child may not necessarily know or remember his birth parent in order for these feelings to occur. In other instances, the child perceives how desperately the adoptive parent wants him to love them. In order to feel they have power and control over the parent, the child withholds what the parent wants most. Finally, some children are so wounded from earlier experiences in life, that they really don't know how to show love. In these instances, the child literally needs to be taught how to feel and express these emotions in ways that feel safe and okay.

Foster children often develop attachments to the families with whom they have lived. When these placements end, it can be incredibly difficult for the child, even though they may be moving to a permanent home. From the child's perspective, the experience of loss teaches them that love hurts, particularly if it is a repeated or familiar event for them. The child can develop a pattern of avoiding feelings of love, for fear of feeling familiar pain all over again.

Experiencing overwhelming joy and love for your adopted child should be expected. Parents should realize, however, that their child may need time before he can allow himself to return that love. He may require even more time before he is able to show it. Foster parents, too, should anticipate that some children will develop loving feelings for them, and this is all right. Know that the love you feel is genuine, and it does not depend upon the child showing love for you to make it real.

This is Not What We Expected

IN SEPTEMBER 2000, DAVID STIRES wrote an article titled, "Sins of Omissions." The article was published in Smart Money magazine, which is not where you would expect to see coverage of adoption issues. Including this article in a financial publication made sense, however, because Stires wrote about the hidden financial costs associated with adoption, particularly when the child turns out to require more support services than the family expected.

In his article, Stires reports that many adoptive parents are surprised, overwhelmed, and angry when their child requires medical, educational, or psychological services that weren't fully disclosed or anticipated during the pre-placement process. He cites the research of Ronald Federici, a developmental neuropsychologist who argues that adoption agencies often withhold this information on purpose. Stires says there is a gamble when adopting a child and that parents need to be alert to all possible scenarios. For example, he wrote:

> *Some industry professionals claim that adoptive parents have no right to expect a perfect child. After all, they say, biological parents essentially roll the dice and pray their genes will combine to produce a healthy baby. But birth parents can argue that at least they know when*

they can eliminate alcoholism or drug addiction as medical risks. Plus, undergoing amniocentesis, routinely recommended for women 35 and older, can detect certain genetic defects.

Stires points out that many parents are suing adoption agencies in an effort to receive financial help in paying for unexpected costs of raising a special needs child. In return, he notes that some adoption agencies require parents to sign a waiver relinquishing their right to sue no matter what happens after the placement.

I worked on a case where the adoptive parents firmly believed that some of their child's problems were known prior to the placement. In their opinion, a conscious decision was made by the placement agency and others not to tell them. They had adopted two brothers, an infant and a school age child, from another country. The older boy increasingly exhibited disturbing behavior, such as doing things that deliberately put his brother in harm's way. When they explored various treatment options for their adopted son, such as attachment-based inpatient programs, they were astounded at some of the costs involved. Even though they kept asking the placement agency for financial or practical assistance, their requests were ignored. Soon, it became clear to these parents that maintaining the older child in the home posed too many risks to the family and they started exploring their options. Only after they asked the director of the placement agency, "What do you think the people in the child's country of origin will say when they find out one of their children ended up in the American foster care system" did they receive financial support by which to address his problems.

Independent of the legal issues involved with this topic, adoption does carry risk factors as well as unforeseen circumstances. It would be a bit dramatic to tell parents, "Pray for the best but expect the worst." Yet, the statement carries an element of truth. I have seen situations where numerous providers warned that a particular child was heading for a life of crime and residential placement. But, he blossomed into a loving, caring child in his adoptive home. I have also seen the other side, where a child who "looks good" on paper turns out to be a parent's worst nightmare.

Realistically, foster and adopted children are at greater risk for emotional and educational struggles. Can we determine which children will have these problems or to what extreme? Of course not. The clues that a child will have some degree of emotional, behavioral, medical, or educational difficulties are usually evident early on. This is why early identification and intervention is so important.

If parents refused to accept these risks, no foster or adoptive homes would exist. Only a small percentage of children in the child welfare system will require extensive, time-consuming, and costly psychological or medical services, and it is not always possible to predict who will.

In order to prepare for the possibility that yours will be a child with special needs, my advice is as follows:

- Read books, take classes, and talk to other foster/adoptive parents before a child is placed in your home. This will help ensure that you have realistic expectations and adequate training to handle any problems your child may present.
- Once you have made the decision to adopt a child, your efforts are best directed to finding ways to help the child rather than to battle with placement agencies. Still, if you believe you are entitled to information, support, or services from the placement agency, consider enlisting the help of an advocate. Let them negotiate with the placement agency while you devote your time to the child.
- If you suspect that your child has or is at risk for emotional, educational, or behavior problems, obtain a competent evaluation. Even if the child's difficulties are relatively minor, it can be useful to establish a baseline from which to compare as he grows older.

- If the evaluation points to emotional or learning delays, seek early intervention. This could include counseling, tutoring, a behavior management plan, or psychiatric care. Addressing problems before they worsen is important.

- Create an extensive support network of friends with whom you can share the joys and frustrations of parenting.

- Three out of four foster parents end up adopting a child placed in their care. Fostering a child may provide you with an introduction to caring for a child, especially if parenting is new to you. When you foster a child, you are also in a position to see the range of his emotional, behavioral, and educational strengths and weaknesses. This will help you develop realistic expectations about what services the child may require as he grows older.

- As you make plans to bring a child into your life, closely examine your financial situation, as well as what services your insurance will cover. Can you realistically afford unexpected expenses? Recent estimates show that it costs well over $250,000 to raise a child for 18 years. If your child requires specialized services, even if only for a short period of time, these costs may rise substantially.

- Be prepared to set aside time just for yourself. Even though a great deal of initial attention needs to be devoted to the bonding and settling-in process when you foster or adopt a child, you need time for you! Especially if yours is a special or high needs child, you will require time and opportunity to recharge your physical and emotional batteries.

> *The difficulty in bonding with the adoptive mother is not so much a matter of trust as it is a matter of loyalty to that first mother.*
>
> — Nancy Verrier,
> "The Primal Wound"

Did the Child Say Goodbye to His Birth Parents?

WHEN A BIRTH PARENT LOSES her legal rights to a child, the court will sometimes permit her to have a "goodbye" or termination session with the child. These meetings are usually supervised by a staff member of the child protection agency or by the child's therapist. The birth parent is instructed to give the child her permission to move forward in life and to stay away from loaded or controversial topics. The goodbye session is highly emotional for both the child and parent, with the child sometimes feeling sad, confused, or overwhelmed. In my experience, some birth parents do an admirable job of ending the relationship with their child while others cause the child further pain.

I remember one instance where a social worker and I supervised a goodbye visit between a birth mother and her six-year-old boy. The child was incredibly depressed and not fully aware of the purpose of the meeting. Unfortunately, the mother was very angry at the social worker, and she was not able to put this aside during the appointment. Toward the end of the session, I placed the boy on his mother's lap and asked her to give him a hug and wish him well. The mother was crying, as was the boy, and she started saying, "Don't forget about me. I'm your real mother. When you get old enough you come and look for me. I'll be waiting." We quickly ended the session, but the boy heard what the mother had said. I still wonder if her words haunt him, all these years later.

Children younger than eight rarely understand the nature of the termination session with their birth parent. Even in situations where the child has only seen his parent infrequently, the notion of a final goodbye meeting will likely be foreign. Too often, termination sessions are held because a birth parent insists on it. Bowing to this pressure, the legal or social service workers will go along with the parent's request, not fully appreciating what impact this will have on the child. In my opinion, termination/goodbye sessions should only be held when the child will realistically benefit from it. At times, the termination meeting really can be therapeutic for the child, providing him with a sense of closure or relief. In other cases, it only serves to increase the stress, anger, or confusion he feels, making it more difficult to successfully transition to a permanent placement.

If you are adopting a child, you will want to find out if he had a goodbye session with the birth parents. If he did, try to find out how this went. Ask if you can talk with the person who supervised the meeting. Ask if written notes were maintained or if a videotape of the session was recorded. It may prove helpful to review this material.

If your child participated in a termination session, you will want to find out what this experience was like for him. Depending on his age and maturity, he may or may not be able to fully articulate this. It will be helpful to ask him if he knew in advance why he was having the meeting and if he can recall what was said. As you discuss the topic, remain sensitive to the role that anger, confusion, grief, and fear may have played for him.

Foster parents may want to share their opinion on whether the child should have a termination session with a birth parent. Some courts will entertain your thoughts on the matter while others will not. Since you know how the child is doing, think about the pros and cons of a meeting with the birth parent one last time. In many instances, for example, I rely heavily on what foster parents have to say about this issue. They have seen how the child reacts before and after visits with the birth parent and they often have a good feel for how a termination session will affect the child. In deciding whether to have a termination session, foster parents can be instrumental in helping others evaluate whether the child has the maturity and mental strength to participate in such a meeting or whether it could cause him too much stress.

Even if your child had a termination session with a birth parent, it is not realistic to expect that he heard from the birth parent what we might believe is important. A parent whose rights were terminated likely had deficits in their ability to be empathic to the child's needs or to put their child's interests above their own. Thus, it is doubtful that your child heard a genuine apology from the parent or an explanation for why things turned out the way they did. Too often, birth parents use the termination session as a time for justifying their actions to the child. For the child, there is little to be gained from hearing this. Instead, he may be wondering why the parent couldn't have done things differently, so that it never had to get to this point.

If you are fostering or preparing to adopt a child who has yet to have a goodbye session with his parent, but you know it will likely happen, there are steps you can take to hopefully make it easier on him.

- Prepare the child for the visit. Depending upon his age, let him know that he will be seeing his parent one last time.
- If you will be taking the child to the visit, don't stray far from the premises. Even though an hour or so may be set aside for the visit, it could be necessary to end it more quickly. You may be needed in order to offer comfort or just to take the child home.
- Build in time to be with the child before and after the visit. He may need lots of reassurance before the visit, as well as comfort after.
- Try not to let the visit occur in places the child considers safe. For example, it may not be best to do the session at the therapist's office, as the office could then become associated with an uncomfortable event in the child's mind.

- Talk with the placement worker about whether you believe the visit should be videotaped. A videotape of the session could be a powerful tool for the child's therapist to use, especially if she is not able to attend the meeting.

- Don't schedule the termination session during times that interfere with the child's other obligations. For example, don't expect the child to go to school after the visit and don't hold the meeting during final's week. Also, try not to hold these meetings during significant dates such as birthdays or holidays.

Call Me Mommy, Not Mrs. Smith

ONE OF THE BENEFITS OF BEING a parent is that the title of "mom" or "dad" is exclusively yours with respect to your child. Parents anxiously await the day their infant starts to articulate the words, "mama" or "dada." Adoptive parents also want their roles acknowledged by their child, and many are proud to be called "mom" or "dad" by their child.

In general, it is easier for adoptive parents to get toddlers to call them "mommy" or "daddy" than it is with older children. Older children may have memories of their biological mother or father, or they may have referred to a foster parent as mom or dad. From the child's perspective, the title of "mom" or "dad" is earned. Many adopted children tell me they feel resentful at having to refer to their parent as "mom" or "dad," especially if doing so conjures up in their mind loyalty conflicts between their adoptive parents and other adults who served a parental role in their lives. In open adoptions, the child may be confused about who to call mom or dad, since he may have two moms or two dads in his life.

Though I understand the need to do so, I find myself taken aback by parents who insist that their adopted children immediately begin calling them "mom" or "dad." I believe it is important to respect a child's feelings in this decision and to perhaps consider alternatives. Some children, for example, call their adoptive parent, "Momma-Sharon" or "Papa-George." For the child, this helps neutralize feelings associated with calling Sharon, "mom" or George, "dad." There is no right answer on this one, but consideration of the child's preference can go a long way toward showing appreciation of their feelings around being adopted.

The terms, "mom" and "dad" also refer to the role an adult plays in a child's life. Therefore, if you are fostering a child, you are the mom or dad at that time. This doesn't mean the child has no other mom or dad or won't call other adults mom or dad in the future. I have little concern about a child referring to a foster parent as mom or dad, unless it is done in a deceitful manner — a child should not be led to believe someone is his birth parent who really isn't.

Birth parents often resent their child referring to a foster parent as "mom" or "dad." Even if the child came up with this on their own, the foster parents are usually blamed. Talking with the social worker or care coordinator about these issues can be helpful. The younger the child, the more likely he will call you "mom" or "dad." If you choose to discourage this, do it in a gentle way that doesn't leave the child feeling he has done something wrong. Sometimes it can be helpful to explain to the child that being a mom or dad is a role, like a teacher or sitter, and that you are serving in this role temporarily.

When Parenthood is Unexpected

WHILE MOST PARENTS END UP FOSTERING or adopting a child because they made a conscious decision to do so, some adults find themselves caring for a child unexpectedly. This is common in situations where the adults know the child in some capacity — such as when he is a relative or friend of the family — and the child suddenly requires out of home placement. In these instances, the foster or adoptive parents may have less ability to maintain psychological distance from the birth parents, because they knew of or witnessed the abuse or neglect as it occurred. For them, knowledge of parental misdeeds is based on first-hand experience, rather than through various written reports. Often, family friends or relatives find themselves in the situation of either taking the child into their home or risk having the child enter the child welfare system and placed in foster care. Decisions must be made quickly as the state may need to immediately place the child.

In many instances, relatives of the birth parent do agree to take the child in, even though doing so may not be best for them or for the child. Frequently, they report feeling a great deal of pressure from other members of the family to care for the child, typically because others view them as the logical choice for placement. They also find that their stress level goes up considerably, especially if they are a single parent, have other children in the home, are elderly, or face the possibility of taking in a sibling group instead of just one child.

When this happens, keep in mind that a "right" or correct decision rarely exists. Instead, there are pros and cons for the friend or relative, as well as for the child. First and foremost, the potential parent must make sure they are able to handle the responsibilities of raising a child. This includes having the energy, time, and money to meet the developmental, emotional, and financial needs of caring for a child, while attending to the other obligations they have. While social service departments can't always give you a realistic timeline, you should find out what expectations they have of you and in what ways you will receive practical, emotional, and financial support. The parent must also assess whether their marriage is strong enough to withstand the added stress and burden of adding a young child or adolescent in the family.

If you suddenly find yourself with the prospect of bringing the child of a friend or family member into your home, stay mindful of the changes that will happen in your life. As an example, much of the content included in this book is not new to many foster or adoptive parents, as they have learned a good deal of it through courses, books, or friends. If fostering or adopting a child is not something you have previously done or considered, you are basically being asked to do a crash course on the topic, often while simultaneously caring for the child. Within a very short period of time, you may likely find yourself being a parent, advocate, and disciplinarian, with all that these roles entail.

By agreeing to raise or care for the child of a friend or family member, the relationship you have with the birth parent may change in substantial ways. The birth parent will likely be forbidden from having unsupervised contact with the child and will therefore be prohibited from coming over to your home. You can expect to sometimes feel tremendous anger at the birth parent because of the dilemma in which you and the child have been placed. If the birth parent is your sibling, the situation can literally pit brother against brother. Suddenly, the issue of where loyalties lie comes up dramatically. If the parent does not work the parameters of their treatment plan, your resentment will likely increase, as you start to recognize that your commitment to care for the child may be for a longer period of time than you anticipated. Throughout the time that you care for the child, his needs and interests must be your primary focus.

In these situations, it is important to obtain counsel and guidance from people who are unfamiliar with all the players on the case. You need the opportunity to discuss the matter with someone who has no investment in any particular outcome. A social worker, therapist, church leader, or a friend who doesn't know the child could all provide useful advice. Above all else, be sure you have ample support or at least know how to get it. While you may not have been ready to assume the role as a parent, this doesn't mean you can't do a good job. But you may need help, support, and guidance along the way.

Adoption Considerations for Couples

T HE IDEA OF A COUPLE CHOOSING to adopt a child brings to mind a variety of stereotypical images. Many people believe that a couple comes to this decision after knowing or experiencing that they cannot give birth to a child of their own. Committed to the notion of having a family, the stereotype continues, the couple embarks on the journey toward adoption with its accompanying home studies, background checks, and agency and travel fees. Eventually, the child arrives and the couple begins a new life as parents.

Certainly, there are elements of truth to this stereotype for many people. In reality, though, many couples adopt a child under different circumstances or for other reasons. I often find that members of a couple have different ideas about adoption with even one partner wanting to adopt more than the other. What becomes especially important over time is the willingness of the couple to discuss with one another their respective thoughts, fantasies, hopes, and fears about adopting. Both persons must be absolutely committed to working as a team when raising a child.

Adopting a child is a major commitment that requires a great deal of work, dedication, and sacrifice. While one or both members of the couple will sometimes have fears and doubts about adopting, maintaining the commitment is crucial for the well-being of the child. In a few cases on which I've worked one member of the couple basically gave into the other member's desire to have a child, without full appreciation of the impact on their relationship. In other instances, couples are suddenly faced with the prospect of adopting the child of a family member, perhaps the child of their own brother or sister. In these cases, the couple feels tremendous pressure from extended family members to adopt the child. This topic was addressed in the previous section.

In anticipation of caring for a child — either through adoption or foster care — it is important to do a realistic assessment of what your day-to-day lives look like. For example, do one or both of you have stressful, demanding, and time-consuming jobs? If so, how might this affect your availability for the child? Let's say there is an emergency at daycare or in school. Is your place of employment close enough for you to leave at a moment's notice and get to the school on time? Do you live in a child-friendly community or will a move elsewhere be something to consider? Most importantly, how will the responsibilities of raising a child affect the time you and your spouse or partner have shared almost exclusively with one another?

A new child, regardless of his age, will command a great deal of the parents' time and energy. Inevitably, this draws attention away from time the couple would typically devote to one another. If both adults feel that their commitment to the child and to one another is strong, weathering the stress of having a new child in the home will prove much easier. If, on the other hand, one partner starts to resent the child or his partner, the tension can greatly affect the relationship, as well as the child's feelings of comfort and safety.

If you and your partner must decide whether to adopt a child from within the family, remember that there is nothing wrong with stepping up to the plate in difficult circumstances and offering to help. Sometimes, even when we have no intention of taking on certain tasks or responsibilities — such as adopting a child — life presents us with these opportunities and challenges. I have seen many examples where the adults — either alone or within a relationship — were aware of a child who needed a permanent home. Even though adoption was not something they wished to pursue, they successfully took on the challenge. Unfortunately, I have also seen marriages end in divorce because the relationship could not sustain the added stress of a new child. Of course, the difficulties experienced by the unsuccessful couples were most likely present before the child arrived. In some instances, the marriage may not have lasted whether the couple adopted a child or not.

QUESTIONS FOR COUPLES TO CONSIDER BEFORE ADOPTING

- In what ways will our daily routines at home and at work change?
- What sacrifices will need to be made by each person; less time at work, fewer nights out with "the boys" or "the girls," taking a job closer to home, fewer hours at the gym, turning the home office into a bedroom, quit smoking, etc?
- How will we afford the added expense of having a child, while attending to our other financial obligations?
- What's likely to happen to our Saturday morning snuggle time or our sex life?
- What changes do we each need to make in our work, school, or social commitments?
- Who will handle transportation for the child to and from school or appointments?
- Can our efforts really be equal or is it more likely that one of us will mostly have to attend to day-to-day parenting?
- How can we make sure we have time just for us?
- Is ours a child-safe and child-friendly community or neighborhood?
- Should we move to a different area?
- Who do we have to rely on to help with babysitting, transportation, and emotional support?
- In what ways are our values and expectations regarding discipline and child-rearing similar and different?
- Do we know other couples who have adopted?
- What can we learn from their experiences?
- If we die, who will be available to take care of our child?

Considerations for Gay and Lesbian Parents

A GAY MAN WHO RECENTLY ADOPTED a four-year-old boy contacted me for consultation on raising his child. He said that shortly after bringing the child home he woke one night to find the boy standing by his bed. The father asked him what was wrong, and the boy said he was afraid and could not sleep. The man asked him if he would feel safer getting into bed with him. The boy replied, "No. I was told you would hurt my butt." The boy had lived in a foster home for two years prior to coming to this adoptive placement. When the foster family learned the boy would be adopted by a gay man, they told him that this man might hurt him.

Much controversy surrounds the issue of parenting by gays and lesbians. Yet, this population continues to foster and adopt children in large and growing numbers. In 2001, an estimated 6 to 10 million gay and lesbian parents lived in the United States, caring for an estimated 14 million children. Although many of these children were born when their parents were in heterosexual relationships, the last decade has seen a sharp rise among gays and lesbians planning and forming families through adoption, foster care, donor insemination, and other means. As of the end of 2003, about two in five public and private adoption agencies have placed children with adoptive parents whom they know to be gay or lesbian. Increasingly, agencies are including content about gay and lesbian parents in their official policies and many agencies are devoting recruitment efforts toward this population. Gays and lesbians who want to foster or adopt a child should no longer focus so much on whether they will be able to, but more on preparation for parenthood.

A 2003 study, "Adoption by Lesbians and Gays: A National Survey of Adoption Agency Policies, Practices, and Attitudes," found that slightly over 60 percent of agencies surveyed indicated a willingness to accept adoption applications from gays and lesbians. Of the agencies surveyed, more than one-third reported having made at least one adoption placement with gays or lesbians in the two-year period studied.

Gays and lesbians who seek to adopt or to become foster parents should be prepared to answer questions about their sexual orientation and behavior to screening agencies. Questions can include "Are you dating" or "Is there a romantic partner in your life" for single persons, or "What would you do if the child saw you having sex" for couples. Agency staff will also ask what steps you will take to discuss homosexuality with the child and assess your understanding of children's knowledge about sex, love, and relationships. You could be asked if you have been in couples counseling, if you have pornographic material in the home, if any of your friends have been charged with committing sex offenses against a child, how you will handle kissing and displays of affection with a same-sex partners in the presence of the child, if you go to gay or lesbian clubs, what social events you will take your child to, and if you have gay or lesbian friends who are parents. The emphasis these agencies place on aspects of your sexual behavior can be somewhat offensive. Yet, it reflects certain stereotypes about homosexuality and there will be time to address the broader realities of your life.

Increasing numbers of studies are examining the impact on children of being raised by a gay man or lesbian. A good overview can be found in the document, "Public Interest Directorate: Research Summary on Lesbian and Gay Parenting," written by Charlotte Patterson and available at www.apa.org. For the most part, studies show that homosexuals' parenting capacity and their children's outcomes are comparable to those of hetero-sexuals. The studies show that children of gays and lesbians have normal relationships with peers and that their relationships with adults of both sexes are satisfactory. In 1995, the American Psychological Association published a report that states, "Not a single study has found children of gay or lesbian parents to be disadvantaged in any significant respect relative to children of heterosexual parents" and concludes that "home environments provided by gay and lesbian parents are as likely as those provided by heterosexual parents to support and enable children's psychosocial growth."

In addition, various studies in recent years have concluded:

- Homosexual parents are no more likely to be emotionally disturbed than their heterosexual counterparts.
- No link has been found between homosexuality and child sexual abuse.
- Homosexual parents have not been shown to be deficient in parenting knowledge, skills, or behavior.
- Homosexual couples establish co-parenting relationships that are at least as effective as their heterosexual counterparts. In fact, lesbian couples tend to share childrearing and domestic responsibilities more equally than heterosexual couples. Lesbian parents of foster and adopted children are generally more involved and display greater parenting skills than do heterosexual fathers.
- Children raised by homosexual parents display no significant differences compared to children raised by heterosexual parents regarding depression, anxiety, self-esteem, conduct problems, intellectual functioning, or many other areas of social and psychological adjustment.
- Children raised by lesbian and gay parents report periodic homophobic teasing that, at times, is stressful. Because these youngsters sometimes experience teasing or ridicule, and yet do not show evidence of increased adjustment difficulties, suggests they possess considerable internal resiliency and/or strong support systems.
- Being raised by homosexual parents does not increase the risk for gender identity problems. Children in lesbian-headed households do not appear to display less traditional sex-typed dress, play, and behavior than children raised by parents who are heterosexual.
- Adolescents and young adults raised in lesbian and gay households are no more likely to self-identify as homosexual than those raised in heterosexual households.

Still, gay and lesbian families will face unique challenges. In fostering or adopting a child, a gay or lesbian parent must be more sensitive to certain developmental and social issues. The child will almost certainly grapple with concepts and notions about relationships and sexuality that may not be true if raised by a non-gay or lesbian parent. Gay and lesbian parents will confront the day-to-day realities of raising a child that all parents do. At the same time, they must be prepared to take into account how their sexual orientation will affect their child's identity, friendships, schooling, and other factors.

To read first-hand accounts from gay and lesbian parents, I recommend the book, "Lesbian and Gay Fostering and Adoption" by Stephen Hicks and Janet McDermott. It features a compilation of 17 essays by gay men and women who have raised foster or adoptive children.

Who Will Tell the Child the Parent is Gay or Lesbian?

In the best-case scenario, the parents would have full control over when and what the child is told about their sexual orientation. But, this is not always the case particularly for older children. Before placement, the child will learn about his new parents from a variety of people, such as a social worker, foster parent, or counselor. During this time, one of these people may tell the child that his new parents are gay or lesbian. Also, if a gay or lesbian couple will be adopting, the child may raise questions on their own about why he is being adopted by two men or two women.

Unfortunately, adoptive parents may not have the opportunity to talk to the person who introduces facts about their sexual orientation to their child. Even if the child was told that they will be fostered or adopted by a gay or lesbian person or couple, it is still important to be prepared to do some clarification for the child. The child should be asked what he knows or believes about homosexuality and what questions he has about it. Young children will most likely hear the news and wonder who is mommy and who is daddy. Older children, on the other hand, will think in terms of how their lives will be affected by having gay or lesbian parents. He'll want to know if he has to tell his friends, if people will tease him, or if he could become gay by living in the home. Ask the child what they were told and be prepared to correct any misinformation.

In preparing to foster or adopt a child, gay or lesbian parents should think through how they will explain their orientation to the child, trusting that it will take the child some time to fully understand the issue. Parents should not give the child too much information on the topic at once, as many children will find the whole concept new and somewhat confusing. In talking to the child, emphasize that the parent's sexual orientation is just one part of the bigger picture. The child still needs to be told about the rules and expectations for living in the home and what their daily life will be like.

The child should be told who else knows the parents are gay or lesbian. For some children, they will wonder if this information is a secret to be kept from the birth parent, social worker, therapist, or teacher. The child should also be given permission to tell or not tell other people. For example, the child can be told, "It is okay if you tell your friend John or his mother. But if you do, I want you to let me know;" or "Your teacher already knows that Sally and I are a couple. She knows you have two moms."

In talking with children about sexual orientation, they must be told that they will encounter people who disapprove or ridicule the child's family. They should be encouraged to talk about this with the parents when it happens, and they should be educated about appropriate ways to respond if this occurs. As a gay man or lesbian, you already know that people can say mean things about your sexual orientation. But, be prepared for a new level of anger when you find out this is being told to the child you are fostering or have adopted. For example, the child's birth parent or siblings might say to the child: "They're not touching you in weird ways are they? You let me know, and I'll try to get you put into another home;" "Your dad's do icky things to each other. I'll bet they do it to you, too;" or "He's a nice father, but he's not like most other men. Don't try to be like him."

Who Will be the Primary Parent?

Despite dramatic changes in gender roles, many still perceive women as the primary caregivers of children. In studies on how mothers and fathers relate to their infants, researchers have found that women mostly interact with the child in a nurturing, calm, and soothing manner, while men are more playful with the child, bouncing him around, holding him in the air, and tickling. No way of relating to the child is better or worse than the other. Both kinds of experiences are important for the child and each contributes to bonding and attachment in its own way.

Some attachment theorists have proposed that infants need a primary parent, even though the parenting may be shared by more than one person. In this line of thinking, the child has one person with whom he interacts the most and who he comes to see as his point person for receiving love, attention, safety, and protection. Many parents insist that they want their child to attach equally to both of them and set off on a course of sharing in the parental role as much as possible. What happens, though, is that parents find their respective strengths and weaknesses along the way and end up relating to the child in a manner that feels most comfortable for them. Along the way, it is natural for a child to go to one parent more often, particularly when she is tired or anxious.

For these and other reasons, gay or lesbian couples should explore what their respective parental roles will be. Each person's temperament can often help determine prospective roles. For example, one member of the couple may simply be more nurturing, more maternal, or more interested in devoting their efforts to caring for a young child. Nothing is wrong with striving for equal participation in parenting. But, in reality each parent naturally gravitates to areas where they have the greatest interest and skill. One member of the couple may therefore assume the role of changing diapers, giving the child a bath, and preparing the food. The other person may find their talent lies in taking the child to the park, engaging in active play, and teaching him certain hobbies or skills.

Your Child's School

I believe that teachers need to know that the parent of a child in their class is gay or lesbian. This information should come from the parent even if the child is in a short-term foster care arrangement. Parents should meet with the teacher, preferably before the child is placed in her class. While the discussion should certainly address other matters of the child's life and education, the parents need to inform the teacher of ways in which sexual orientation might affect the child at school. This includes:

- Acknowledging which adults will be permitted to pick the child up from school, obtain information regarding the child's progress, or call to speak with the teacher.
- Find out if the teacher knows other gay or lesbian parents.
- Encouraging sensitivity on the teacher's part around Mother's Day and Father's Day projects, as well as other family-based discussions or activities.
- Asking the teacher how they will deal with any derogatory comments about homosexuality directed at the child by other students.
- Finding out what the sex education curriculum includes and whether it addresses homosexuality in any manner.
- As a gay or lesbian parent, consider helping out in your child's class or volunteer to assist on field trips. Parents often report that these efforts go a long way toward reducing stereotypes and negative attitudes about their family by both children and adults.

I am happy with my daughter and she is very much a part of the family, not just my biological family but the extended lesbian and gay "family." There are issues around her having learning difficulties and she attends a special school where there are various professionals involved. Somewhere in the reams of paperwork it is written that I am a "homosexual"!

— Stephen Hicks & Janet McDermott,
"Lesbian and Gay Fostering and Adoption"

When You are Dating

Gay men and lesbians are often not sure how to address the issue of adopted or foster kids with their dating partners. When and how to introduce the child and partner can sometimes feel quite stressful. Gay men, in particular, report finding partners who are confused or turned off by the prospect of a potential partner raising a child. Part of this reaction may reflect that gay men, like other males in society, can internalize the message that gay parents can't be trusted or shouldn't be raising children. Gay men, especially if single, also provide foster care or adopt children at a much lower rate than lesbians. Thus, the notion may be foreign to a dating partner, simply because he has never met a gay parent before.

Particularly if you are providing foster care, new partners should be told that these children can sometimes present odd, confusing, or challenging behaviors. In addition, the person you are dating needs to know that children command a great deal of your time, energy, and attention. New partners should know it is not as simple as you getting a babysitter every time the two of you want to go out. The new person in your life will therefore need to take a close look at whether they want to be with someone who has the responsibility of caring for a child. If the relationship becomes serious, your partner will need to be told that he may be subject to a criminal background check by the agency that places children in your care. Issues of trust may be triggered and require the two of you to share very personal information early in your relationship.

If it looks like the relationship is becoming serious, your new partner will have to examine their feelings about being a co-parent. Depending upon the level of your foster or adopted children's need, your partner will have to recognize the role they will play in setting limits, enforcing consequences, helping with homework, attending school functions, and dealing with problematic behaviors. In some instances, your new partner may be expected to attend classes on caring for high-needs children. If you provide foster care services through an agency, you must find out their policies pertaining to dating. For example, do they require you to let them know about this, particularly if your partner will interact with the child?

In the event that you enter into a long-term commitment with a partner, members of the child's treatment team may not accept him or her. While you may believe your partner should be able to attend treatment or education meetings, the placement agency may not agree. A conflict may ensue between you and the agency as well as between you and your partner. Some of the difficulty will ease over time, as the treatment team comes to realize that your partner is genuinely committed to you and the child.

False Allegations

One of the realities of providing care or treatment for abused or neglected children is the risk that the child will allege you have hurt them or approached them sexually. Most placement agencies have detailed proce-dures for dealing with these allegations because they occur somewhat frequently. Some agencies will investigate the allegation before removing the child from your care, while others will place the child elsewhere while they conduct their interviews and investigation. The experience can be very disturbing and stressful often resulting in parents refusing to care for any more children or to limit which children they will accept.

Children make false allegations of physical or sexual abuse for a variety reasons. Some children use it as a manipulative ploy to get out of a placement they don't like or to get even with a parent who has angered them. This occurs more often with older children and adolescents. Other children make false allegations with no ill-intent. Instead, a parent's behavior may simply be perceived as confusing or threatening. Because of a background that might have included physical abuse, sexual exploitation, or other boundary violations, the child associates a parent's behavior with those times. For example, a child may see a parent naked; the parent may walk in on the child while he is getting dressed; the parent may touch a child on the leg; or the parent may raise their voice at the child in anger. These innocent acts can be translated in the child's mind as the parent attempting to seduce or hurt them. In some instances, the child may have been hurt or exploited in other placements and fears the same will happen with you.

While no parent wants to have false allegations of abuse made against them, gay and lesbian parents are often more sensitized to the effects or implications. Gay men and lesbians recognize that there are many people who hold stereotypes that homosexuals sexually abuse children or that gays and lesbians should not care for children. Because of this, gay and lesbian parents fear, rightly so, that there is a greater risk the child will be believed when he makes a false allegation.

At the risk of sounding too alarming, I really encourage all foster and adoptive parents — regardless of sexual orientation — to entertain the notion that a false allegation could be filed against you. At a minimum, you need to have a plan in place for how you will handle this if it arises. The child could suddenly be taken from your home, you could be prohibited from having unsupervised contact with him, and people who were once supportive of you may appear to turn a mistrustful eye your direction. If you have a support network of other foster or adoptive parents, ask if any of them have had allegations filed against them. Find out how they dealt with it, from both a practical and emotional standpoint. You could even consider asking the placement agency in advance how they approach these allegations when they arise.

The risk that a child will make a false allegation against you can not be eliminated. Still, there are steps you can take to reduce this possibility and to effectively handle it if it occurs:

Maintain a good reputation. When people in your neighborhood and community know you to be an honest and trustworthy person, they are less likely to believe false allegations made against you.

Use history as a predictor. Before a child is placed in your home, find out if he has made allegations of abuse about other parents or providers. Find out if the allegations were substantiated or not. If the allegations were not substantiated, try to obtain as many facts as possible.

Obtain documentation. If your child has made false allegations against anyone in the past, ask for a copy of the letter that deemed the report unsubstantiated. This documentation may help you in the investigation process, by demonstrating that the child has made such assertions in the past.

Be aware of boundaries. People have different ideas about what kind of behavior is "too close." You may be a hug and touch kind of person, but others around you may not. Be sensitive to how your child perceives closeness by you. Also, recognize that when you raise your voice, the child could misperceive that you are angry and about to hurt them.

Know the child's background. It is important to know if the child was ever hurt or exploited in a prior foster or adoptive home. If so, they may believe you will do the same. If the child you care for was physically abused, try to use non-threatening approaches to discipline. If the child you care for was sexually abused, be conscious of the ways you touch the child. It may prove necessary to have two adults in the home at all times or never to be alone in a room with the child with the door closed.

Cooperate with the investigation. If a social worker, detective, or placement worker alerts you of the allegation, offer your full cooperation. You will be provided with the opportunity to share your side of the story and your perspective of the events.

Follow-through. If the allegation is deemed to be false, you may be asked if you are willing to have the child returned to your home. Consult with a friend, therapist, or placement worker about this choice, as you will likely have feelings of anger and betrayal that could negatively impact your ability to provide the child with what he needs.

Discuss the issue with your child. If the child is returned to your home, it will be important to discuss the allegation — what motivated it, and its consequences for the child, you, and the family. A therapist, social worker, or other neutral party may help the process. Hopefully, the child will appreciate that these kinds of statements can greatly affect other people in profound ways. If the allegation was the result of a misunderstanding of circumstances by the child, this should be clarified for her. If the allegation was malicious or manipulative in its intent, the child must recognize that this can impact whether people believe the things he says in the future.

Choosing Services for the Child or Family

Many gay and lesbian parents contact me for consultation specifically because they want to learn how best to raise a child, while taking into account how their sexual orientation might affect the arrangement. Some of these parents have had fears or concerns about the ways their sexual orientation might influence the child as he grows older. Thus, they are seeking advice for being the best gay or lesbian parent they can be. Other parents with whom I have consulted have been reluctant to tell me they are gay or lesbian. Single men and women are often the most reluctant. In exploring this, the parents tell me that they either had negative experiences with other providers, or they feared I would judge them if they disclosed their sexual orientation too soon. Word-of-mouth referrals can alleviate any worries you might have about how a provider will react to learning you are gay or lesbian. By talking with other parents, you can find out if they know of providers who won't let sexual orientation issues interfere with the work that needs to be done.

Earlier in this section, I referenced the 2003 study, "Adoption by Lesbians and Gays: A National Survey of Adoption Agency Policies, Practices, and Attitudes." The text can be found by visiting www.adoptioninstitute.org. In reviewing this study, I was struck by the finding that adoption agencies that focus on placing children with special needs were more likely to make outreach efforts to gays and lesbians. Because these children are often more difficult to place, perhaps the agencies that specialize in these kinds of placements want to broaden the pool of prospective homes as much as possible. But, this also suggests that a large number of gay and lesbian parents stand to raise children who are at greater risk of presenting with complex medical, educational, social service, developmental, and/or mental health needs. In order to obtain the most competent and effective services for these children, the parents need to trust that the providers with whom they work are not willing to let their feelings about sexual orientation interfere.

Particularly with providers with whom you will have an ongoing relationship, I believe it is fair to have a candid discussion with them about sexual orientation. This discussion can include finding out if they have worked with other gay or lesbian families, if they believe their attitudes could limit their effectiveness, or if they believe the child could receive confusing or mixed messages in working with them. In larger cities, many gay and lesbian parents seek the services of gay- or lesbian-identified doctors, therapists and educators. While it can be good to have this option, a gay practitioner will not necessarily be skilled in the areas of parenting that need the most attention. This is one of the reasons why a screening interview with the provider can be so important.

In talking with a child's therapist, parents should ask how they plan to handle discussions of sexual orientation with the child. For example, explore with the therapist how she will respond to questions the child asks her about homosexuality, as well as what she might say if the child expresses disapproval of his parents' sexual orientation. Older children may particularly have questions or feelings about their parents' sexual orientation that they would rather discuss with a neutral person than with the parent. As the parent, you need to know how the therapist will address these issues and to what extent they will likely share this information with you if it comes up.

RESOURCES

ON THE WEB

ACLU Fact Sheet on Lesbian and Gay Parenting
www.aclu.org (use search function)

Gay and Lesbian Parenting Website
www.proudparenting.com

PART TWO

Settling In:
Your New Family

Defining Family Job Descriptions

E VERYONE IN A FAMILY HAS A JOB to do. In its simplest form, your job is to be a parent, while the child's job is to be a child. This means that parents assume authority and command in the house. For their part, children need to play, behave responsibly, and attend to their obligations at school. These concepts seem so obvious to many parents, that you may wonder why it's being stated here. I find many children in foster care or adoption systems require guidance around roles and boundaries, with emphasis placed on what it actually means to be a parent or child.

It is quite common for many foster and adopted children to grow up to act in ways that are termed, *parentified*. These children were forced to sacrifice aspects of their childhood, having to act more grown up than most children their age. This is typically seen in situations in which a child had to care for younger siblings due to the neglect or unavailability of a parent. I also see it with children who, because of neglect or abandonment, had to spend a great deal of their time focusing on basic survival needs, perhaps wondering where they would next sleep or when they might eat again. Children who were physically abused often lose the spontaneity and creativity associated with play. Some children never learned to play because no one ever showed or offered them outlets for play such as toys or crayons. Sexually abused children may have been put in a role of being a partner for the abuser, a situation that can leave the child feeling or behaving more grown-up than they really are.

THINGS TO HAVE IN THE HOUSE

- Building blocks
- Lego's
- Tinker Toys
- Human and animal figures
- Paper, crayons, and pens
- Boardgames: Candyland, Chutes and Ladders, Trouble, Connect Four
- Dolls and stuffed animals
- Bathtoys
- Marbles (for children over five)
- Yo-yo
- Children's music: CDs or tapes
- Puzzles
- As few electronic games as possible

Play is important to a child's development. Play encourages a child to use their imagination and to think about the world around them. Too often, foster children tell me they didn't have much time to play because of other demands. Regardless of the child's age, I believe parents should have a variety of toys and play items in the house. Even teenagers appreciate having access to drawing materials, yo-yo's, an Etch-a-Sketch, a slinky, and board games. I'm often struck by the number of teenagers who come into my office and want to play Candyland, which the manufacturer subtitles, "A child's first game." Don't expect your child to necessarily play with all of the toys. Sometimes, it is enough to establish for the child that the house is a playful environment, with ample opportunity for fun, laughter, creativity, and silliness.

Remind children that all members of the household need to work as part of a team to make the house a good place to live. Therefore, each person has duties, which might include: cooking, cleaning, bill paying, feeding the animals, homework or laundry. It is easy for kids to feel they are the only ones who are burdened with responsibility. When you make clear that everyone in the house plays a part, the child will feel more included in a collaborative effort.

I also encourage parents to have children's storybooks in the house. Many children who were abused or neglected never had the chance to read or be read to. Thus, they don't always know about Mickey Mouse, Snow White, Care Bears, Curious George, Sponge Bob, Power Rangers, Alice in Wonderland or Ernie and Bert. Again, just because a child may be in grade school — or even an adolescent — they can still take delight in reading or hearing these stories. The child may not always gravitate to storybooks, but having them communicates that the house is a child-friendly and play-friendly environment.

CHILDREN'S BOOKS TO HAVE IN THE HOUSE

- "Curious George" by H.A. Rey
- "Love You Forever" by Robert N. Munsch
- "No More Water in the Bathtub" by Tedd Arnold
- "The Magic School Bus" by Joanna Cole
- "I'll Always Love You" by Hans Wilhelm
- "Seeing Stars" by Sharleen Collicott
- "What Newt Could do for Turtle" by Jonathan London
- "Frog and Toad are Friends" by Arnold Lobel

The Parent as Coach

THE JOB DUTY MOST PARENTS share in common is that of coach. In a lot of ways, the same holds true for the therapist. But, parents serve in the role of coach each day. In educating a child about life, shaping their behavior, enforcing consequences, and celebrating their accomplishments, we are preparing children for what it means to live in broader society. Eventually, your child will be required to negotiate the demands of the social world without having you by his side. All that you have taught him to that point will need to be put in action.

Keeping the perspective that you are the child's coach can help you to maintain your diligence, particularly when he is defiant and oppositional. If you back down when your child challenges you, he receives the message that he can do the same everywhere else. What happens, though, when he starts his first job and the boss asks him to do something he doesn't want to do? He won't keep his job for long after telling his boss, "No, I don't want to. You can't make me."

The examples are endless, but it all comes back to the same theme. When you teach a child basic rules for the home and school, most of these principles are the same in the workplace or in the broader world.

Is the Child Giving You Reasons or Excuses?

For all of us, there are times we need to provide an explanation for our actions. This might include telling our boss why we were late, informing someone why we took something without asking first, or letting the officer know why we were driving over the speed limit. In some instances, our efforts are designed to inform another person of why we did something. At other times, we're basically offering an excuse, with the hope that we won't be punished. Naturally, children do the same thing. One of our key jobs as parents and providers is to make sure the child knows the difference between a reason and an excuse.

Too often, foster and adopted children grew up in families where excuses were used to justify actions. Maybe the child's birth mother made excuses for why she couldn't complete a treatment plan, or an abuser made an excuse for why he harmed the child. When a child hears a parent make excuses for their actions, he learns that it buys them time and that they are not taking responsibility for their actions. If a child grows up in a home where excuses are used to justify actions, he too can start to do the same, almost as a habit.

When your child offers his explanation for an action, you can ask: "Tell me what the word 'reason' means. Now, tell me what the word 'excuse' means." This way, you'll know if the child can tell the difference between the two. If not, you may need to educate him on the two definitions. Next, you can say: "Tell me again why you did what you did. Then, I want you to tell me whether you are giving me a reason or an excuse." This lets your child know you are not easily fooled or manipulated. It also gives him the chance to be truthful with you about his reasons for doing or not doing something.

Facilitating the Parent-Child Bond

In addition to establishing authority in the house, parents have one other crucial job: To bond with their child. This is true even for foster parents, as it is important to strive for having a genuine and meaningful relationship with the child, regardless of how long he will be in your home. Adopted and foster children frequently tell me that it takes them more than a year to feel safe in their new home. Adopted children, in particular, tell me it takes them even longer to believe or trust that their adoptive parents won't give them away, as their birth parents did. In light of this, parents should take the initiative early in the relationship to begin the bonding process.

Some children are averse to touch. Particularly with abused and neglected children, touch may not feel safe. Use your intuition on this one. For example, some children cringe or pull away when a parent squeezes their shoulder while talking, pull them in for a hug, or stroke their hair. If this happens, it may be enough to simply say to the child, "It doesn't look like you want me touching you. Did that bother you when I squeezed your shoulder? Remember that I won't hurt you. I just want to let you know I think you're great!"

Some children will not allow hugs or other significant body contact between themselves and their parents. Instead of forcing touch on the child — or trying to convince them that touch is all right — approach touch in safe and subtle ways. For example, a toddler may not let you hold him, but he may permit you to rub his toes or wash his hair when he bathes. With older children, they may let you work on their hair, pat them hello or goodbye, or they might permit you to tap their hand to get their attention. In short, parents should find ways of having physical contact with their child. Touch is soothing and reminds us that we're human. In many cultures, touch is used as a form of communication. Don't permit a child create a situation where you never have any physical contact. But you should not force physical contact on a child even though your intentions may be loving and sincere.

STEPS FOR FACILITATING BONDING

- Frequent touch: Hugs, cuddling, a squeeze on the shoulder when talking, rubbing the child's head, massage, tickling, washing the child's back, carrying the child, butterfly kisses, snuggling up and watching a movie, playing "This Little Piggy," brushing the child's hair
- Talking to the child at eye level, with eye contact
- Reading stories together
- Playing together
- Taking walks
- Doing homework together
- Dressing the child
- Making the child a special meal
- Bedtime rituals, such as reading a story or talking about your days
- Exercise together
- Napping together
- Wrestling
- Put lotion on child's face, feet, back
- Face painting
- Living room dancing
- Sharing a snack from the same dish
- Doing a chore together
- Telling the child about your life
- Snowball fights
- Singing songs together

When Your Child Feels Like a Thing, Not a Person

F OR MANY CHILDREN, IT IS BAD enough that they had to deal with abuse or neglect in their birth family. When they enter the child welfare system, many are not necessarily relieved or grateful. Our child welfare system is imperfect. Children may end up in multiple placements, they can end up living with families who don't treat them well, they can have several social workers or treatment coordinators, and they may have to face the prospect of an uncertain future for many months or years. The impact of this is that it can leave the child feeling more like an object than a person. This is especially true for children who were physically or sexually abused, as these acts are inherently dehumanizing for a child.

Often, children tell me that parents and members of their treatment team have a perception of them based on what is written in the various social service reports. From their perspective, it is as if the only thing that matters to others about their lives is what is included in their placement file. A 15-year-old boy, for example, recently listed for me some of the allegations that have been made against him by therapists and foster parents, much of which he said were not true. He feared that I would believe that he was a homicidal sexual perpetrator. He was relieved when I informed him that I had not read the records associated with his life and wanted to learn about him from him. He later told me that this is one of the first times he felt that someone was treating him more like a person than a treatment case.

The challenge for parents and providers is to help the child recognize and appreciate that he is indeed a person and that he will not be treated as an object in our care. A child who has had to deal with a lot of change and uncertainty may have a difficult time trusting this, so we must keep reminding them of their worth.

Children who feel they've been treated as objects often develop a variety of psychological coping mechanisms in order to deal with these feelings. This can include trying not to have any feelings at all. From the child's perspective, if they cut off or ignore their feelings, they don't have to experience the pain, sadness, or anger of their situation. Our task, therefore, is to gently help them start to feel their emotions again, in the context of being with someone who won't hurt or exploit them. For too many children, their experiences have taught them that love hurts or that trusting others leads to betrayal.

In your home, these children need a great deal of empathy. They need to know that there are people who understand how confusing and sad their experiences have been. When I interview children, I will often ask them if they believe anyone in their lives can truly understand what their experiences have felt like to them. Sadly, many of these children say, "no." Frequently, when I interview a child or adolescent who has lived in a variety of homes or treatment settings — and therefore had a number of therapists — I ask, "With all the counselors you have seen, do you feel that any of them have truly understood what your experiences have been like?" Every now and then, the client will identify one provider they say did understand. More often than not, though, the children tell me that no one 'gets it.' Certainly, this increases the isolation they feel, which in turn makes them feel more dehumanized.

I encourage parents to talk with their child about what it is or was like to be in foster care. Ask him to share his happy and unhappy memories. Encourage him to talk with you about the foster parents he had, other kids with whom he lived, teachers, pets, and the places he lived. Find out who he felt close to and how it was for him to leave these people. Remind him of your interest in knowing what it was like for him before he came to your home. This demonstrates a genuine interest for the life your child has experienced and can lessen the isolation he may feel.

Explaining Household Rules to Children

C ERTAINLY, YOU WILL WANT TO MAKE a good impression on the child you bring into your home. Parents don't want to be seen by their child as mean, and they want him to feel comfortable. Particularly for children coming into a home from an abusive or neglectful situation, new parents tend to go easy on the child, not wanting to add to the stress and trauma he has already experienced.

Yet, household rules should be made clear to children early on in the placement. Parents should identify the top four or five rules they want their child to know about and follow. These rules should be the ones that parents are willing to enforce at all times, without exception. The rules should be presented to the child shortly after he arrives in their home. Posting these rules on the refrigerator, on a bulletin board, or in the child's room may prove helpful. Examples might include:

- You must wash your hands and face before dinner.
- Your school clothes need to be ready the night before.
- You cannot watch TV during the week.
- You are responsible for keeping your bathroom clean.
- You must make your bed before you leave for school.
- You should be in your bed no later than 8 p.m. on school nights.
- You are not allowed to answer the phone.
- You must feed the cat before you have breakfast.
- You cannot go outside without asking.
- You can only play with electronic games for 15 minutes a day.

Over time, additional rules can be clarified and enforced for the child, but avoid over-loading the child with too many rules at once. Also, do not assume that a child knows to obey basic rules, such as "brush your teeth before bed," "don't talk to strangers in public," or "don't slam doors." You may need to check to make sure they understand what you are asking and can complete the process without your help or supervision.

Starting off with firm and strict rules is typically better than with loose and unstructured ones. It is easier to loosen rules that are too strict than it is to tighten rules that are too loose. Enforcing rules also immediately sets the tone in the household that the parents are ultimately in control. If the child is not defiant or oppositional, rules can be modified. But if the child is defiant, parents will be glad they took control early on. In fact, I counsel parents to tell their children upon arrival, "If you don't know if it is okay to do something, ask first."

Parents shouldn't try to identify all the rules and expectations as soon as the child arrives. In some instances, you won't even think to tell the child of a rule until a particular event happens. For example, you may have the expectation that children not play on one side of the house because of your vegetable garden. One day, you look outside and guess what? They're playing in the tomato bed. When this occurs, gently remind him how you want things done in the future, taking care not to make him feel bad for doing something he didn't know he should not have done.

Rules help children feel safe. They also communicate that boundaries are important at home, in school, and in society. A child may not like a certain rule, and older children may claim that a particular rule didn't apply in their previous placement. Yet, parents establish authority by clearly identifying rules to children while removing some of the ambiguity commonly felt by foster and adoptive children. Early discussions of rules can also help avert power struggles between the child and parent, in that the parent can say, "Remember, we discussed this issue right after you arrived here."

Couples and family members who have lived together for a while don't always have to think about what is or is not permissible in the home. But a child entering this family does not know these rules. Often a foster or adopted child acts or behaves in a way that is surprising or stunning to the new parent. For example, the child may eat with their hands instead of a fork, use the bathroom with the door open, or hit the family pet when angry. If the parent responds in an alarming or dramatic manner, the child may feel ashamed, believing something is wrong with him instead of his behavior. If rules are made clear early on, these kinds of difficult situations can be avoided.

If there are other children in the home, they may not need as much structure and limitation as the new child does. Thus, the rules they must follow may not be as strict, making the new child feel that your rules are unfair. In these instances, remind him that the other children have rules of their own to follow. Also, tell him that the other children already demonstrated through their behavior that they do not need strict rules. You can say, "When you show me that you are able to go outside without leaving the yard, I'll no longer require you to ask me first. But we'll need to practice this a few times."

> ### *You win psychological tug-of-war not by pulling harder, but by dropping the rope.*

You should decide in advance the consequences for breaking a rule. This way, if the child violates a rule you have set, you won't have to decide on a moment's notice what the sanction will be. Preferably, tell your child in advance what a likely consequence will be for disobeying a rule. For example, you can say, "If I see that you leave the yard without asking me, then I will change the rule to where you can't leave the house without asking me." Then, if the child leaves the yard, immediately implement the new rule. Consequences are most effective when they are given immediately after a violation, without a lecture or judgment.

Ultimately, the consequences you give should be meaningful to the child. The consequence should make him behave differently or lead to other choices in the future. Unfortunately, some children seem immune to the consequences they are given. A parent can take away TV time, make him stay in the house all weekend, cut his allowance, or make him scrub the toilet and some children don't seem bothered by it. In turn, this can leave the parent wondering if the child is learning anything by receiving the consequence.

You can't force the consequence to have a significant impact on the child. Nor can you ensure that the child will not break the rule in the future. Still, it is important to deliver consequences consistently after each violation. Use your own life as an example. If you get a ticket for speeding but are not bothered by it, it doesn't matter. You still have to pay the ticket and if you get caught speeding again, you will receive another one. Maybe you don't care about getting tickets and having increases in your automobile insurance premium. But, you know these consequences will be applied if you don't stop speeding. Since one of our primary jobs is to prepare children for the real world, we must help them learn that society is often very swift and effective at implementing consequences for misbehavior.

RULES FOR MAKING RULES

- Identify the major rules of the house early on.
- Maintain eye contact with your child when identifying the rules.
- Get at eye-level with small children.
- Remind your child to ask you before he does something he is not sure is okay.
- Ask your child what he thinks should be included on the rules list.
- Let your child know that you have rules to follow also.
- Periodically remind your child of the household rules.
- Post some of the rules on a bulletin board or refrigerator.
- Explain your reasons for each rule, emphasizing that the rule is in place to keep them or others safe or to maintain order in the home.
- Let your child know that some rules will be modified over time. Tell him that new ones will be added as needed.
- If your child breaks a rule, ask him to tell you what rule was broken before you re-state it for him.
- Remind your child that there are certain rules just for him. Others in the household may not be required to follow those rules.

Your foster children should be aware of planned consequences. Don't hesitate to post established consequences, both positive and negative, on your refrigerator door or in your foster children's rooms. Consequences shouldn't be surprises. In fairness to your foster children, they should be aware of what they will get for behaving well and what they will lose for misbehavior.

— Christena Baker, et. al.,
"Rebuilding Children's Lives"

A child needs to know where she begins, what she needs to take responsibility for, and what she does not need to take responsibility for. If she knows that the world requires her to take responsibility for her own personhood and life, then she can learn to live up to those requirements and get along well in life.

— Henry Cloud and John Townsend,
"Boundaries with Kids"

Contracting with Your Child for Good Behavior

WHEN PROVIDING THERAPY to a child, I will ask that he agree to a verbal contract. The contract states simply:

1) The child believes there are parts of his life he is unhappy with or that need to be improved.
2) He is willing to work hard in therapy.
3) He is willing to work toward changing behaviors that cause him or his family stress or confusion.

In turn, I agree that I will take him seriously, that I will not hurt him, and that I will not give up on him. In essence, I communicate to the child that ours will be a collaborative effort geared toward helping him have a more rewarding and satisfying life or family experience.

Contracts in therapy ensure that the child is consenting to working on their issues. Contracts can also serve as a motivator for the child. I will remind him about our agreement periodically during therapy. This reinforces his hard work while reminding him that we are working toward a mutual goal. Children view our contract as an acknowledgement that we have a relationship with one another, one based on joint effort. Particularly during challenging times in therapy, the contract reminds the child that we have both committed to do what is needed to achieve the goal of helping him have a better life.

Contracting with a child also helps reduce feelings of shame they often experience when they are brought to therapy. In establishing the contract, I tell the child: "I will work hard and your parents will work hard. We will be here with you throughout, because we want to see you make it. But who else needs to work hard?" This communicates to the child that he and I are part of a team that is working together to make his life better. I tell the child, "We will all work together toward healing your heart. But we can't do it for you and I'm not willing to work harder than you. You have to be an active partic-ipant. Are you willing?" Even with highly resistant or oppositional children, I find that most are willing to agree to the verbal contract. I may have to make frequent reminders about our agreement as the therapy goes on, but getting to that initial point of cooperation is actually easier than one might think.

Parents may find contracting useful as well. A contract takes the emphasis away from the child seeing the parents as demanding, bossy, and mean. Instead, parental requests can be reframed as, "We want the mood in this house to feel a certain way. We want to strive to have our home be a happy and loving place. To this end, there is work we all must do. As parents, we will promise not to nag you to brush your teeth before bed. You agree to brush your teeth the first time you are asked" or "I promise not to raise my voice with you when I get angry or frustrated. You agree to ask me before

---

A JUDGE'S HOME DISCIPLINE

Feuding couples that appear before Chandlee Johnson Kuhn, chief judge of Delaware's Family Court, may be able to plead ignorance. But her daughters cannot. A binder of carefully written rules at their house includes prohibitions on everything from running indoors to lighting candles without a parent. When a child breaks a rule, Judge Kuhn lets her present her case and makes sure both sides agree on the facts. If it's a first offense, she offers leniency; but after that, she holds firm. As punishment, she might take away a playdate, or multiple playdates for more serious violations. When her daughters, 9 and 12, are battling each other, she prods them to talk through their disagreements; if they cannot, they get disciplined for a "fighting infraction."

— Wall Street Journal, June 24, 2004

---

you play with the dog." Parents can then ask the child if he agrees to commit to the contract.

When these agreements are established within the family, parents can remind the child about the ways that he is and he is not following the contract. Contracts therefore make it easier for parents to find positive things about the child's behavior that they can acknowledge. If parents need to remind the child about the ways he is not following the terms of their agreement, the child is less likely to interpret this as meaning that he is bad. Instead, the focus is on the agreements he made but has not kept.

Recently, I consulted with a couple in the process of adopting a 15-year-old girl. The girl was removed from her birth home two years earlier. When I met with the girl and her adoptive parents, she told her new parents and I that she had no intention of loving them and planned to move out after she turned 18. Nonetheless, the parents were firm in their commitment and agreed to go ahead with the adoption. I framed the work I did with this family around establishing contracts. This approach modeled for the girl that she was not expected to love her parents or explore whatever feelings she had pertaining to her life. But, it was pointed out to her that she would have to follow firm rules and expectations in the home. She was reminded that she would be given opportunities for greater independence if she complied with household rules and consequences if she did not cooperate. This approach ended up working well for the family. The parents lessened the expectations they had that the child would interact with them in loving and intimate ways, and she felt less pressure to be someone she didn't want to be. Still, they agreed to work in a collaborative manner toward the goal of having this be a safe placement for her, where the majority of the expectations were made clear.

In making contracts with children, I encourage parents to be serious, yet playful. Parents should clearly spell out their agreements to the child. This might include:

- I will make sure you have breakfast and dinner each day.
- I will make sure you have pencils and paper for doing your homework.
- I will make sure you have clean clothes for school.
- I will make sure to tuck you into bed each night.

The child is asked to agree to:

- Do what is asked the first time I am told.
- Finish my homework before watching TV.
- Not leave the table until I am excused.
- Put my toys away before going to bed.
- Not use the phone after 8 p.m.
- Use a napkin when eating.
- Hang the towel up after bathing.

Learned Helplessness in Children

IN THE EARLY DAYS OF PSYCHOLOGICAL research, rats were placed in boxes from which they could not escape. The rats would run around the box, climbing walls and desperately looking for a way out. Eventually, the rats gave up. They sat in the corner, stopped eating and drinking, and soon died. The researchers then altered the experiment. They repeated the procedures, but before the rats died, they removed one of the walls, thereby permitting an avenue of escape for the rats. What they found, though, was that the rats did not move toward the exit. Instead, once they had given up and were in the corner, it seemed they had decided that nothing they could do would help them escape. Their experiences had taught them they were helpless to change their circumstances. The condition was termed "learned helplessness."

While learned helplessness is not a diagnosis, the symptoms of the condition are common for many children who have experienced abuse or neglect. It also manifests in children who experience a great deal of frustration and betrayal, as in situations where they have to frequently change homes, don't get to see their siblings regularly, or where prospects for adoption keep falling through.

When these children arrive for mental health treatment, they appear depressed and withdrawn. Many are prescribed antidepressant medications to help counter their sadness and despair. Unfortunately, the medication is not always helpful. Talk therapy proves somewhat limiting as these children often have little interest or motivation for talking about their past and exploring ways to move beyond their grief and loss issues. Quite often, these cases are discouraging for therapists and parents, as it seems that nothing they do motivates the child.

Our challenge in these instances is to do what we can to instill hopefulness and confidence in the child. Since the root of learned helplessness is not feeling in control, anything we can do to help the child feel he has mastery over his life will be helpful. Parents should provide the child with opportunities for success and achievement such as sports, dance, karate, or with their schoolwork. At the same time, we must communicate to the child an understanding and appreciation of the level of despair they feel. This can be difficult, especially when we want to believe we can provide the child with solutions for their troubles, but their sadness seems insurmountable.

A child in this state constantly struggles with whether to simply give up. This self-doubt can result in social withdrawal, sudden academic failure, acting out, substance use, sexual activity, or in the worse case, attempts at suicide. These feelings are also at the root of conditions such as eating disorders.

It is common for these children to feel we or others have given up on them. Some of this can be detoured when we communicate our faith in their ability to pull through a challenging time. With work and patience, many of these children can identify the despair they feel. A 14-year-old boy with whom I worked once said, "I just feel defeated, and I feel like giving up." In therapy, I will sometimes show children video excerpts from interviews with famous athletes or others who also faced the temptation to give up at one point in their lives, but who persevered and made good things happen for themselves.

When providing therapy for these children, I will sometimes educate them about the concept of learned helplessness. Clearly, this is easier to do with an older child or teenager than with a youngster. One of my primary goals is to get the child to focus on the word, *learned*. Cognitive psychology has been instrumental in demonstrating what has been learned can be unlearned and that acquired behavior can be given up. Viewed from this perspective, learned helplessness is acquired, based on a history of maladaptive and troubling experiences. It can be modified when we provide the child with alternative experiences, as well as the means for thinking about his past and present life.

Children and Pets in the Home

CHILDREN REACT DIFFERENTLY TO SEEING pets or animals in their new home largely based on their previous experiences with animals. If you have animals in your home, learn about the child's previous experiences with them. Parents should set firm limits about what kind of contact the child can have with the animals in the home, at least initially. Parents should tell the child not to approach or touch the animals without their permission or supervision. This rule benefits both the safety of the child and the animal. Over time, if the child demonstrates the ability to interact with the animal in a safe and nurturing manner, the restrictions can be loosened.

Children who have been neglected or abused frequently hurt or bother animals. Often the child feels helpless to do anything to stop the hurt they are experiencing and so they play it out with beings younger or weaker than they. Hurting animals also gives children a sense of control over something more vulnerable than they as well as a means for expressing their anger and rage. Many children grew up in homes where animals were abused, tortured, or killed. Sadly, some children have had to witness sexual activity between humans and animals.

The extent to which a child can hurt or torment an animal should never be underestimated. While some kids will provoke the animal, by pulling its tail or poking it in the face, others resort to more extreme forms of cruelty. Some children will even kill the animal with little remorse.

Many pet owners treat their animals like a human member of the family with the animal receiving lots of love, attention, and affection. A child who was abused or neglected can find this confusing. They may even resent the love and attention given to the animal. By hurting the animal, the child believes he is eliminating his competition. He may also recognize that hurting the animal is a way of getting back at you when he is angry.

Pets provide children with great opportunities for learning about unconditional love and responsibility. We must still make sure the child has the ability and maturity to interact with the animal in safe and appropriate ways. In some instances, we may need to show the child how to hold, stroke, and approach the animals. Many children make great strides in their emotional health when given an animal to take care of. Having a pet reinforces for the child that he is needed and depended on, a wonderful feeling for many kids.

Often, I will bring my small dog to the office with me. I will hold him and show the children how he likes to be petted. Children who are otherwise shy or oppositional will sometimes open up more, telling me about animals they have known in their lives. A variety of therapeutic horsing programs are designed to teach children responsibility, caregiving, nurturing, and empathy. In the process of working with the animal, the child develops feelings of competence and mastery, which in turn helps him to feel better about himself.

Helping the Night Feel Safe for Children

NIGHTTIME CAN BE SCARY for children. Some children have vague fears, such as monsters, which really have no basis in reality. For them, a few reassurances from a parent at night can help diminish these fears. Others may need the parents to do a closet check, add a nightlight, or to keep the door open. Children who have experienced trauma in their lives have greater difficulty at night than most children do. The dark and quiet of night intensifies the fears they have. Some fear that someone will break into the house and hurt them or their family. One adopted boy with whom I work stacked pillows in front of his window. It took him over a year before he was able to tell his adoptive mother and me that he feared his birthmother would break in and kidnap him.

A NOTE REGARDING BATHROOMS

A good number of children who were sexually abused had this occur in bathrooms. For example, the abuser may have perpetrated on the child while he was bathing. Because of this, many children develop fears of bathrooms. Particularly with very young children, they may urinate or defecate in rooms other than the bathroom, as a result of their fears. Others will refuse to let the bathroom door be open when they are inside, while some will refuse to let the door be closed. I've seen many cases where the child insists a parent stay in the bathroom with him, as it is the only way he feels safe in there. While you do not need to ask your child if bad things happened in the bathroom, be prepared for the possibility that he may have scary feelings regarding that room. If this occurs, take steps to help the child feel more comfortable about the bathroom. This can include making sure he has a few favorite toys or items in the room; assuring him that the lock is secure; putting an intercom in there, if necessary; adding brighter lights; covering the window; and placing a battery-operated recorder for him to play comforting music.

Many children report that bad memories come to them at night partly because of the lowered interference from noises and activities. Some children have nightmares or night terrors about real or imaginary things. These children toss and turn through much of the night, even if they don't wake up. Some will sweat, urinate in the bed, or even wake up on the floor. More so than older children, young kids will sometimes wander into their parent's bedroom. You should have a policy and strategy for dealing with this before it occurs. Otherwise, the comments you make or the behaviors you show in response may come across as rejecting or confusing for the child. In other instances, the child may start coming to your room every night and refuse to sleep alone.

For many children, the trauma they experienced occurred when they were in bed. This might have included sexual abuse, listening to their parents fight, or hearing loud parties. Rather than having the bed feel like a safe place, some children retreated to their rooms to escape the chaos happening elsewhere in the family. Others were sent to their rooms while the parents used drugs, had sex, or were away from the home.

When I interview children, many tell me they have difficulty sleeping. Yet, when I ask the foster or adoptive parents how well the child is sleeping, they say 'fine.' I have thus learned that children do not always tell their parents when they are having trouble sleeping. Similarly, there may not be any clues to suggest that the child is not sleeping well at night.

Rituals before bed can be a good way to help children feel safer and more secure at night. This can include:

- Spend a few moments with the child talking about your days.
- Read to your child before he falls asleep.
- Use visualization; tell your child a story of him traveling to an exciting place, through space, or to some fantasy place.
- Put a tape or CD player by his bed that plays soft music or children's tunes.
- Put glow-in-the-dark shapes on the ceiling above his bed.
- Put a dream catcher above the bed.
- Place a flashlight by the side of his bed.
- Use one or more nightlights.
- Position the bed away from the window.
- Have your child decide how to decorate the room; this will help it to feel more like a protected space.
- Offer to do a middle-of-the-night check on him, letting him know you'll leave proof, such as a note or special toy.
- If you have an alarm system in the house, let the child set it at night.

Two Main Principles

Not everyone needs to know your child is adopted.
There is no right time to tell a child he is adopted.

Talking with Children About Adoption

SOME ADOPTIVE PARENTS DON'T want other people to know their child is adopted. One adoptive father said to me, "People say she looks like me. So why should I tell people she's adopted?" Telling other people that a child is adopted is a personal decision. If the child is of the same nationality or skin color as you, it is easier. But, if the child looks different people will sometimes stare and some will ask intrusive questions. Parents should practice responses to these questions. No one has a right to inquire into aspects of your private life, and at times you may need to say, "Excuse me, I don't have time to talk right now," "I really do not want to discuss this," "That's not something you need to concern yourself with," "You can ask my child that question when she is older," or "It's really much too complicated to get into right now."

Many adopted and foster children feel betrayed when others know about their status. To them, they feel this is a private matter. Many get angry when

---

WHO NEEDS TO KNOW YOUR CHILD IS ADOPTED?

- Physicians
- Teachers
- Counselors
- Close family members
- Family friends

their parents or others volunteer to people that they are adopted or in foster care. Parents should remind their child that they will respect their wishes, except in instances where the other person needs to be informed.

Parents frequently ask when they should tell their child that he is adopted. In general, telling a child he is adopted is more of a process than an event. Talking to a child about adoption starts when he is quite young, often continuing until he is a teenager or adult. For young children, reading story books about adoption can prove helpful. You can also show them maps or photographs of the place they were born. Researchers tell us that children have favorable views about adoption prior to age seven or eight. After that age, as they develop the ability to grasp complex concepts, they may feel more ambivalent about it.

Adoption Talks with Children

Decide what you will share. Before talking with your child about his adoption, sit down with your partner or a friend and decide what information you believe should and should not be shared. This way, if your child asks an uncomfortable question, you will have prepared the kind of responses you want to give.

Set the right tone. If you are relaxed and comfortable in talking with your child about his adoption, he will feel more at ease.

Don't say it all at once. Young children cannot grasp all the concepts and details associated with adoption. To a three-year-old, you might say, "We went to China and brought you to our home. They sent us pictures of you before we ever met you." When the child is four, you can add more details such as, "Your mommy was too ill to take care of you. So they started looking for a family for you. We wanted a child at that time and that is when we found out about you." As the child grows older, they can grasp the more-complicated reasons they were placed for adoption.

CHILDREN'S BOOKS ON ADOPTION

- "Tell Me Again About the Night I Was Born" by Jamie Lee Curtis
- "The Day We Met You" by Phoebe Koehler
- "Oliver: A Story About Adoption" By Lois Wickstrom
- "Lucy's Feet" By Stephanie Stein
- "Brian was Adopted" by Doris Sanford

Welcome your child's questions. If you show a genuine interest in the questions your child raises, he will come to know that you are willing to be open and honest with him. It will also help him feel it is safe to ask questions in the future.

You have time. However you choose to talk to your young child about adoption, know that you will have other opportunities for discussing this topic. As your child grows older, he will ask more questions. By late childhood, your child will be able to grasp concepts they really didn't understand when they were younger. As long as you convey that the topic of adoption is always open for discussion, your child will believe it is all right to ask questions as they feel the need to.

Many children who enter the foster care system or who are placed for adoption do so because of the irresponsible behavior of one or both parents. Parental rights are often terminated because of substance abuse, physical abuse, prostitution, sexual abuse, neglect, or criminal behavior.

Adoptive parents in particular sometimes struggle with how much of the truth should be shared about the child's history. Parents will ask me, "Do I tell her she was sexually abused as an infant?" "Do I tell him his mother left him in a trash can?" "Should my child be told that his father is alive, but in prison for murder?" "Do I tell him that his mother was raped?" "Do I tell her that her mother fought for her in court, but lost?" or "Does my child need to know how horrible the conditions were in her country of origin?"

Unfortunately, there is no correct answer to any of the above. But, children should be provided with some of the truth about their background. This information should be told to them at a level that is appropriate for their age. It doesn't make sense, for example, to tell a young child he was sexually abused. This information may hold more importance, however, in his preadolescent years when he is dealing with issues of sexuality. Ultimately, parents must ask themselves whether revealing certain information stands to make the child's life better or cause unnecessary distress.

Sherrie Eldridge, author of "Twenty Things Adopted Kids Wish Their Parents Knew," writes: "Your child, at the appropriate age, can actually benefit from hearing painful information about his past because he will know that you are telling him the honest, gut-level truth. Kids are geniuses at detecting untruths. This giving of information doesn't have so much to do with the truth about his past as it does with his relationship with you and himself. He is learning to trust you at a deeper level and he is also developing self-esteem. He is possibly having some of the ugliest and most painful information about his past revealed by you, yet at the same time you are demonstrating that you love him just as he is."

Reviewing the Records

Prior to an adoptive placement, parents may receive an extensive collection of documents pertaining to their child's history. This may include psychological evaluations, social service narratives, school records, legal records, and medical records. Parents often find the information contained in these reports overwhelming, and at times, contradictory. I had a case in which a boy had been in foster care in three different states. This meant that the adoptive parents were only provided with a portion of the available records. It took months of investigation to gather records and to put the pieces together. When they finally collected what they could, his adoptive mother told me that it was almost as if the data pertained to two or three different children since much of it contained contrasting information about the child.

Parents should ensure that their child does not find these documents. The papers should always be kept in a secure place, such as a locked drawer or safety deposit box. In addition, your beneficiaries need to know what you want done with this material in the event of your death.

There are times when it can be helpful and therapeutic for a child to learn what is contained in the placement file. I frequently review the contents of the placement file with the child in therapy, using it as a means of educating him, while learning about the thoughts he carries about his story. Often, the child will clarify details in the records, such as the extent of the abuse he experienced, whether he saw a parent using drugs, or to whom he turned to for comfort. I find it is a powerful therapeutic tool, but one that must be used in a sensitive manner and at a time when the child can withstand the emotions that will inevitably arise. In reviewing these records with children in therapy, I typically find that they are excited and motivated about the process. In a lot of ways, I'm basically doing detective work, as the child has a history that pre-dates coming to his new family or to my office. Even if the child has no conscious memories of his past, my experience finds that they appreciate having the chance to be part of the exploration.

Consider some precautions regardless of whether the child is informed about the contents of his placement file in therapy or at home. First, don't let the child read the reports at random. Instead, pick which documents should be reviewed first and which should be postponed or kept from the child altogether. Parents should also anticipate that their child will ask questions for which they'll have no answers and that they may not fully understand some diagnostic terms. Children often react with anger when they read these reports, so don't let the child read everything all at once. Finally, always explore the child's thoughts and feelings about what they are reading.

Do I Tell My Child the Full Truth about His Past?

Even though there are no right answers to this question, I do believe there are some basic guidelines to follow:

What is your intent? Before disclosing information about your child's history, or that of his biological parents, ask yourself what your intention is. Is the goal to inform the child's understanding of his background, to sour his opinion of his biological family, to make him like you more? In short, in what ways might the information you have help or hurt your child's experience of being adopted or in foster care?

Will he find out anyway? If someone other than you is likely to reveal information about his history, then consider telling the story yourself. If a child finds out about their biological family or previous history from a social worker, extended family member, written report, or through some other means, he may come to doubt your truthfulness and sincerity.

Use it to educate. Even though we may not feel comfortable telling a child some of the brutal or ugly facts of their past, we may have little choice. Details should be revealed in a manner that educates him about responsibility, choices, and consequences. Don't try to paint the child's biological family in a negative light, but we can point out how his mother or father made choices that had consequences for their child. For example, the child can be told, "Your mother stayed addicted to drugs. Instead of choosing to get the help she needed, she kept using. She then couldn't care for a baby. This is why we always talk to you about consequences of your actions. Your mother wasn't a bad person, but she made poor choices. We try to make good choices for ourselves, and we want you to make good choices in your life. When we make bad choices, other people sometimes end up getting hurt."

Be sincere. Don't feel you have to hide your feelings about your child's past. If your child was hurt in some way, it is all right to let him know some of how you feel. Your child will be looking to you for guidance on how to react. As long as it is genuine, I am fine with a parent saying, "Your mother permitted her boyfriend to do things to you that I believe are really sick. We don't need to go into all the details, but I think you were hurt in some pretty disgusting ways. It makes me really angry, because I don't believe anyone should ever hurt a child. It makes me sad, thinking of how scared you must have felt. Trust that I will never let anyone hurt you."

RESOURCES

FURTHER READING

Talking with Children About Adoption (book)
Mary Watkins and Susan Fisher

ON THE WEB

Talking to Your Child About Adoption (article)
www.adopting.org/talk.html

Ask about the classroom environment. This includes such details as how many children are in the class, the mix of boys and girls, the predominant personality types, and what special needs exist in this group of children. Ask also about her teaching styles: Do children work alone or in groups? How much time must they spend sitting and listening? Do they do lots of paperwork? What kinds of hands-on learning experiences do they have? Then ask about how your child is functioning in this environment.

— W. Sears & L. Thompson,
"The ADD Book"

You and Your Child's Education

CLOSE CONTACT BETWEEN PARENTS and teachers is recommended even under the best of circumstances. But let's face it, many parents know little about their child's school environment, and most don't go to the school on a regular basis unless invited by the teacher or principal. When you have a foster or adopted child, frequent contact with the teacher, principal, and other school staff (e.g., yard officers, nurse, aides, or counselors) is important.

I believe that teachers should know if one of their students is adopted or living in foster care. He or she can then observe the child, paying close attention to issues such as social skills, adherence to rules and boundaries, and teasing. Since it is common for foster and adopted children to find themselves in a new school environment in the middle of the term, they may or may not want to explain to the other students their circumstances. This includes the teacher. Others may look or speak differently than the rest of the student body, becoming vulnerable to provocation or teasing. With children who have had to change schools often, they may approach social relations with reserve, having learned not to get too close to people, lest they move again. Frequently, foster kids tell me they are teased for residing in foster care, but rarely do they tell the adults about this. You should therefore consider asking your child if he is being teased. If so, report this to the teacher and insist on knowing what steps the school will take to deal with this.

I know that some foster care agencies limit what parents can tell teachers about the children in their care. While you should respect this, there are times when the rules need to be modified. Certainly, you will want to discuss this with the care coordinator before you disclose details about the child's life. As an example, a treatment foster parent recently told me she has a nine-year-old girl in her care with a long history of making false allegations of sexual abuse by parents and other adults in her life. Because of her indiscriminate attachment, the child seeks out the attention of adult males. This school year, her teacher is a man. Sure enough, the girl's seat is right next to the teacher and she takes advantage of opportunities to be close to or to touch him. Even though the teacher needs to exercise his own boundaries in his classroom, it could be helpful for him to know some of the allegations this girl has made against others. The rules of the placement agency, however, prohibit this parent from providing the teacher with these details about the girl's past.

Some children, because of cultural differences or because of their abusive and neglectful backgrounds, never learned basic school or social skills. They therefore find themselves feeling and behaving in a manner that sets them apart from the other students. For children who have significantly delayed social skills, parents and teachers may need to discuss whether more emphasis should be placed on the child's interpersonal relations over academics. Viewed from this perspective, the child is supported and encouraged to interact with other kids through sports, music, or clubs, while academic progress is not overly emphasized. The idea behind this approach is that some kids can catch up on academic delays, but may not be as able when it comes to peer relations. Realistically, some children cannot make it in a regular school setting, at least until their behavior settles down, given that they never learned how to function in such an environment. Home schooling or placement in a small, private school may then be recommended.

No child wants to feel different from kids their age. Yet, foster and adopted children are sometimes different from their peers in noteworthy ways. While it should be the child's choice to disclose their foster or adopted status to their schoolmates, parents and teachers should pay attention to the ways foster or adopted children stand out in the school setting. This may include:

- Being of a different race or culture than the other children
- Being older than the other students due to being held back a grade
- Having to leave class to take medication
- Having to leave class to see the school counselor
- Receiving full-time or adjunct special education services
- Conflict with authority, especially with female teachers
- Having attention difficulties in class
- Having to leave school to attend foster-care related duties, such as counseling, evaluations, treatment team meetings, or visits with parents

By discussing your child's foster or adopted status with teachers, you can also help sensitize them to some of the issues this population of children may have to deal with. As an example, a foster parent reported to me that the nine-year-old boy she was caring for started crying when doing his homework one night. When she asked him what was wrong, he couldn't really say. She then looked at his homework assignment, where the class assignment was to ask the parents how they came up with the child's name. Because this boy had no contact with his birth mother, he couldn't complete the assignment. The foster parent discussed the issue with the teacher, who agreed that it may not be a good idea to keep this activity in the curriculum.

Medication Issues in the School

Given the prevalence of psychiatric disorders in foster and adoptive populations, there is a good chance that your child could be prescribed medication for attention, activity, or behavior problems. While some medications can be given once in the morning, others may be needed at lunch or before the child leaves from school. Find out your school's policy regarding administering medication to children. Most schools will cooperate with you, but they may require you to fill out specific forms or request a written order from the child's psychiatrist.

While some parents prefer that teachers or others not know their child is taking medication, my opinion is that teachers should have this information. Since children are in school for such a significant part of their days, teachers are an excellent source of information regarding the child's mood and behavior. The teacher can let you know if the child appears ill, is having a difficult time focusing his attention, or is too hyperactive. As I write about later in this book, parents should provide their child's psychiatrist with a symptom log. The psychiatrist will often use the log to judge how well a medication is working. It is useful if the child's teacher could also maintain a symptom log, especially during the first few weeks that the child is taking a new medication. The psychiatrist will then have data from the home and school.

I find that teachers are more receptive to observing the child and reporting about his behavior when they are told why he is on medication and what symptoms the medication is supposed to treat. This doesn't mean you have to provide the teacher with a crash course on child psychiatry. Instead, try saying something such as, "Tommy has a hard time focusing in class, especially in the late afternoon. When this happens, he usually becomes disruptive to the other students. His psychiatrist believes that this pill, taken with his lunch, should solve some of this. It will be helpful if you can let me know if you observe Tommy being too inattentive or disruptive after lunch."

Determining Your Child's Education Needs

As a foster or adoptive parent, you play a key role in helping to determine your child's academic strengths and weaknesses, as well as his educational needs. It is common for children in the child welfare system to attend different schools, given that they may live in more than one home over the course of their placement. The stress and adjustment responses associated with changing schools and homes can greatly impair a child's learning. Even if you are told that your child is performing at the 6th grade level, I encourage you to find out if this is really true. You can gauge your child's ability as you help him with his homework, have him read to you, and listen to what he says about his feelings about school. A good number of children I evaluate are significantly delayed in their learning, yet this has gone undetected for quite some time. Unfortunately, because so much attention has been directed to safety and placement issues, awareness of their academic strengths and weaknesses often falls by the wayside.

By federal law, public schools have the obligation to determine whether children are performing at grade level. For a variety of reasons, many children who need special help or services are not identified in a timely manner. Particularly in smaller communities, teachers may be reluctant to recommend special evaluations or services for children, given how few resources there are. Once it becomes clear to a teacher or school psychologist that a student may require assessment for special services, it can sometimes take months before the child is evaluated.

As a parent, you have the right to ask the schools to evaluate your child's grade level performance. But, don't expect your request to be acted on at once. More likely, you will need to remind the school of your request and stay on top of their progress. I would say that more often than not, the parents with whom I work have to assume a proactive role in getting their child evaluated.

You also have the right to seek an independent evaluation of your own. Obtaining an evaluation for the child on your own may be the best option, particularly for children who attend large schools or who live in districts where special education services are limited. You will likely have to pay for this service, unless you can convince the child's insurance carrier or placement agency to cover the costs. A psychologist or educational specialist can conduct the evaluation. If you obtain an independent evaluation of your child, request a written report that summarizes the tests administered, lists the specific scores, and offers detailed recommendations. The school is not obligated to abide by the recommendations put forth by an outside evaluator. Yet, many districts will take your requests more seriously if you can prove to them that an outside evaluation substantiates that your child has learning problems or requires extra attention or services in class. Other tips to consider:

- Get everything in writing. If you request an evaluation for your child and the school says "yes" or "no," make sure you have written proof.

- After all calls and meetings, write a summary letter and send it to each person. Offer them the opportunity to correct anything included in the letter.

- Before a child can receive special education services for a learning disability, classroom interventions must have been attempted. It is important for you to be aware what interventions are being used with your child and how progress is monitored and assessed.

- If an Individualized Educational Plan (IEP) is developed for your child, you are entitled to due process if there are points of disagreement.

- Make sure the IEP is being followed. Schedule periodic teacher conferences to keep updated on your child's progress.

- Be involved in the decisions made about your child. If one-to-one tutoring is not offered as an option, but you think it could help, ask if it can be provided.

- When a child is placed in your home, find out if he had an IEP in his previous school. If so, make sure this document transferred with him.

Does a Child Have a Learning Disability Forever?

IDENTIFYING AND TRACKING A LEARNING disorder can be tricky. For some children, evidence of a learning disorder may not show up until the later grades, when the work becomes somewhat more challenging. For others, they may excel in certain areas, but fall behind in one subject, such as reading, writing, or arithmetic. At times, it is not always clear if the child has an actual learning disorder, or if there are broader intellectual deficits. This is why it is important for the child to receive a comprehensive educational assessment if there are any questions about his ability to learn. Early intervention is more productive at addressing the underlying problems than is waiting until the child's struggles become unbearable.

It is difficult to determine if a particular child will continue to have a learning disorder in adulthood. Although learning disabilities often have a biological basis, this does not mean that improvement is not possible. In addition to biological factors, other factors involved in the development of learning disabilities may include poor early language development, poor phonics instruction, poor mathematics instruction, and poor instruction in writing or spelling. Most learning disorders do persist as a child grows older, but that doesn't mean the child can't have a productive and happy life. Instead, he may need to make accommodations. When consulting with parents and teachers, I often recommend that they identify a child's strengths and place more emphasis in those areas than in trying so hard to bolster the weaker areas.

Whether a child's learning disorder will continue into adulthood depends upon a variety of factors, such as:

- The age with which the disability first appeared
- The type of learning disorder
- The child's response to interventions
- The child's self-confidence and level of motivation
- Teacher and family expectations
- The child's general cognitive abilities

The most effective interventions for children with learning disabilities are multifaceted. Typically, this includes the use of cognitive, linguistic, and cognitive-behavioral methods. While the use of these techniques does not guarantee that the learning disability won't continue to adulthood, they do help maximize opportunities for the child to learn how to cope with limitations he may have in areas of reading, writing, arithmetic, or language.

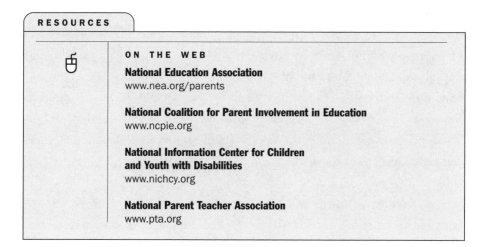

RESOURCES

ON THE WEB

National Education Association
www.nea.org/parents

National Coalition for Parent Involvement in Education
www.ncpie.org

National Information Center for Children and Youth with Disabilities
www.nichcy.org

National Parent Teacher Association
www.pta.org

Middle childhood is often the period when being adopted is first seen as a problem. This is when the youngster begins to reflect on the meaning of being adopted — which often leads to feelings of confusion, and to feeling odd or different. And this is when the child, because of his growing capacity for logical thought, begins to realize that there's a flip side to his beloved adoption story — that in order to be "chosen," he first had to be given away.

— David Brodzinsky,
"Being Adopted"

How Children View Adoption

D AVID BRODZINSKY HAS DONE A GREAT deal of research on the experience of adoption by children. Brodzinsky has been instrumental in pointing out that children understand and relate to being adopted in different ways, based on their age and cognitive development. Because children understand relationships differently as they age, a five-year-old may appear ambivalent about his adoption. When he turns eight, though, he may react quite differently. As Brodzinsky notes, young children view a family as the group of people who live together. By age eight, children understand the difference between a biological family and a non-biological family. Around age eight children also start to grasp the concept of being "given away."

A good number of foster and adopted children are referred for counseling between the ages 7 and 11. Typically, counseling is sometimes recommended at this age because the child is behaving in more anxious or defiant ways than he once did. Children at this age are often dealing with feelings of loss and grief that were not present at earlier stages of life. Also at this age, thoughts — and for some children, memories — of their birth family increase. Some children hold a fantasy that their birth parents will come find them, while others develop elaborate stories about the identity of their birth parents. Children who are particularly anxious will sometimes fear that someone will take them from their adoptive family. The confusing feelings that often develop in middle childhood can result in some foster or adopted children acting in defiant ways at home or in school.

When children reach middle school age, they are more focused on peer relationships. At this age, children do not want to be seen as different from other children. For a child who is in foster care or who is adopted, they may fear that other children will tease them because of their status. A child who at one point was quite open about being adopted may suddenly be afraid that others will find out about this information. As a parent, this can take you aback as the child gets angry when you talk to others about his adopted status.

In the book, "The Psychology of Adoption," Brodzinsky writes:

> *Adopted children also experience 'status loss' associated with being different. These various losses often leave the adoptee feeling incomplete, alienated, disconnected, abandoned, or unwanted. Furthermore, the sense of loss typically leads to a characteristic pattern of emotional and behavioral reactions commonly associated with grieving ... What has been called pathogenic in the adopted child's behavior is nothing more than the unrecognized manifestation of an adaptive grieving process.*

In my experience, parents are not necessarily insensitive to these issues. What becomes difficult, though, is that many children do not perceive that the parents are taking the matter as seriously as they are. Identity and loss are so paramount for the child, that it influences most aspects of his behavior, identity, and adjustment to being in the family. Children do not always have the words or ability to effectively communicate how these issues and themes affect their inner world. It thus becomes our challenge to approach the topic in a manner that feels supportive and non-judgmental to the child.

If you suspect your child's attitudes or behaviors may be influenced by their feelings about being adopted or in foster care, try asking the following questions:

- Sometimes children get angry because they were adopted or are in foster care. Do you think some of your anger could be because of this?
- Foster or adopted children can feel different from other kids. Sometimes, kids tease them because of it. Are kids giving you a hard time because you are in foster care or adopted?
- How many of your friends know you are adopted or in foster care? Is this something you have been trying to keep secret? What are you worried will happen if they find out?
- You used to ask a lot of questions about your birth family, but you don't anymore. Is this because I answered all your questions, or do you just not want to talk about it? How often are you thinking about your birth family? Can you give me a few examples of what you're thinking?
- I get the impression that you think I haven't been up front with you about your adoption. Are there questions you have for me based on the kinds of things we've talked about already?
- I'll bet you're angry that the families you met before coming here didn't adopt you. I don't know why they didn't adopt you. But it may have something to do with them, not just you. Anyhow, I know you're upset and I still consider you my special boy.

Adolescent Perspective

Teenagers have their own unique struggles with being adopted or living in foster care. Particularly for those in foster care, they start to believe that no one will ever adopt them. Sometimes they'll ask to be returned to their birth family, saying that they are old enough to take care of or protect themselves. For teenagers who are adopted, they develop further questions about their identity. Adopted teenagers, for example, may ask themselves, "In what ways am I like my adopted parents, and in what ways am I like my birth parents?" I find that some of the adolescents with whom I work are scared to death of behaving as their birth parents did. I consistently hear comments such as, "I won't use drugs and make the choices she did;" "I won't ever put a man before the needs of my children;" or "I'm not sure I even know how to act different than my mom did."

Lois Melina, author of "Raising Adopted Children," writes, "If the task of the preschooler is to understand *how* adoption happens and the task of the child in middle school is to explore *why* it happened and what it says about her that she was adopted, the task of the adolescent is to determine how adoption has shaped her in specific ways." I would add that teenagers also struggle with whether or not the adults around them truly 'get' what it has been like to feel somewhat removed, different, or as an outsider within one or more families. Whether the root cause is the self-centered nature of adolescence or the teenager's more-sophisticated brain, I find that many foster and adopted adolescents – more so than younger children — look for validation of their emotional experience. Certainly, empathy is something most children crave. The need for it intensifies during the teenage years.

As an example, there was a 15-year-boy with whom I worked whose mother left him and his sister with a family friend when he was a very young child. She told them she would come back for them but never did. His life since then has been one of living in multiple foster homes, while always fearing and hoping he would get adopted. One day he told me that he wanted to hunt his birth mother down. He told me he was going to hold a knife to her throat and ask her why she left him. As we talked about the issue, I offered that he may not be so interested in his mother's explanation. Oh sure, I know the boy has several questions. But what I heard in his anger was him expressing the desire for his birth mother to know how difficult his life has been since she left them. Does he want some answers? Sure he does. In a more pronounced way, he longs for his mother to hold him, comfort him, and truly understand what a difficult life he has had since the day she left.

While school-age children may feel anger toward those who could not care for them, teenagers often feel a greater sense of betrayal. The teenage mind is more sophisticated than that of a child and the teen may know more information about their relinquishment than when they were younger. Unlike a younger child, a teenager may take a logical or rational perspective on their biological parents, asking questions such as, "If she couldn't take care of me, why didn't she give me to someone else in the family," or "I'll probably go back to them anyhow, so why not let me live there now?"

As teenagers start to address and explore issues of identity, they examine the ways their looks, attitudes, beliefs, and values are similar or different from those of their family members. This is probably most pronounced in cases of international adoption, where the child may want to return to the country of origin to see other people who look like him. I heard an interview recently with a 16-year-old Korean adoptee. She was preparing to make her first trip back to Korea, in order to meet her birth mother. During the interview, she stated that she had certainly seen other Asian people here in the United States. For her, though, it was important to go back to Korea to be with, as she said, her "own people."

Even though there is the stereotype that adolescence is a time of rebellion, research indicates that most adolescents share the values of their parents. At the same time, the adolescent must make sense out of new ways of thinking or behaving, using his peer group as a gauge. This is why psychologists place so much emphasis on parent-child communication during the teenage years. Clearly, adolescents need to be exposed to a variety of perspectives. That is what a good portion of the teenage years are all about. Yet, it appears that teenagers take much of what they see and learn about the outside world and compare it to the values and ideals on which they were raised.

Developmentally, adolescence is a time of separation and individuation. Children go through their first phase of individuation at around age two, when they start to detach from the close bond with the mother and venture into the broader world of family, friends, and daycare. Similarly, adolescence is a time of psychologically moving away from the family and developing more extensive interests in friendships and activities that may not include one's family.

If the teen experienced neglect, abuse, or other forms of disruption in infancy, the initial separation and individuation phase may have been a time of stress. Children who experienced a lot of change in their lives at age two — due to divorce or foster placement, for example — tend to have a more difficult time with transitions as they grow older. They may become quite anxious when confronted with change, or they may get irritable and prone to aggression. Inevitably, as they come face to face with the transitions of moving from childhood to adolescence, they can experience low self-esteem, problems with family members, or school failure.

We therefore need to permit teenagers the opportunity to separate from the family and test the waters of freedom and pre-adulthood. With adolescents in foster care, this may be limited by circumstances if the teen requires a great deal of supervision and isn't permitted the opportunities of their peers. With teenagers who are adopted, parents often fear that their child's natural tendency toward separation is a threat to the relationship that has been developed. This can be a delicate balance for the child and the parents to negotiate.

While many adopted teens struggle with trying to figure out whether they are more like their birth or adoptive parents, the adoptive parents may experience related fears. This can be especially true if the child experiments with drugs, exhibits erratic behavior, or engages in early sexual activity. National studies consistently reveal that upwards of 70 percent of teenagers in any given community use alcohol or drugs at least once before turning 18. The question for all parents, therefore, is not so much *if* their child will use. Instead, parents need to look at the likely circumstances the child will be in when they try alcohol and drugs, as well as what choices they are likely to make about subsequent use. If your child has a genetic predisposition toward substance abuse, it is vital that you have a talk with her about this reality long before she finds herself in the settings where drugs and alcohol are available.

In adolescence, many teenagers turn their mental attention toward finding their birth families. This is particularly true of foster children, who often live in the same community of their family members. With few exceptions, studies indicate that the majority of foster children return to their families after they turn 18. Some of this stems from the fact that they haven't been adopted and therefore don't always have a solid foundation by which to venture into adulthood. Adopted teens, on the other hand, often think about whether they want to search for birth family members. When they do, most adopted teens are more interested in reuniting with siblings than with their mother or father. The adopted teens whom I interview often tell me that their heart-felt loyalties are to their adoptive parents. Yet, curiosity about their genealogy, family history, and reasons behind the initial relinquishment sometimes beg to be answered. When they have a biological sibling, they indicate to me a tremendous pull to find this person, stating that it feels as if part of them is missing.

These issues and dynamics bring a whole new dimension to the teenager's therapeutic needs. For parents and providers, it can be difficult trying to determine which aspects of the teenager's behaviors are age-typical versus which are motivated by adoption or foster care concerns. Independent of foster care or adoption issues, adolescence is a confusing time, and one that is often filled with mystery or confusion. Just to make matters worse, many psychiatric disorders don't start to manifest until adolescence or early adulthood. Thus, some of the behavioral changes some teenagers exhibit may be indications of a budding psychiatric disorder. If the teenager starts acting in ways that are markedly different from when they were children, it may be necessary to explore whether there are organic causes for this, particularly if he has a history of mental illness in his birth family.

If the teenager is in counseling, the therapist needs to carefully evaluate whether to employ family therapy approaches or only see the teen alone. Also, the therapist must examine how they will handle issues of confidentiality. As I indicate elsewhere in this book, my preference is to work on a family therapy model whenever possible. Realistically, though, it is sometimes best to work with adolescents alone, perhaps only meeting with the parents periodically. Coming to a decision about which approach to use on a particular case can be quite a challenge. Parents should trust the judgment of the therapist on this one, though it is acceptable to ask for an explanation as to why one approach will be used over the other.

RESOURCES

FURTHER READING

The Psychology of Adoption (book)
Brodzinsky and Schecter; Authors

Children's Adjustment to Adoption (book)
Brodzinsky, Smith, & Brodzinsky; Authors

When babies have already attached to a birth mother or foster mother, they are likely to come into the adoptive home already grieving for that primary bond. And because they are preverbal, their grieving can look like other problems, usually physical, that cause the adoptive parents great anxiety.

— David Brodzinsky,
"Being Adopted"

Your Child's Real and Imagined Ghosts

By the time a child is placed in a foster or adoptive home, they may have developed relationships with several people, including social workers, a counselor, a Guardian ad litem, a Court Appointed Special Advocate, an attorney, and at least one other foster parent or family. Often, these persons have played more of a significant and vital role in the child's life than did his own birth family members. When a child is then placed in a new home — permanent or not — they may lose these relationships. We should keep in mind, however, that the child rarely loses his thoughts and memories of the time he had with these people.

While new foster or adoptive parents will meet their child's placement or social worker, they don't usually meet the other providers who have worked with their child. Though this is something you may have little control over, I encourage you to meet —or at least speak by phone with — these people. On the one hand, you will get different perspectives on your child's history and personality. More importantly, meeting these people helps add continuity to the child's life. The child is often shouldered with the task of educating the new parents about his prior providers and family members. These people have likely known and worked with the child for a substantial period of time, and the child has developed significant attachments to them.

When new parents take the time to meet or speak with some of these people, it helps the child feel his parents are interested in the life he had before coming to the new home. But, care should be taken when speaking with foster parents who asked for the child to be removed from their home. While they may offer good feedback or warnings, they could still be feeling angered by the child and attempt to influence you in negative ways.

Some agencies have policies on what kind of contact foster parents can and cannot have with the children who leave their care. Typically, post-placement contact is discouraged or prohibited for a specified period of time once the child leaves their home. From a practical standpoint, I understand why these conditions are imposed on foster parents. But, for the child, the restrictions do not always make sense. Some children may need the opportunity to bond with the next parents they are placed with, free from the confusion of having the other family in their life. But, it goes against the nature of children's attachments to leave one home and be prevented from contact with the adults who previously cared for them. Also, the foster parents with whom the child lived often have crucial information about the child's history, behavior, and emotions that gets lost when he leaves their home. This sets up a situation where the new parents must figure out on their own what works best in raising the child, without the benefit of hearing the experience of the previous family.

When I conduct a psychological evaluation on a foster child, I always ask the foster parents, "What do the next parents need to know about raising and caring for this child?" I then integrate their comments into the written report. This way, if these parents don't get the opportunity to speak with the next family, their thoughts about what the child requires at home are at least documented. Creating a Life Book or adding content to an existing one can be a good means of communicating your information about the foster child. Subsequent parents would love to read about your experiences and observations, as it can only help them understand and know the child in a better way.

Parents should also maintain awareness of the manner in which the child is affected by thoughts or memories about the birth family. Children often tell me it feels like their new families want them to ignore or forget about their birth family. This is most pronounced when new parents prevent an adopted child from having contact with his siblings. Some parents mistakenly believe that if the child doesn't talk about his birth family, he is not thinking about them. Yet, when I ask foster or adoptive parents to ask their child, "How often do you think about your birth family," the amount given by the child is a bit startling. When I evaluate or counsel children, I often discover that they are secretly yearning for their birth mother, father, grandparent, or sibling. Unfortunately, they feel they must keep this to themselves. The child then feels isolated and disconnected from the people who want to love and bond with him.

In my clinical work with foster and adopted children, I find that many live in a world surrounded by ghosts. Whether they have conscious memories of their birth family or not, children tell me they frequently think about why they were relinquished, what problems their parents had, who their birth fathers were, and whether their birth mothers think of them. Those with younger siblings with whom they have little or no contact frequently tell me they spend a great deal of time worrying about them. Regardless of how reality-based these thoughts are — and I tend to find that the child's thoughts are sometimes dominated more by fantasy than truth — they have tremendous influence over the child's life.

Parents differ in their readiness to talk with children about these ghosts. Some adoptive parents, for example, feel threatened by the fact their child thinks about birth family members. These parents tell me it is important that their child maintain loyalty only to them, and to discuss the birth mother, siblings, or other relations may threaten that. I don't believe it needs to be a daily discussion, but I do think foster and adoptive parents should talk with their child about their biological family. This provides not only validation for the child about his history but also ensures that he doesn't feel the need to hide or deny feelings of loss, grief, and longing. These discussions can also lessen the child's conflicts of loyalty. Too often, children tell me they imagine their birth parents want them to act or behave in one way, while their foster or adoptive parents expect them to behave in another. This is not only confusing for the child, but kids sometimes tell me they give in more readily to the imagined wishes of their birth parents.

An exercise I sometimes use with children in therapy often proves useful. I will ask, "Have you ever seen those cartoons where there is a devil on one side of the character's head and an angel on the other?" Inevitably, children have seen this image, as it is quite common. I then say, "I wonder if your life ever feels like that, where you have your birth mother on one side of you and your foster/adoptive mother on the other side. Like in the cartoons, your birth mom may be giving you one message, while your foster/adoptive mom is giving you another." I then ask the child to expand on this notion, requesting that he give me examples. As I discuss this with the child, his foster or adoptive parent is in the room. One girl I used this exercise with said to me, "I feel like my birth mom wants me to be a bad girl, like her. This mom wants me to be perfect." I asked her to expand on this, telling me in specific language what she thinks both mothers would say to her.

I then move to a discussion with the child about the ways she feels caught in the middle between the wishes of each parent. In some instances, I will bring in another therapist to help me in a role play with the child. I'll have the foster/adoptive parent take hold of one of the child's hands, while the therapist holds the other. They stand on each side of her and begin to gently tug her in opposite directions. I tell the child to pretend that the therapist is her birth mother. The two moms then talk to the child, simultaneously, each voicing what each wants or expects of her. I stand behind the child, instructing her to tell each parent how she feels about what they're saying to her.

I did this exercise with a nine-year-old boy several years ago. He had lived with his birthmother until he was six, at which point he was adopted by his current mother. During the role play, his adoptive mom was saying to him, "Be loyal to me. I'm your mom. I'm the one who keeps you safe. I'm the one who gives you a good home. Be loyal to me." The therapist playing his birth mother said, "No, be loyal to me. I'm your *real* mom. I'm the one you should stay true to. Maybe I couldn't take care of you, but I'm your real mom." While they were doing this, the boy was trying to loosen the grip they each had on his hands, and he was crying.

Soon, the boy broke free from the surrogate birth mom, fell to floor and began kicking her. He then started yelling, "You're not my mom. You didn't take care of me. What about the time you put me in a tub of hot water? What about the time you beat me? What about the times you left me alone?" He continued to list several things his birth mother had done to him when he lived with her as a young child. As he did this, his adoptive mother and I looked at one another, nonverbally acknowledging that we were unaware of some of the events he was detailing to his surrogate birthmother.

The example demonstrates that this boy had many memories of living with his birthmother. As the therapist, I was aware of some of them. His adoptive mother, with whom he had lived for three years, knew some of it too. Yet, as he kicked the therapist who played his birthmother, and told her all the things "she" had done to harm him, we found out he had a wealth of experiences and feelings that he hadn't yet shared with either of us.

Understanding Sibling Relationships

A BOUT 65 TO 85 PERCENT of children entering the foster care system have at least one sibling. Thirty percent of children in foster care have four siblings or more. In 1995, about 75 percent of siblings were separated when they entered foster care. Most placement agencies have policies that specify the importance of trying to place siblings together. Realistically, though, this may not be feasible, particularly if there are a lot of siblings or if the siblings are extremely aggressive to one another.

Particularly in instances of neglect, the time siblings spend together in their early years is often greater than the time they spend with their parents. Sibling relationships are complex and last a lifetime, often longer than most marriages and many parent-child relationships. As I stated earlier in this book, many foster and adopted children hold stronger desires to be with their siblings than may be true with regard to their birth parents.

I am frequently asked to evaluate sibling pairs or groups and to make recommendations as to whether they should be placed together or separately. The request often comes amid dissent or strong disagreement among members of the children's treatment team. Assessments of this nature typically include a range of procedures, such as reviewing case files, interviewing all members of the children's treatment team, and observing the children alone and then together. These are incredibly challenging evaluations, as the implications are tremendous. More often than not, the siblings genuinely want to reside together. The struggle is in determining if this is really in their best interests.

Some people feel siblings should be separated in situations where one sibling has highly pronounced medical or psychological needs, where one sibling has a history of perpetrating on another, or where there are so many siblings that it is doubtful one home could be found for all of them. When the sibling group has suffered tremendous neglect, some professionals argue that it is not fair to place them together. Instead, they believe each child should be in a separate placement where they can finally get the love and attention they missed out on in earlier times of life. While these are appropriate considerations, the unique dynamics of each sibling pair or group should be considered.

Sibling relations also exert considerable influence on individual development and attachment behavior, particularly in early childhood and adolescence. Sibling relations assist children in developing both a private and public identity. Within the family, children teach one another the values and norms of the family. From sibling relations, children learn, in part, how to make and maintain intimate relationships. For example, when a child shows concern over the anxiety of a sibling and attempt to alleviate this stress through getting a favorite toy or talking to the sibling, this suggests an understanding of the other's feelings and ideas about how to comfort the other. Through these interactions, children learn about feelings, intentions, and needs of persons other than themselves as well as the social rules of the family in which they are growing up. Over time, these skills greatly influence the development of one's personality.

Older siblings are often supplemental attachment figures and caregivers for younger siblings. Common situations in which this relationship could occur include when the older child recognizes potential danger to the younger sibling, in a cooperative family system where the older sibling is asked to help or relieve the parent in caregiving while the parent is doing another task, and in family systems where the adults are unwilling or unable to carry out the parental role appropriately. In some instances, younger siblings have more significant bonds to an older sibling — who provided more of the caretaking than did the parent — than to the actual parent. Unfortunately, the reverse may not be true. Instead, the older sibling — to whom the attachment has formed — may resent the demands and responsibilities associated with this role.

In many cultures, older siblings are expected to take care of younger siblings. If neglect occurs in the family, this culturally-sanctioned dynamic gets intensified. The important thing to keep in mind is that caregiving by one sibling to another is not always maladaptive. Especially if you are fostering or adopting a child from another culture, it is useful to find out whether this hierarchy of caregiving is common in the child's background.

When siblings with a reciprocal caregiving dynamic enter a foster or adoptive home, conflict can arise when the parents try to assume ultimate authority. With children as young as three and as old as 17, I have seen tremendous resentment when the new parent insists on relieving — for lack of a better word — the older child of their caregiving responsibilities. This can set up a situation in which the parent and older child enter into a power struggle. I worked on one case where, as soon as the foster mother diapered the baby, the four-year-old sister walked over and ripped the diaper off. She then told the mother in no uncertain terms that her sister only wears cloth diapers!

Issues related to trust are common for foster and adopted children. They may therefore believe that the only ally they have is another sibling, while adults are beings to be feared. When the sibling pair or group comes into your home, there may be little reason to trust you. If an older sibling is accustomed to the protective role for a younger brother or sister, they could feel the need to intensify this around you. Innocent acts on your part can suddenly be perceived as a threat to the older child. To counter this, he may do things to detour you from the younger sibling, such as arguing with you or trying to direct all your attention to him. In extreme cases, he may allege to others you have tried to hurt the younger child.

According to the National Adoption Information Clearinghouse, a greater number of former foster children are searching for their siblings than are searching for their biological parents. They are suing child welfare agencies in order to get them to release information, and they are winning. As I noted earlier in this book, more foster and adopted children initiate searches for siblings than for birth parents.

At least 10 states have programs, laws, or policies that promote sibling placements. In California, for example, former Governor Gray Davis signed a bill that contains provisions aimed at facilitating post-adoptive contact between siblings who are not placed together. Under the law, recommendations for sibling visitation are to be included in children's adoption case plans. In New York and Massachusetts, judges have ruled that child welfare agencies must try at all costs to keep sibling groups together. The Massachusetts decision added that brothers and sisters should be raised together, even half-brothers and sisters, "unless there are compelling reasons for separating them."

What the Studies Suggest

There are generally mixed results when reviewing the issue of sibling placement in child welfare systems. Some researchers suggest that placing siblings in the same home increases the risk of disruption. Other researchers report no association between outcome and sibling placement. For example, Barth found that sibling placements (33 percent) were no more likely to disrupt than single-child placements (35 percent). But, sibling placements for children 15 and older tended to be more disruptive than single-child placements. Other studies suggest that problems in sibling placements occur only when other children live in the home.

Some researchers found sibling placement for older children tied to reduced risk of disruption. For example, one researcher reported that children who were placed alone disrupted at the rate of 10 percent compared to 5 percent for children placed with siblings. Of the children placed by themselves in that study, 11 percent had siblings placed in other adoptive homes. Of the separated siblings, over 90 percent were believed to have moderate to severe behavior or emotional problems.

In her study, attachment researcher Mary Ainsworth found that sibling ties are important for resolving feelings of grief. She wrote, "We found evidence that both feelings of responsibility in caring for others in the family and/or a sense of family solidarity were important factors in the successful resolution of mourning the loss of a family member." Viewed from this perspective, sibling relations provide children in the welfare system with a sense of permanence they otherwise may not have.

In New Mexico, a subgroup of Children's Court Attorneys host a series of panels that include adolescents and adults who have gone through the foster care system. Typically, many panel members have at least one sibling, and they are asked to address the placement issue. At one of these forums, I was asked to give a talk to the audience. Before I presented, I listened to what the panel of former foster children had to say. With only one exception, the panel members agreed that siblings should be kept together at placement. Those panel members who had lived with their siblings in foster care generally appreciated it, while those who were separated expressed tremendous anger and resentment at the courts.

In an article that summarizes the research on sibling placement, Gloria Hochman notes:

- When children are separated because of sibling rivalry, it teaches them that the way to deal with conflict is to walk away from it, not work it out. Siblings who remain together learn how to resolve their differences and develop stronger relationships.
- The responsibility felt by an older child for younger siblings is not necessarily negative.
- Even a needy child does not necessarily benefit from being the only child in a family.

- When a sibling is removed from the home because of behavior problems, remaining children get the message that the same thing can happen to them.
- Removing a sibling from a foster home because he has abused his sibling does not guarantee that the abuse will not continue in another environment. Therapy may be a more appropriate intervention.

By and large, I am a proponent of keeping siblings together. But, this doesn't mean that siblings should be placed in the same home in all circumstances. A careful consideration must be made of the dynamics in the children's lives. If siblings are separated, parents should do what they can to support and encourage contact between the children. Too often, I evaluate or treat children who have siblings with whom they are not permitted contact. The anger, grief, and confusion they experience are tremendous. Certainly, situations arise where one sibling should not have the opportunity to contact their brother or sister at will. This is especially true if the parents are concerned that the sibling may cause further problems or distress for the child or the family in which he resides.

I rarely encounter a situation in which I believe contact between siblings should be prohibited at all times. When that occurs, the wishes of the parents have often overruled the needs of the child or recommendations of the placement agency. As noted, circumstances exist when a sibling should not have unrestricted contact with a brother or sister, or even to know the address or phone number for their sibling. Still, compromises can be made, such as using a neutral party to communicate messages.

Defining and Discussing Personal and Family Values

V ALUES ARE THE BELIEFS, standards, and principles we hold about how to act and behave in the world. Each of us has values about our lives and behaviors. We also hold values about other people. Some values people hold include:

- People should not hurt other people
- People should not hurt pets
- Always respect adults
- Do not swear in public
- Don't take things that do not belong to you
- Let your guest decide what activity you will engage in
- All laws should be obeyed
- Go as far as you can with your education
- Parenting is more important than having a career
- Be on time for appointments and obligations

Values are most often formed within the family. As children grow older, the values of the family don't need to be stated or identified too often, because the child likely becomes familiar with expectations within the family.

When you bring a child into your home — particularly an older child — they may not share your values. In some instances, the values of the child's birth family may be quite different from yours and reflect attitudes or beliefs you find wrong, offensive, or even shocking. For some, their behavior reflects the values they hold. They may not have internalized commonly shared values such as don't steal, don't disrespect adults, don't hit other people, and don't lie or cheat. As mentioned earlier, the child may believe it's his role to care for a younger sibling. This may go against your own beliefs on the topic, creating conflict between you and the child.

Values, culture, and tradition can be closely linked. Some parenting styles are based strongly on the expectations or norms of certain regions or communities. This sometimes bumps into the beliefs of our broader society about safe child rearing. As an example, some cultures approve of spanking children. When Protective Services steps in and alleges child abuse, the parent can find this somewhat confusing. In many cultures, it is expected that children will eventually take care of their parents. You may bring a child into your home that holds this belief, while you think the child should focus on his own life.

Parents should talk about values with the children in their home and explain the reasons behind their values. Your job is not necessarily to convince the child that your points of view are correct. Instead, by discussing values you can hopefully help the child develop a broader perspective of the world, which teaches them how the actions and beliefs of one person can affect those of another. If you have adopted from abroad, you may play a part in educating your child about the norms of the country's culture. As the child ages, he will likely examine his Western values and those of their homeland, asking which best reflect their own attitudes and beliefs.

In some instances, we are not always sure why we hold our values or beliefs. When a child challenges our beliefs, we can then become frustrated, simply because we hope or believe that others should share our views. Reflecting upon values and their development may prove useful. For example, are your values similar or different from those of your parents? If they differ, how did this evolution occur? Was it because of your life experience or do you tell yourself that your parents were simply naïve?

It may be appropriate to talk with the child about the values held in his birth family. Out of loyalty, the child may insist that the values of his birth parents are more justified than what you have to offer. He may struggle with questions such as, "Am I more like my family or more like yours?" If this occurs, remind the child that these kinds of issues are not black and white. Ultimately, we come to have the beliefs we do based on what is modeled for us and what we experience in the world. Values develop over time and they can change. Try talking about this with your child. Who knows, your child may get you to more closely examine some of the beliefs you hold and why it is you do.

Children, Parents, and Food

NOTHING PUTS SOME PARENTS into a stir faster than the food issues their foster or adopted kids offer. As an example, parents have reported the following scenarios to me:

- She digs in the trashcan, looking for something to eat.
- He would sit at the table and eat with his hands. Even with soup, he'd stick his fingers in the bowl and pull out the vegetables one by one.
- There was this horrible smell coming from his room. After two weeks, I finally found the source. He had been stashing egg sandwiches under his pillow.
- I keep finding food in the strangest places. He'll leave piles of it in the corner. I find cookies and muffins in between the cushions on the couch. I've even found food in the bathroom.
- He always has to have something in his mouth. Gum, suckers, gummy bears, jawbreakers. Even at night, I have to check his mouth to make sure he's not sucking on something.
- I've never seen a kid eat so much. He doesn't eat to feel full. He eats until all the food in the pot is gone. He can't stand it if there are leftovers.
- I walked in one day and she was eating dry food out of the cat's bowl. I had noticed the cat seemed to be eating a lot lately. It wasn't the cat, though. It was the girl!

First off, keep in mind that rejection of your food is not necessarily a rejection of you. Second, let's explore the meaning food can hold for people. Food is associated with nurturing and survival. We all require it and we all have one or two favorite food items that we turn to for comfort. Mine is macaroni and cheese. Given the vulnerability many foster and adopted children feel, self-soothing with food is an important survival mechanism for them. Some of these children grew up in neglectful or impoverished environments where food was not always available. Some children literally had to go through trashcans to find something to eat, or stash food in hiding places to ensure food for the next day. Some were never taught appropriate means of feeding oneself, let alone basic table manners. For children who grew up poor, stealing food was a means of survival.

The challenge in dealing with a child who has issues around food is to show respect for the meaning behind their habits or behaviors while gently demonstrating that they don't need to act the same way around food in their new home. If your child requires something in his mouth at all times,

IDENTIFYING YOUR FOOD RULES

- Can your child help themselves to any food item in the kitchen?
- Which meals must be eaten at the table?
- Can your child start eating immediately, or do they have to wait until all persons are served?
- Does your child have to say a prayer before eating?
- Can your child eat while watching TV? Playing in their room?
- Can your child automatically have second helpings?
- What are your rules about candy and sweets?
- Is your child expected to help with food preparation?
- Can your child swap lunch items with other kids at school?
- What are the rules when you go out to eat at a restaurant?
- Can your child have soda at a friend's house?
- Will you do a random search of his bedroom looking for food? If you find food, what will the consequence be?

and you want to discourage this, start out slow. Tell him he can't have anything in his mouth at night. Over time, wean him away from these items during school hours, during play and the rest of the day. Most importantly, don't communicate to your child that something is bad or strange about him because of his food habits. If the child's behavior around food and eating is really bizarre, try saying, "This is the way we do it in this house."

Sadly, many children do not grow up with the ready access to food that most of us take for granted. Some of this may be economic, while children from orphanages are often limited to only one or two meals a day. When the child comes to your home, the availability of food can be overwhelming. Coupled with poor eating habits, the child may not understand that there are rules, norms, and expectations with regard to eating. You will need to educate him about the standards in your home, as well as in the larger society. For some children, it can help to have a small table where snacks are readily available. Similarly, you can give younger children a small apron or purse in which they can carry dry snacks. These steps can have a tremendous effect at reducing the anxiety some children have about food.

ANGER PROBLEMS ASSOCIATED WITH TEEN WEIGHT GAINS

Teenagers with problems managing anger are more likely to be overweight than those who manage anger appropriately, William H. Mueler, Ph.D., said in a poster presentation at a conference on cardiovascular disease... "It's not just 'anger in' or 'anger out,'" Dr. Mueller said. "We're suggesting that it is important to look at the emotional health of kids. It's beyond just diet and exercise. If they feel good about resolving interpersonal stress and learn to decrease conflict, these skills will spill over into their general lifestyle."

— Family Practice News, July 15, 2004

Teaching food and eating habits is often like communicating other values. Let children know what the expectations are in his new home. This may entail showing them how to use a napkin, how to hold a fork, how to eat soup, or how to chew with their mouth closed. Early on, talk about rules pertaining to food and eating. Don't assume all children know these rules. In some situations, you may need to do daily or random room searches to find out if your child is sneaking or hoarding food. Decide in advance if you will give a consequence for finding food or whether you will simply remove what you find.

Teaching Boundaries

I T IS NATURAL TO ASSUME that a 10-year-old child will act and behave as most children his age do. With many children who were abused or neglected, they may not have developed the skill or maturity of others their age. Especially if you are bringing a child into your home who grew up with neglect or who lived in multiple placements, find out early on if he fully understands basic rules, such as:

- Don't hit other children
- Don't talk to strangers
- Look both ways before crossing the street
- Don't pull the dog's tail
- Don't communicate your needs by having a tantrum

These seem like basic concepts, yet some children do not understand them. In many cases, the children with whom I work have an emotional age that is much younger than their chronological age. Because of this, they failed to learn skills and techniques for getting by in the world that other children their age have mostly mastered. In some instances, this is little more than a nuisance for the parents. In other situations, though, it has tremendous implications for the child's ability to exercise good judgment.

One way to explore these issues with a child in a safe manner is to play the game, "What would you do if...?" Here, the parent poses questions about a variety of low- and high-risk situations in which kids can find themselves. After the child responds, the parent then talks with the child about their answer. The parent can then support and validate the good choices the child makes while providing reasons for modifying choices that may not be as good. A lot of times, parents will need to educate the child about why a different course of action is best or about the bad things that can happen if the better choice is not followed. Thinking of every situation is not possible. But, by playing the game, the parent and child start a dialog that will hopefully continue over time.

As an example, let's say you ask the child, "What would you do if you're in a public restroom at the urinal and a man stands next to you?" The best response is for the child to indicate that he would finish using the bathroom, wash his hands, and leave. Some children might say, "I would stare down at him." This is where you talk with the child about why this is not the best course of action, pointing out that it is rude, it is inappropriate, and other people should not do the same.

WHAT WOULD YOU DO IF...

- Someone offers you $10 to take a paper bag to the person standing across the street?
- An older person asks you to touch them under their clothes?
- You and I become separated in a large store or at the mall?
- A stranger comes to you and says I told him to bring you home?
- Someone you don't know asks you to give him your address?
- An adult tries to start a conversation with you in a public restroom?
- A stranger offers to give you a ride home?
- A neighbor you don't know too well invites you inside for cookies?
- Somebody tells you something but asks you not to tell me?
- Somebody calls and asks you who is home?

For a child with indiscriminate attachment, you can ask, "Is it okay to stand close to a man you don't know too well or sit on his lap?" I use this example, only because too often children who come to my office for an evaluation — children I have never met —freely tug on me, sit on me, or want to wrestle with me. Certainly, I am not going to hurt or exploit them, but these are not behaviors they should be exhibiting with an unfamiliar adult male. It isn't necessary to talk with the child about all the ways they could be exploited by getting close to strangers. But they should be educated about appropriate boundaries.

Aiming for One Big, Happy Family

WHEN PARENTS CHOOSE TO ADOPT or foster a child, the children who already live in the home can experience mixed reactions. In general, younger children are more receptive to having a new child in the home, though they can become a bit jealous and territorial at first. Pre-adolescent and teenage children can appear indifferent to having new children in the home. For them, they mostly want the child to leave their belongings alone and to not embarrass them in front of their friends.

If the new foster or adopted child is oppositional, demanding, or aggressive, the children who already live in the home naturally become resentful. Particularly for the older child, he may have very little patience for the child's behaviors and will communicate to the parents that he wants the disruptive behaviors stopped immediately. In many cases, the older child will take advantage of the opportunities they have to be away from the home, simply because they don't want to hear or put up with the new child's words or actions. This puts the parents in a tough bind, as they try to strike a balance between the loyalties to the child already in the home, versus the commitment made to the new child.

Parents feel added stress and disappointment if they hope all the children in the home get along, but it does not work out that way. In some instances, the foster or adopted child can command so much of the parent's time that the child already in the home comes to resent them, as well as the new child. It is not uncommon for this to create stress between the parents and their older children. Their children may blame them for bringing the child into the home and nothing short of "giving him back" seems to hold the potential for resolve. Even though adolescence is a time for psychologically distancing oneself from the parents, this process can be accelerated or become more intensified if the older child resents his parents for bringing a new child into the home.

When there are other children in the home, consider the following:

- If you know that the child you will be bringing to your home has a history of oppositional or aggressive behavior, tell the other children of this in advance. This will decrease the likelihood they will be surprised or caught off guard when the child presents with defiant attitudes or behaviors.

- If your older child is staying away from home or is reluctant to bring their friends over, try to arrange for times they can be home when the disruptive child is away. Encourage the older child to bring their friends over, for example, when the other child is at school, on respite, or at some other activity. It can be helpful to do this on a schedule, such that your child knows the other child will be out of the home on certain days or at certain times.

- Remind the older child that it is not their role to solve the problems that the younger child creates. Let them know you will do what you can to help the child control annoying or destructive behaviors. Give the older child permission to set appropriate limits, such as keeping their bedroom and bathroom doors closed. If the new child persists in entering the older child's room, consider whether you will permit that child to put a lock on their door. If you do, make sure you have a key and remind them of your right to enter their room.

- Make time to participate in activities that are fun and familiar to the older child. This may require placing the younger child in respite care or with a sitter if his presence will diminish the good time the older child might have. Don't let the stress of having a new child in the home interfere with your familiar traditions and activities.

- Don't fall into the trap of believing that all children in the home should be treated equally at all times. The new child will often point out all the privileges the other children in the home have that he doesn't. Remind him that the other children have the privileges they do because they demonstrated trust, maturity, and responsibility. Let him know that once he does the same, he will have similar opportunities.

- Permit the older child to share with you any frustrations he has about the younger child's presence or behaviors. Encourage him to talk with you about these feelings and to not say mean things to the younger child. While you may have an appreciation for some of the new child's struggles, and how this may contribute to his behavior, your older child may not care. Instead of just trying to explain and justify the new child's behavior, let the older child know you are aware of how bothered or troubled he is by the changes in the home.

- Offer to let the older child come to family therapy. Maybe he doesn't want to participate in the therapy on a regular basis, but expressing his frustration or anger to a neutral party may prove helpful. The therapist will also be able to reinforce for your child that you are doing all you can to make the home a pleasant place to be for all members of the family.

The Blame Game Children Play

P ARENTS BECOME QUITE ANNOYED when a child constantly blames others for the things for which he should take responsibility. With young children, we almost expect to hear, "He started it!" But when a child refuses to acknowledge the part he played in wrong or disturbing behaviors, it leaves parents wondering if he can ever admit to a wrong-doing.

Children who grew up in chaotic homes often use blame simply because it was modeled for them by adults. At the time the social services department becomes involved with the family, they may request that the birth parents complete a treatment plan before the child can be returned home. Too often, the parents make excuses for why they can't comply with the treatment plan: *I don't have a car, my boss won't let me, it was raining that day, I forgot to make the call, the results of the drug test are wrong, I couldn't find the building, I overslept,* and *I shouldn't have to do all this.* The child therefore spends a lengthy amount of time in foster care or may even be placed for adoption. What this tells us is that child probably lived in an environment where people did not take responsibility for their actions. Many times, they may have gotten away with it. Also, we have to question whether anyone ever held the child accountable for his actions.

Society demands that we each take responsibility for our actions. If I don't pay my phone bill, I have no phone service. If I don't pay my mortgage, I'll lose my home. If I take something from the store without paying for it, I'll be arrested. The same thing applies to children, and especially to adolescents. If a teenager thinks she can blame others for using drugs, skipping classes, or getting pregnant, she is mistaken. Our job is to teach children to take responsibility for their actions, in order to prepare them for making decisions in life.

If your child blames others for his actions, recognize that it may be his way of trying to divert the topic from the issue at hand. Try not to let the discussion go too far from your main point. Even if he says, "I can't do it. I don't have a pencil," remind him that he still needs to do his homework. Don't get trapped into arguing about whether he has a pencil or not. Blaming is less effective when the person listening to the excuses simply refuses to accept them.

When possible, try to use real world examples for your child. Children often feel that they are burdened by rules that no one else has to follow. Granted, you and I don't typically have to return home or get to bed by a certain time, but we certainly have a lot of rules to follow. Let your child know that rules help bring order to homes, schools, and society. When we follow rules, we demonstrate that we are able to take responsibility. If all we did was blame others when things go wrong, it is doubtful that others would see us as trustworthy. The same is true with young children.

In addition to the stress of attempting to control their child's behavior, these parents feel enormous guilt and shame. They intended to adopt a hurt child and nurture him into a whole person. Instead, they are less parents than jailers, less nurturing than controlling, less accepting than rejecting, less loving than hating … into this mix, add a child who can be completely charming and engaging to all outsiders, and it is a small wonder these parents feel insane. The same child who put his fist through a wall and pulled a knife on Mom, is a charming, helpful, compliant child in respite care.

— Gregory Keck and Regina Kupecky,
"Adopting the Hurt Child"

Everyone Else Thinks He's Wonderful

MANY PARENTS REPORT FEELING like they get the raw end of the deal from their child. These parents report that their child does everything he can to create power struggles and to put the family in a bad mood. But only at home. When their child is with relatives or neighbors, some parents say they are told their child is respectful, cooperative, and friendly. The parents wonder if it was really their child these people spent time with.

Selective behavior in different settings is common to almost all children. But I do find that children who can make life miserable for everyone at home, can keep it together and put on a good show outside of the home. For one thing, the child is not as invested in controlling the dynamics outside of the home. They know their stay with a relative or neighbor will be short, and little will be gained from battling these people. But, children with traumatic backgrounds do feel the need to control the environment in their own home which helps them feel safe and in control.

If a child acts respectful in one environment, but not another, they probably have some idea of what they're doing and can likely be taught ways of modifying their behavior. But, parents should make sure the child is not trying to make the parent feel like he is going crazy. For seriously disturbed children, they want their primary parent to feel bad and inadequate. It is much easier, from the child's perspective, to control and dominate a parent who feels ineffective, than one who feels in control.

While it will take some practice, try to remain calm when your child is acting defiant and oppositional. When the child perceives that his actions are not bothering you, he may try a different strategy. If all you do is get angry and yell, you already know the child's behavior will not stop. At times, it can be helpful to try a paradoxical strategy, such as, "Oh come on, you can scream louder than that;" "You only threw the clothes on the floor from one drawer. Aren't you going to do the same with the clothes in the other drawer;" "Hey, you learned a new swear word. Good for you! I'll bet you know them all now;" or "Boy, I'm really angry too. Here, I'll scream with you!"

In some instances, tolerance and limit-setting are the only options available to the parents. Parents may need to take active steps to make sure they're not getting sucked into the child's game by arguing back, getting mad, or acting out of control. If the child breaks a rule, it must be met with a consequence. Rather than deciding on the consequence at the time, parents should choose them in advance. This information should be communicated to the child during calmer times.

Children who are oppositional and argumentative can take an enormous toll on parents and others in the home. For them, they feel so angry or bad about themselves that they cannot tolerate a relaxed, happy, or comfortable atmosphere. You don't want to set up an "us vs. them" dynamic in the home, but the family should acknowledge the ongoing stress. The couple should seek professional consultation, if necessary, on ways of managing defiant and difficult behaviors in children. The family should place the child in respite care or with a friend, while they do things to strengthen their bond.

If the problems go unaddressed, the child ends up feeling — and likely being — in control of the mood of the household, while the parents feel defeated and exhausted. Many parents, out of chronic frustration, end up sending the child to a different foster home or to a residential setting. While this may ultimately be what the child requires, it does nothing to address the core issues the child is dealing with and makes him feel even more like an object than a person.

> *The little boy grew. He grew and he grew and he grew. He grew until he was nine years old. And he never wanted to come in for dinner, he never wanted to take a bath, and when grandma visited he always said bad words. Sometimes his mother wanted to sell him to the zoo!*
>
> — Robert Munsch,
> "Love You Forever"

What You Need to Know about the Child's Birth Family

F OSTER AND ADOPTIVE PARENTS often question to what extent they need to concern themselves with aspects of the child's birth family. Foster parents are sometimes told it is not their role to know much about the child's family, while many adoptive parents want to focus more on the here and now than on the past. Because open adoption is more common than it once was, the amount of information parents have about their children's birth families and backgrounds can vary considerably.

In my opinion, parents should have as much information as possible about a child's origins. Not only does this allow parents to better understand the various behaviors and personality of the child but also to provide the child with the support and empathy he may require. When you have all the obtainable details about your child's background, you can approach parenting from a position of strength. Many of the parents I work with who adopted from abroad tell me they feel as if they are raising a mystery child. At times, this adds to the stress or confusion they feel about their child's behavior or history.

Most of us can look at aspects of our own personality and behavior and see how it is similar to that of our parents or siblings. Increasingly, genetic science informs us that temperament, personality traits, and behavioral styles run in families, just like hair and eye color. Parents may benefit from knowing whether a child's behavior is a feature of his genetic temperament rather than a learned response. For example, the child's natural temperament may simply be more impulsive, moody, or risk-taking than the new family in which he will be raised. By recognizing that the child is behaving in a manner that fits with his basic style, we are less apt to think the child has some kind of disorder.

Parents should keep in mind that psychiatric conditions also run in families. Conditions include depressive, anxiety, learning, and substance abuse disorders, as well as Attention-Deficit/Hyperactivity Disorder. When parents know in advance that their child has these risk factors in his family of origin, they can be more sensitive to the possibility that these conditions are showing up. The parent can also take precautionary steps early on as a way of minimizing the chances that any of these conditions will handicap or limit their child. For example, if you know that the child's birth mother or father had learning disorders, you can insist that he receives an evaluation if he is having trouble in school.

Too often, foster and adopted children come to us as puzzles to be solved – especially in the case of international adoptions where parents may have little or no information about the child's genetic history. In these instances, we often do a lot of guessing as we try to figure out the child's needs. For example, if the child was born premature or with low birth

BLAME IT ON YOUR MOM

Roots of Adult Diseases Trace Back to Womb

The importance of getting a good start in life long has been conventional wisdom — not to mention the foundation for an entire industry offering torrents of advice to pregnant women. Get ready for even more opportunities to blame mom for what ails you. From osteoporosis to cancers and cardiovascular disease, the evidence keeps flooding in: The roots of adult diseases stretch back to childhood, infancy and even the womb. And it has nothing to do with genes…

…The first studies of 'fetal programming' found that men who weigh less than 5.5 pounds at birth have, on average, a 50 percent greater chance of dying of heart disease than men with a higher birth weight, even accounting for other cardiovascular risks. Other researchers have confirmed the link between low birth weight and both cardiovascular disease and type-2 diabetes. A U.S. study, for instance, found that women born weighing less than 5.5 pounds had a 23 percent higher risk of cardiovascular disease than women born bigger…

You can't turn back the calendar and avoid that childhood bout with strep, or get mom to eat better while she was pregnant with you. But you can play defense. If you were born small for your length, you are at greater risk of type-2 diabetes and should keep your weight down. If as a newborn you had a scrawny abdomen, your liver may be too small to effectively clear cholesterol from your blood, so be extra vigilant about cholesterol levels.

—Sharon Begley, Wall Street Journal, 09/17/04

weight, the birth mother may have smoked cigarettes during her pregnancy. If the child's birth parents did not graduate high school, this may indicate they had learning disabilities. By thinking about the child's development in these ways, parents are better prepared to seek appropriate services for the child.

You may have little control over what information will be given to you about a child you will adopt or foster. Even if you are about to adopt a child and you enter the full disclosure process, some states will permit you to look through the child's file, but they will not allow you to keep personal copies of the documents. Given how overwhelming the content or paperwork will be, it is doubtful you will be able to remember key information. In these instances, obtain written permission to periodically review the file.

Children, Families, and Holidays

F OR MANY PEOPLE, HOLIDAYS are associated with thoughts of togetherness, happiness, rest, and celebration. Even if we don't do anything special on certain holidays, we still appreciate having time off work and hopefully getting some relaxation. For the most part, children don't pay much attention to holidays except the major ones like Christmas and Thanksgiving. To them, the other holidays are just opportunities to have time off from school.

Generalizations can't be made about what holidays might mean to foster and adopted children. It is still an area that requires some review. Adopted children from abroad will likely need to have details explained to them about many of our holidays. For example, they will need to be told why we dress up on Halloween, eat turkey on Thanksgiving, hunt for eggs on Easter, watch fireworks on the Fourth of July, or hand out cards on Valentine's Day.

Parents should try to explore the child's thoughts, feelings, and experiences about holidays. If the child had an abusive or neglectful background, the holidays may not have been a happy time for him. As an example, some children experience ritualized forms of abuse around Halloween. If the child's birth family was chaotic, family gatherings may have resulted in conflict or excessive use of alcohol, drug abuse, or violence.

Many adoptive parents choose to raise their child in the religion of the family. In some cases, this may mean the child is introduced to new religious beliefs, traditions, and holidays for the first time. Alternately, the child may be expected to assume a different religious identity from one he previously held. Parents should remember that religious beliefs differ greatly from one another. Some religions only require that the members believe in a certain God or higher power and that they attend certain services, such as church on Sunday. Other religions — such as Judaism — encompass broader aspects of the person's daily life and include a variety of additional holidays, rituals, and traditions. If you bring a child into your home, for example, and expect them to assume a Jewish identity, you may be asking him to make substantial changes to how he views himself and the world around him. Parents should be sensitive to the willingness of the child to relinquish his identity from his past as he moves toward assuming a new one.

PART THREE

Emotional Issues: Providing Your Child With Opportunities for Growth and Healing

In many cases, parents can come up with creative strategies to allow children to act their emotional rather than chronological age. Kids who have missed out on an important developmental stage need safe and appropriate ways to make it up.

— Foster Cline and Cathy Helding,
"Can This Child be Saved"

Children's Chronological vs. Developmental Age

Trauma, abuse, loss and abandonment take their toll on emotional development. It is natural for children to regress to earlier stages of development during stress. After a particularly disturbing event, a seven-year-old child might suddenly be unwilling to sleep alone, start bedwetting, be fearful of being away from a parent, refuse to go to school, or start sucking his thumb. Usually, with parental support and encouragement, the child eventually returns to more age-typical behavior.

Parents should not underestimate the role life experience plays in a child's psychological development. Even though a child's body keeps on growing, his emotional maturity may not advance at the same rate. In my experience, the developmental age of the child becomes most clear during moments of stress and tension. For example, one family with whom I once worked adopted a 9-year-old girl. Like most children her age, she played with dolls, engaged in fantasy play with her friends, and started to notice boys in a whole new way. Once, when I confronted her in therapy over behavior she had shown in my waiting room, the nine-year-old girl buried her face in her mother's shoulder. She became increasingly angry, started hitting her mother's arm, and said, "I hate you. I'm not going to do what you want. I don't like you. You can't make me." I asked her mom, "What age does this look like to you?" The mother replied, "She's behaving like a three-year-old, which she usually does when angry." This helped us both appreciate that this child regresses to the age of a toddler during times of conflict. Rather than judge this or see it as something negative, we learned our interventions with this child would be more effective if we responded to her at her emotional age.

Emotional immaturity is not a disorder. Instead, it results when children are denied the more age-appropriate and age-typical experiences of childhood. When a young child constantly directs his attention and efforts to basic needs, such as safety or security, it interferes with normal development. Children learn to think about the world around them primarily through play. This is how children start to learn about mastery and limitations. In relationships with others their age, the child also learns about sharing, emotions, and cooperation. If a child is struggling with issues of abuse, neglect, or chaos in his immediate environment, the learning he must do gets put on hold. These children also fail to learn adaptive ways for getting their needs met, as often it is not modeled for or shown to them. Instead, they might learn that the only way to get attention is through rage, aggression, or throwing a tantrum.

Disruptions and trauma in early childhood can result in attachment disturbances which have lifelong implications for how the child feels about himself and others. Some psychologists have offered that "attachment disorder" is actually a manifestation of Posttraumatic Stress Disorder. Viewed from this perspective, the child becomes overwhelmed with confusing experiences and emotions. The biological response is to seek assurance from the primary care provider. Yet, if the child's parent is abusive, intoxicated, or absent, the child remains in a state of fear or trauma. If this state continues over time, the child does not learn how to get his needs met by others or even how to self-soothe in an effective way. In

---

RE-PARENTING TECHNIQUES

- Curl up together and read stories.
- Tuck him into bed at night.
- Wash his back or hair in the tub.
- Make projects together: Models, holiday crafts, costumes, etc.
- Sing lullaby songs, either to or with your child.
- Bounce him on your lap. Otherwise, roll around together in bed or on the floor.
- Tickle one another.
- Talk with him about your day and remind him how happy you are to be home with him.
- Keep him by your side as much as possible, particularly in stores or out in public.

---

many respects, his emotional development is brought to a halt, even though the demands of his environment may not accommodate this reality.

A common complaint I hear from parents is, "He can't tolerate it if I say, 'no.'" Similarly, when I ask some of the children that I evaluate what makes them mad, they often say, "When I don't get my own way." At a very young age, children are used to getting their way. Infants don't usually make demands on us except for things they genuinely need: feeding, changing, holding, and soothing. We don't typically say "no" to an infant, unless she is doing something dangerous like putting an object in her mouth or trying to crawl too far from us.

As the child ages, though, we find ourselves saying "no" with greater frequency. Children begin exercising their newfound skills in ways that aren't always safe or in their best interests. Over time, the child learns that limit setting by adults is one of the realities of the world. Though they may not always like it, the shaping process of early childhood results in most children being able to tolerate the restrictions that parents and the broader world imposes on them.

If a child did not receive adequate parenting in early childhood, he may not have internalized these messages. For many children in chaotic or neglectful environments, no one ever set limits on their behavior. Alternately, the child may have learned through experience that having a tantrum results in getting what he initially wanted. Thus, the child fails to outgrow the self-centeredness of infancy. When he finally finds himself in a home or setting where limits are enforced, he becomes angry and resentful, likely because he was used to getting his own way. In response, he may start a tantrum, become aggressive, or challenge the parents in other ways.

A major role for foster and adoptive parents, therefore, is facilitating their child's psychological growth and development. Parents must be aware that chronological age and emotional age are often quite different for these children. This is one of the reasons the child may prefer to play or have more in common with younger children, or even have no skill at all for interacting appropriately with his peers. In many instances, the child actually needs to be re-parented. True, it isn't possible to put a school-age child back in diapers and start over. But, parents can interact with their child in ways that provide him with experiences and feelings denied to him at earlier stages of his life. Parents should not shy away from these techniques, believing their child will find them silly or childish. Some of my suggestions require age-appropriate modifications, and some can't realistically be used with older children, such as teenagers. Be playful and creative.

If a child is asked to do something for which he doesn't have the skill or maturity, he starts to feel bad about himself. In turn, he may withdraw or act out. The parents then become frustrated and angry, wondering if he is just being oppositional. Soon after a child comes into your home, it should become clear what he can and cannot do with regard to his abilities and maturity. You can then modify your requests, gearing it to his emotional age. For example, if you ask a 10-year-old boy who has 10-year-old maturity to feed the dog, most likely the dog will be fed. But, you wouldn't ask a five-year-old boy to feed the dog, at least not without your supervision and guidance. If your child has the emotional age of a five-year-old, try saying, "Here, let's feed the dog. You hold the bowl and I'll pour the food in." As another example, you wouldn't ask a five-year-old to clean their room and expect them to do it all on their own. Instead, you might say, "Let's go clean your room. Put your toys in this box and then we can make the bed together." At times, you may need to make requests of an older child with the language you would use with one who is much younger.

Therapeutic parenting specialist, Nancy Thomas discourages parents from permitting their child to engage in activities requiring responsibility until they can demonstrate the ability and maturity to do so. For example, most 12-year-old children can walk to the local park or corner market without parental supervision. But for children with disrupted or traumatic backgrounds, parents must be absolutely sure their child can do these activities in a responsible way. In other words, can you be reasonably sure your child won't talk to strangers, will come right home, will return home on time, and will not venture beyond their destination without checking with you?

Many children do manage to compensate for deficits in their maturity level as they grow older. But, this isn't to say there aren't consequences. These children are often perceived as odd by other kids and therefore teased a lot. Teachers or coaches may also find their behaviors confusing, thereby doing things to make the child feel like an outcast. An eight-year-girl I recently evaluated, for example, carries a small stuffed animal with her for security. Not surprisingly, some of the kids in her class have been teasing her about this.

What I tend to find is that most children eventually discover their natural talents and interests. Slowly, they start to feel a sense of mastery, as they direct their efforts toward activities they find rewarding and satisfying. This is one of the reasons I place a lot of emphasis on trying to help children identify interests and goals. If some of this is in place by the time they finish high school, their chances for getting off to a good start in adulthood are increased.

The Role of Shame

Child development theory emphasizes that all infants, between 18 and 36 months, confront the stage of *autonomy versus shame*. As the child grows older and develops greater abilities for expression, movement, and mastery, his efforts can either be supported, thwarted, or ignored by his primary caregiver. For example, infants naturally learn to crawl, stand, walk, and slowly have greater control of their bodies and actions. When parents cheer and celebrate these milestones, the child emerges from this stage sure of himself, elated with his new found control. If, on the other hand, the young child's excitement is met with anger or frustration — picture the scenario of a child crawling out of his mother's sight and in her fear, she spanks or yells at him, asking, "How could you do that?" — he grows to feel bad about himself. Over time, this becomes the roots of shame.

Shame is with us throughout our lives. As William Pollack notes, it begins to be experienced very early on, and is perhaps one of our most primitive feelings. Pollack writes: "Infants show the precursors to shame — physical responses such as painful blushing and "heat" — when their vocalizations for parental response or gestures for recognition go largely unacknowledged." Shame, therefore, plays an important part in developmental attachment. When a caregiver is mostly responsive to her infant child's cues, he grows to develop trust in others and eventually, a secure attachment. If his cues are ignored, however, the risk for attachment disturbance is high. Coupled with the role shame plays in infancy, the child is at risk for having chronic feelings of inadequacy throughout his life.

Shame differs from guilt in many ways. Guilt is typically felt in response to something we do: lie, hurt somebody, take something that is not ours, cheat or break a rule. Guilt therefore socializes. In feeling guilt, the hope is that we will choose to alter our behavior in the future. Shame, on the other hand, is less about what you *did* and more about who you *are*. Shame has a much more inward focus, and as such, leads shameful parties to feel poorly about themselves, rather than simply the actions they have taken. Shame — particularly in children — often leads to withdrawal from others, aggression, and interpersonal conflict. A child who feels shame will sometimes attack or strike out to other people, seek power and perfection, or emotionally shut down.

I am frequently intrigued by the amount of shameful feelings my clients struggle with. By nature of the fact that they were abused, abandoned, or neglected, something bad happened *to them*. They did not cause the trauma. Instead, they suffered because of the choices, carelessness, inadequacy, or mental disturbance of the person who should have taken care of them. From their perspective, however, many feel as if *they* did something wrong. Intellectually, they can identify the ways that their parents dropped the ball in the caregiving department. Still, they struggle with the feeling that they somehow contributed to their circumstances.

Is this somewhat irrational? Sure it is. Yet, it is common for all of us. Think about the times you thought things could have turned out different, "If only I…" We all have a tendency to develop a form of magical thinking about bad things that happen. It is when it becomes excessively self-blaming or self-punishing that it stands to interfere with healthy psychological development.

As an example, I was talking with a 15-year-old client recently about the struggles he is having in school. Soon, it became clear that all the bad feelings he has about himself were channeled into our discussion about his academic performance. He started out with, "I just don't know how to learn. I'll never do well in school. I don't know why I even try." This led to a discussion of the deeper feelings he has that he is somehow defective or deficient because his mother abandoned him when he was five. Our conversation about his performance in school therefore moved to one of him expressing self-hatred and anger over the abandonment by his mother, something he never had any control over.

Tantrums as a Form of Communication

Six months after she was placed with them, the parents of a nine-year-old adopted girl I was seeing took her to Washington, D.C., for a family vacation. Shortly after arriving in the hotel room, the girl proceeded to have a tantrum, tossing clothes around the room, sticking socks in the toilet, throwing rolls of toilet paper, and pulling towels off the shelf. Once she was reasonably calm, the child's adopted father tried talking with her, to find out what she was feeling. As it turned out, this girl was overwhelmed and angry. Having spent all of her life in New Mexico, she was unfamiliar with plane rides, escalators, elevators, large numbers of people, and busy cities. When her father offered that she find another way of expressing her feelings, she replied, "This is what I do. It's how I show I'm angry."

Some children use tantrums as a form of communication simply because they were never taught alternatives. Be it that they witnessed violence or aggression, experienced severe abuse or neglect, or that they just weren't shown how to express feelings in an appropriate manner, these children act out their feelings. As written above, the anger and aggression some children exhibit can be a manifestation of the shame they feel about themselves. In essence, their behavior may be their way of communicating, "I feel bad about myself. I'm mad because of it. I will try to control you so I can feel stronger or more powerful."

The challenge for the parents, therefore, is to both recognize that the child may be trying to tell you something — even if it is to say, "I'm feeling out of control and this is how I try to regain control" — and also that the child needs to be taught other means of expressing feelings. The comments you say to a child during these moments can go a long way toward defusing the situation, as well as minimizing the chances he will feel even worse about himself.

Even though a child experiencing a tantrum looks out of control, the tantrum is often the way he tries to feel in control. During the tantrum, parents should remain patient, calm, and tolerant of the child's behavior. If the child is potentially harmful to himself, others, or property, the parent should try holding the child as he rages. One foster mother I know lets her child rage in the middle of the living room floor while she sits off to the side. She says there is plenty of room, the child doesn't hurt herself or damage anything, and it solves things more quickly than if she tried to get the girl to show her feelings or control her behavior in other ways.

Ultimately, what we need to communicate to children during these times is:

- I can handle your emotions.
- I am stronger than your emotions.
- I am not afraid of your emotions.

In children, anger can serve as a mask for profound hurt, loss, and low self-esteem. For some children, they simply do not feel good about themselves, and they are angry because of it. When parents or teachers yell at them, if other kids avoid them, or if a parent says "no" to them, this increases the anger they feel, creating a vicious cycle. Children who have experienced a lot of loss or change in their lives need their parents to offer support and empathy. Though it can be hard to do this when the child is raging, hugs and talking during the cooling-off phase can help in the long run.

Particularly if the child grew up in a chaotic family, he may be accustomed to seeing what amounts to adult tantrum behavior. Most likely, though, this was never followed up with a discussion about why the adult was angry, or how their actions made others feel. Talking with your child about their tantrum, soon after it is over, is important. In doing so, your goal is to communicate your understanding of what it is the child wants or how they felt. At the same time, you use the opportunity to educate your child about less disruptive ways of communicating his wants, needs, or feelings. This helps the child appreciate that his actions are sometimes unsettling for other people. It is also your chance to remind them that he (hopefully) didn't get what he wanted by having the tantrum.

Children sometimes have tantrums that are within their control, while others have little control over behavior that results from fear or frustration. Knowing the child's history can sometimes give us clues as to whether his actions are deliberate or simply beyond his ability to fully contain. If your child suffered severe trauma and/or was born with neurological distur-bance, the likelihood that the tantrums are out of their full control increases. Children whose mothers consumed alcohol, drugs, or tobacco during the pregnancy, for example, typically have difficulty regulating their mood and emotions. When angry or frustrated, it is not uncommon for these children to respond in exaggerated or dramatic ways.

If the child has a tantrum in response to your limit-setting, or because he did not get his way, then this suggests an immature response style that is likely manipulative. As tiring as it can be, if you respond in a consistent manner each time your child behaves this way, refusing to give in to his wishes or demands, the behavior will eventually subside. This is best managed by establishing firm limits, making clear the choices he has, and enforcing consequences for misbehavior. Parents should not engage the child in a discussion about their behavior during or immediately following a tantrum but should talk after he calms down. Tell him why you believe he had the tantrum. For example, you could say: "You were really mad at me for saying 'no,' weren't you?" "You didn't think I was being fair when I told you to stop playing, huh?" or "It's hard for you to let me be in control sometimes, isn't it?" After offering empathic statements such as these, remind the child about other ways he can express his anger with you. This can include: "It is okay to tell me that you are mad at me," "If you get angry and need to go to your room to be alone for a while, that is fine," "Did you notice that after all that yelling and screaming I still didn't let you have the ice cream you wanted? But it is still okay that you were angry about that."

HELPING CHILDREN RELEASE THEIR RAGE: AN EXERCISE

I like to take all those old socks with holes in them and put them in a big box with all those socks with a missing pair. I then tie two or three of them together. The child is instructed to throw the socks real hard into the driveway or at a tree. They can yell or scream, but they are told to channel their anger through those socks.

- A pillow fight is a good way to release anger. Though it seems a bit aggressive at first, the parties inevitably have a good time, and rarely will someone get hurt. Just make sure the room is big enough!
- Save those old phone books! The angry child can be directed to tear them up as a means of releasing anger.
- Tell your child to take a walk! To the end of the driveway, to the corner and back or around the backyard.
- Have the child lie across your lap, as you sit on the couch. Have the child kick their feet up and down, into the couch, while you safely hold them.
- If a child feels someone did them wrong, have them draw it on a piece of paper or to write down what happened.
- Sometimes kids need to cool off, rather than engage in a physical action. At times, have them sit quietly on the floor, legs folded and hands in their lap for two- to three minutes. Have them face the wall to minimize distractions and ask them to breathe deeply.

If, on the other hand, your child's tantrums come out of nowhere, last for more than 15 minutes, and the child seems mentally or physically uncontrollable, this may indicate a neurological cause. These children do not have the ability to stop their behavior or curb their impulses when angry, frightened, or frustrated. In these cases, children may require neuropsychological or medical evaluations. Some medications are effective at helping to reduce violent and aggressive behavior in children.

Pay attention to what sets your child into a tantrum. If you can predict the triggers, you will be in a better position to divert it before it starts. Above all else, the safety of the child and those around him must be your first priority. As the parent, you have an obligation to protect your child, yourself, your property, and other children or animals in the home. Too often, I see parents try to manage their child's aggressive tantrums on their own. In many instances, they get physically injured. If your child, particularly if he is bigger or stronger than you, is prone to violent tantrums, have a plan in place that may include calling a friend, calling the police, taking him to the hospital, or doing whatever you need to in order to protect yourself and those around you.

Building Children's Confidence

Whenever parents ask my advice on raising children, I usually point out the importance of building a child's confidence. Children who do best at managing the challenges of school, peers, and society are those who are somewhat sure of themselves, able to set appropriate limits with others, and who recognize their own personal worth in comparison to others.

Feeling confident still requires that the child respect other people, both peers and adults. Having confidence in oneself simply means believing that you are just as good and worthy as others. When children have confidence in their abilities, they can stand up to someone who may be bullying them, therefore feeling less like a victim. Kids who have confidence are more likely to raise their hand in class to answer questions, therefore enhancing their learning. Kids who have confidence are also more willing to take appropriate risks, finding their strengths, interests, and talents in the process.

Foster and adopted children are at high risk for feelings of shame and inferiority. When we strive to find ways of boosting their confidence and self-esteem, we counter the negative messages these children may have internalized.

Tips for Confidence Building

Remind your child of his talents. Try not to do this by comparing him to other kids. Instead, emphasize your awareness of his different abilities. This can be in sports, academics, music, art, or even personality. Every now and then, say things such as, "You're obviously paying attention really well in school. I'm so proud of the grades you bring home," "It's great, the way you catch that ball. You track it with your eyes all the way as it heads toward you," "The pictures you draw are incredible. I want to hang all of them in my office."

Catch your child being good. Kids need to be told when they're doing well. Unfortunately, we often do the opposite. When your child is exhibiting respectful and appropriate behavior, tell her! "You look like you're doing a great job of concentrating on that homework," "I appreciate that you're playing quietly. It allows me to focus on my paperwork," "Thank you for taking out the trash when I asked without giving me a hard time. I like that kind of behavior," "You made it home last night right on schedule. Thank you for coming in when we agreed that you would."

Provide opportunities for success. Some children simply have a more challenging time in a whole lot of areas than other kids do. For them, schoolwork seems more difficult, they can't make or keep friends, and they aren't good at sports. These children usually end up feeling bad about themselves. Maybe you can't change the problems they are having at school or with their peers. Instead, try to find things they can do that are helpful to you or others. Even the simplest activities can improve their self-esteem. Examples include: Helping you cook a meal, putting gas in the car for you at the filling station, donating old toys or clothes to a thrift store, volunteering at the animal shelter for a few hours on the weekend, washing the neighbor's car, researching a topic on the Internet, donating a proportion of their allowance to a local charity, or walking the dog.

Teach the word, "no." Children need to learn that adults don't say, "no" just to be mean and depriving. Instead, children should recognize that we all must set limits with other people at times. As children grow older, they will learn other ways of establishing boundaries with people. But, early on they need to understand that it is all right to say, "no," "Stop it," "I don't like that," or "Quit doing that" when someone is acting in a way they don't like. Teach your child to say, "I don't like it when you talk to me like that" to siblings or family members who make them mad. Tell them that they can say, "no," or "Stop it" if another kid touches them, teases them, or tries to bully them.

Anger that adoptees have built up over the years can erupt as uncontrollable rage. There is the unexpressed anger that they are adopted; anger that they are different; anger that they are powerless to know their origins; anger that they cannot express their real feelings in a family climate of denial.

— Betty Jean Lifton,
"Journey of the Adopted Self"

I was angry at my adoptive mom for not exploring the subject of adoption with me. I was angry that the subject of adoption made her uncomfortable ... Because she was unable to help me process my loss and grief, I ended up blaming her for it. She was not responsible for my losses, but I needed her to 'hear' the deepest cries of my heart.

— Sherrie Eldridge,
"Twenty Things Adopted Kids Wish Their Adoptive Parents Knew"

TELL ME THE STORY OF YOUR LIFE: AN EXERCISE

As I've written elsewhere in this book, I work on a systems model with children. This means I rarely see a child in counseling without his parents in the room. Only when I first start providing therapy to the child will I meet with him alone. I will usually meet with the child for an hour or two alone and then all subsequent sessions are with the child and parents. When meeting with the child alone, I will ask him to tell me the story of his life, encouraging him to take as much time as he needs and to tell me as much detail as he knows. Later, I tell the child that I will ask him to do this exercise again, but with his foster or adoptive parents in the room.

With the parents present, I remind the child of what I told him, and I ask him to once again tell me the story of his life. I instruct the parents to sit quietly and to not offer any corrections, questions, or clarifications. I will usually have the child look at me with his back to his parents. That way, he can focus on the story and not look at their nonverbal cues or reactions to what he is saying. More often than not, the child tells me a story filled with many gaps. There may be long stretches of time with absent memories, even if it is only their infant years. Still, I will ask, "Tell me what you think was happening to you when you were a baby."

Frequently, children have a distorted or inaccurate view of what happened in their lives or why things occurred as they did. This can be surprising for parents who at times find themselves questioning why a child believes the things he does.

I once asked a 13-year-old boy to share with me the story of his life, first with me alone and then with his adoptive mother in the room. He told me that his birth mother was a prostitute and that his father was a homeless man. He said his father gathered up enough money to buy sex from his mother and that he was conceived. He then added that his mother couldn't take care of him and left him in a dumpster, where he was later found. As the boy was re-telling this story, his adoptive mother's face was filled with shock and surprise. Ignoring my request to stay quiet and let the boy tell his story, she asked him, "Where on earth did you get all that?" I had to stop her and remind her that it didn't matter. Even though she had told him his birth and adoption story many years before, this is the story he carried in his mind. In turn, it is the story that affects how he perceives his own identity, history, and worth.

As the therapy progresses, I let parents know they can provide the child with answers to questions or more accurate details about their lives. But, initially, it is quite useful to hear what the child thinks and believes, as this has a tremendous influence over his view of himself.

Children and Prenatal Exposure to Toxins

> *Research on attachment suggests that caregivers with certain characteristics can promote positive outcomes for children who are prenatally exposed to alcohol or drugs.*
>
> — Madelyn Freundlich,
> "Adoption and Prenatal Alcohol and Drug Exposure"

Scope of the Problem

IN A STUDY OF 10 HOSPITALS, an estimated 1,200 of the 4,000 drug-exposed infants born in 1989 were placed in foster care. Even if the drug-exposed infants remain in the care of their families after birth, many enter the child welfare system later, because of the chaotic and often dangerous environment associated with parental alcohol or drug abuse. A report from the U.S. House of Representatives Select Committee on Children, Youth and Families found that "increasing numbers of infants are being born drug-exposed, placing them at particular risk of the multiple problems that lead to out-of-home care."

Families abusing alcohol and other drugs, whose children are placed in foster homes, are more likely than other families with children in foster care to include mothers with less education, to be poorly housed, and to receive government assistance prior to placement. Additionally, children from families in which alcohol and other drugs are abused are more likely to enter the foster care system at a younger age than those placed from the general population. The median age of children placed in foster care because of parental drug use is 4.7 years, as compared to 7.5 years for other children.

Children from homes in which substance abuse occurs may be at higher risk for multiple foster care placements. These children often exhibit difficult and frustrating behaviors, requiring greater skills and caretaking on the part of foster parents. Long-term, single placements are uncommon for most children in foster care. However, children who have the wide assortment of behavioral problems frequently associated with families in which substance abuse occurs seem to be harder to place and at higher risk for multiple placements. Consequently, infants from families in which alcohol or other drugs are abused can represent a special challenge to the child welfare system.

One of the things that complicate this picture is that courts and child protection agencies are typically faced with timelines for reunification that are not consistent with the literature on substance abuse recovery. Recent research out of UCLA, for example, suggests that it takes upwards of six months for a body to achieve physiological recovery from long-term use of alcohol or drugs. Not until then, these researchers argue, can the individual start to address the *psychological* aspects of their addiction. Depending on the causes and contributing factors to the addiction — to include genetics, primary support system, family history, and personal motivation — it can take over one year before an individual is able to stay on a path that leads to long-term recovery.

Rarely are the courts going to allow a child to remain in out-of-home placement for this duration of time. Therefore, parents are often referred for services that cannot adequately address the root cause of their addiction. Maybe they can maintain three to four months of recovery — long enough for the child to be returned to their care — only to return to substance use in the future, which then starts a repeat of the original cycle.

The inadequacy of the ability of our communities to address these issues is especially important when one considers that a fairly high proportion of children are returned to foster care placements after reunification with their biological parents. Current estimates find 32 percent of children previously placed in foster care re-enter the system, compared to only 2 percent of children who are adopted. Research also shows that reunification is twice as likely for parents who do not use drugs compared to substance abusing parents. In New York state, it is estimated that half of the children reunited with parents with substance abusing backgrounds return to the foster care system within four months.

A study by the National Committee to Prevent Child Abuse found that 80 percent of the states identified parental substance abuse as one of the most prevalent problems in families reported for child maltreatment. Experts now estimate that 500,000 to 750,000 infants are born each year that have been exposed to one or more illicit drugs in utero. When the legal drugs — alcohol and tobacco — are added, the figure rises to considerably more than one million substance exposed infants.

Infants enter foster care more than any other age group and most enter foster care because of parental substance abuse. Children of substance-abusing parents stay in foster care longer than children who are referred for other reasons. Unless the parents work a vigorous treatment plan, which often includes some form of drug or alcohol treatment, their child likely will eventually be placed for adoption. This means that a significant number of children who are adopted — both within the United States and from abroad — come to their homes with prenatal alcohol or drug exposure as a risk factor.

While the research indicates that some of these children do not show any long-term developmental delay, others experience a multitude of behavioral, learning, and neurological problems throughout childhood. Some of the most common problems cited include:

- Disturbed sleep/wake cycles
- Poor fine motor control
- Hyperactivity
- Language delays
- Attention problems
- Learning disabilities
- Poor impulse control
- Difficulties with abstract reasoning
- Memory impairment
- Poor judgment
- Impaired adaptive functioning

Research into this area also shows it does make a difference which substances a mother was using during pregnancy, as well as how long she used them. The most common physical effect on children is low birth weight and small head size. The most common behavioral effect is that the child becomes easily overwhelmed by various stimuli, such as bright lights, loud noises, or sudden and unfamiliar touch. In infancy, these children are often difficult to soothe and many seem anxious and frightened. Over time, the child may develop a fearful or cautious approach to his environment, which interferes with his ability to learn about the world by interacting with it in meaningful ways. The manner in which the primary caregivers respond to the child's mood and behavior have profound effects on his long-term attachment pattern.

Alcohol

Research implicates alcohol in a wide range of perinatal effects including:

- An increased risk of spontaneous abortion and stillbirth
- Shorter gestation periods
- Reduced birth size and weight

Alcohol exposure is one of the leading causes of mental retardation in the United States, as well as learning, speech, and behavioral problems. When a pregnant mother consumes alcohol, the risk of miscarriage, premature delivery, and birth complications rise. Alcohol kills neurons in the fetal brain and it can affect the way the brain develops.

Researchers normally divide the long-term effects of prenatal exposure to alcohol into two categories:

- Fetal Alcohol Syndrome (FAS)
- Alcohol-Related Birth Defects, sometimes called Fetal Alcohol Effects (FAE)

To meet the criteria for Fetal Alcohol Syndrome, one sign from each of these three categories must be present:

- Prenatal and/or postnatal growth retardation (weight, length, and/or head circumference below the tenth percentile corrected for gestational age)
- Central nervous system involvement (indications of neurological abnormality, developmental delay, or intellectual impairment)
- Facial abnormalities (with at least two of the following signs: head circumference below the third percentile; narrow eye slits; flat and long upper lip; underdeveloped midface; and flattened nose bridge)

Other physical abnormalities associated with FAS include cardiovascular problems, cardiac murmurs, kidney troubles, respiratory dysfunction, hernias, and shortened fingers. Delayed motor development is also common, and children with FAS often have impaired vision and/or hearing.

Fetal Alcohol Syndrome annually affects between 1.3 and 2.2 children per 1,000 live births in North America— between 16,000 and 22,000 children per year.

Most children with FAS never catch up in size or cognitive ability, relative to their non-affected peers. Because of this, they will likely require special education services throughout childhood. Studies show that children with FAS had IQ scores ranging from normal to severely mentally retarded, with an average score of 65 – five points below the level marking mental retardation.

Researchers have estimated that, among the children prenatally exposed to alcohol, the number suffering potentially severe developmental effects without diagnostic signs of FAS is twice the number of those with FAS indicators.

These effects include:

- Alcohol-related features (alcohol dysmorphia)
- Growth retardation
- Cognitive deficits
- Attention and memory deficits
- Distractibility
- Poor organizational skills
- Inflexible approach to problem solving

Tobacco and Marijuana

Women who smoke cigarettes during pregnancy often have babies with low birth weight. Children born to mothers who smoked during pregnancy are at greater risk of developing hyperactivity, language and motor skills deficits, and impaired cognitive function. Some studies suggest that these children have lower IQ scores, as well as health conditions such as asthma.

Despite the growing use of cocaine and amphetamines, marijuana remains the most widely used illicit drug. Rates of newborns prenatally exposed to marijuana have been estimated at levels from 3 to almost 20 percent, which would indicate that every year women give birth to between 125,000 and 835,000 children prenatally exposed to marijuana. Studies that have examined the effects of prenatal marijuana exposure indicate that these children are at greater risk of having behavioral problems, as well as verbal and memory deficits.

Cocaine

Prenatal exposure to cocaine increases the risk of preterm delivery, smaller-than-normal head size, low birth weight, and low scores on the Apgar, which assesses the overall condition of newborns. Long-term studies on the effects of cocaine yield mixed results. Some studies indicate that 30 to 40 percent of a sample of cocaine-exposed children had language development and attention problems through at least their fourth year of life. The American Medical Association, however, cautions that the data from these studies is too fragmented to allow any clear predictions about the effects of prenatal cocaine exposure.

Brain Development and Behavior

When I evaluate children whose birth mothers used alcohol, drugs, or tobacco, I typically find evidence of mild to moderate impairment to the frontal region of the brain, the prefrontal cortex. The frontal lobes are located right behind the forehead and continue to grow throughout childhood. They are not fully developed until early adulthood.

The frontal lobes are responsible for executive functions such as:

- Our ability to use logic
- Sizing up potential risks
- Short term memory
- Sound decisions and judgment
- Impulse control
- Mental reasoning
- Cause and effect thinking

Deficits of this nature are incredibly frustrating for parents. They result in children failing to exhibit age-typical behaviors in school, at home, or in the community. Most of these parents tell me their child lacks the ability to exercise good judgment. In a crude way, the frontal lobes are directly responsible for those behaviors that we couch under the term, *common sense*. One father told me recently that he was riding a bicycle with his 13-year-old adopted daughter and she kept going through stop signs without looking. An adoptive mother told me that her eight-year-old son goes up to any dog he sees, without any awareness of the potential for danger. The frontal lobes play a main part in these kinds of decision-making operations.

While a lack of common sense can be tolerated in some situations, failure to exercise good judgment can result in harm to the child. Without a logical assessment of the risks or benefits of one's actions, the consequences may be life threatening or result in severe sanctions. As children grow and mature, we hope they are able to recognize situations that may be unsafe or dangerous and to take the appropriate action.

If your child's birthmother consumed alcohol, drugs, or tobacco while pregnant, it is important for you to ask the psychologist who evaluates him to provide you with data pertaining to frontal lobe functioning. If frontal lobe impairment is identified, it tells you that the child may appear to have Attention-Deficit/Hyperactivity Disorder. ADHD, however, is typically responsive to medications and interventions that have little effect on frontal lobe impairment. Thus, an alternative course of treatment may be required.

Prognosis and Interventions

It is difficult to predict which children will experience learning, memory, or behavior problems as a result of prenatal exposure to toxins. Studies conducted with adoptive parents who are raising children with these risk factors show a range of outcomes. Some adoptive parents report that their child has only slight problems in these areas while others report significant impairments. This suggests that parents should not rule out adopting a child just because the birth mother used alcohol, drugs, or tobacco. Rather, the child's current health and behavior must be considered, as well as his responsiveness to therapeutic and educational interventions.

The single most potent factor influencing developmental outcome turns out to be the cultural environment of the child, as expressed in socioeconomic status and parental education level. Simply put, the poor suffer the conse-quences of vulnerable birth status more than those of higher income. The developmental deficits that normalize by school age in most children tend to persist longer in those from low income families.

COMMON BEHAVIORAL EFFECTS
FOLLOWING PRENATAL DRUG EXPOSURE

Effect	Alcohol	Cocaine	Heroin	Nicotine
Hyperactivity	■	■	■	■
Attention Deficits	■	■	■	■
Aggressiveness	■		■	
Impulsivity	■	■	■	■
Cognitive Delays	■		■	■
Learning Disorders	■		■	■
Sleep Problems	■			
Feeding Difficulties	■	■		
Irritability	■	■		
Fine Motor Impairment	■			
Mental Retardation	■			
Physical Deformities	■			
Difficulty Adjusting to New Situations	■	■	■	

If you are raising an infant who was exposed to toxins, you should obtain frequent medical and developmental evaluations, particularly if the child shows some of the above symptoms. We know that early intervention services can go a long way toward detouring problematic behaviors, such as tantrums, learning delays, or inattention. Even if the child does not qualify for special services, you may want to hire or work with a developmental specialist who can teach you techniques for promoting good behavior, attention, and learning. All or most children do well with parental efforts that provide structure, boundaries, clear messages, and strategies to reduce stress or anxiety. Children with neurological vulnerability because of prenatal toxin exposure will require this structure more frequently and by all or most of their caregivers.

A question many parents ask is whether to tell a child his birth parents used alcohol or drugs. I believe children should eventually be told, but in words that are appropriate for their age and cognitive development. As previously mentioned, children learn about the consequences of drug use in profound ways when they appreciate that substance use impaired the ability of their birth parent to take care of them. As mentioned earlier, your child has a high statistical risk of using alcohol or drugs, just by nature of being a teenager in today's society. It is therefore important for you to have frank and candid discussions about substance use, at least by the time he is 12. Many federally funded websites offer excellent tips for parents on talking with their children about alcohol, tobacco, and drug use.

Most experts agree that some people are genetically vulnerable to addiction. This doesn't tell us who will or will not actually use drugs or alcohol but shows that certain people will not be able to use drugs or alcohol recreationally. Instead, they are "wired" to become addicted if they use. By talking with an older child or adolescent about drug use, addictions, and the actions of their birth parents, you can hopefully help them to appreciate that they could be at genetic risk of having their drug or alcohol use get out of control. If your child has a genetic predisposition to substance use, education and intervention on your part will need to be done early and often.

RESOURCES

FURTHER READING

What's Going on in There: How the Brain and Mind Develop in the First Five Years of Life (book)
Lise Eliot

Talking with Kids About Drugs and Alcohol
www.talkingwithkids.org

What You Need to Know About Attachment

D URING WORLD WAR II, WHEN the Nazi's were bombing London on a daily basis, it was a tremendously stressful time for many children. One parent, usually the father, was typically away amid chronic hunger and poverty. Each day, children would often see dead bodies being carried away. In order to counter the ill effects on children, some people proposed giving parents the choice of having their kids reside in an orphanage in the countryside, noting that the Nazi's did not have enough bombs to attack the city and the rural areas. Some parents took advantage of this, which meant the children did not reside with either parent.

The children who lived in the orphanages ended up dying at a higher rate than the children who remained in the city, even though their surroundings were cleaner and they had adequate meals. At first, some people thought the children were dying because of disease. They ordered the orphanage painted and thoroughly cleaned. Still, the children kept wasting away and dying. Eventually, a consultant was hired who instructed all members of the staff — nurses, doctors, and janitors — to stop cleaning and to give the children more attention throughout the day. Each member of the staff was told to periodically touch the children and to try to spend time with them. After this was initiated, the death rate among the children returned to normal rates.

When the war ended and children were assessed, it was also discovered that the children who moved to the country had more symptoms of trauma than those who stayed in London. The researchers concluded that being away from the parents was more stressful for the children than being surrounded by death, bombings and hunger. Findings such as this highlighted the importance a parent plays in their child's life and development, particularly the primary caregiver, who is usually the child's mother.

In the summer of 2004, terrorists overtook a school in Russia, holding over 1,000 hostages. Unfortunately, many of the children were killed, as were the adults who were held with them. For some of the children, a parent or grandparent survived the ordeal with them, while others did not. Attachment and trauma theory tells us that the children who had a guardian with them should fare better psychologically than the other children, even in light of all the other horrors they witnessed.

We had a case in New Mexico where a mother beat her toddler with a shoe until he could not speak or use his hands or arms. The child was placed in foster care and the mother's legal rights were terminated. Through rehabilitation, it took more than one year for the child to gain enough strength in his fingers in order to use a Ouija Board to spell out words, since he still couldn't communicate verbally. When asked what he wanted, the first word he spelled out was MOM. This was startling for many members of his care team, who felt that he would want nothing to do with the person who caused his injuries and disability. Yet, even through his suffering, the child communicated his interest in wanting his mother. This is not an isolated story and it highlights the importance of "mother" for the young child, even when it is the mother who is contributing to the stress, abuse, or trauma the child is experiencing.

I remember a foster mother once telling me that the nine-year-old child she was caring for desperately wanted to be returned to his mother, even though she had beat him horribly. She said he reminded her of the family dog she had when she was growing up, noting, "My brother was always mean to that dog. He would yell at him, throw things at him, and sometimes kick him. But that dog kept coming back to him."

The importance and meaning of the parent-child relationship is at the heart of the word, attachment. While early theories and observations focused primarily on the role of the mother and her infant, we now know that a child can develop an attachment to any caregiver, biological or not. Some schools of thought suggest that attachment forms while the mother is pregnant with her child. Viewed from this perspective, attachment is a biological process, designed to orient the child to his main caregiver once he is born. Even if true, children can certainly develop an attachment and bond to persons other than the mother, as demonstrated consistently in circumstances where the biological mother is permanently or temporarily absent from the child's life. Cross-cultural observations certainly confirm that children can attach to someone other than the primary mother and do just fine psychologically.

As many researchers have noted, attachment bears a lot of similarity to the instinctual imprinting of young animals. Attachment behavior — the seeking of a primary source for comfort and security, especially during times of stress — is prominent in every species of bird or mammal whose survival depends heavily on parental care. It is also universal among all cultures. While a parent may immediately form an intense bond with her child, the process is a bit slower in reverse. It takes about six months before a baby begins to bond with his parent, accelerating for the next 12 months. This is not to diminish the importance of the caregiver during those first few months of life. Rather, in humans and in animals, attachment behavior corresponds with the onset of locomotion. As some have suggested, babies may not need to feel attached until they reach the point when they are capable of crawling on their own.

Infants are born with the capacity to signal their needs for warmth, food, touch, changing and greater comfort. They do this in a variety of ways, to include smiling, eye contact, sucking, wiggling, crying, and reaching. This cycle is referred to as the "attachment system" and it works as follows: The child experiences stress, either from internal cues (I'm hot, cold, wet, or afraid) or external cues (The light is too bright, that sound was too loud, something or someone is causing me pain). The child activates his attachment cues (smiling, reaching, or crying]. If the mother responds, the stress is alleviated and the attachment cues stop. If the mother does not respond, the child's level of stress increases, as do the attachment cues (whining turns into crying; crying turns into screaming; subtle body movements turn into thrashing).

Infants elicit this engagement from a small number of caregivers, which usually includes the primary person, such as the mother, who takes care of him. When the child's caregivers are mostly responsive to his needs, it helps him feel safe. This means that the caregivers accurately perceive that he needs to be held, changed, fed, or played with. When an adult says to an infant, "Oh, you must be hungry," "That must have hurt," bounces the child on her lap as he smiles, or even when she changes a diaper, she communicates to the child that she understands how he feels and what it is he needs. Much of the interaction between an infant and his caregiver is intuitive. Babies can't state what they need and so they require the caregiver to read these signals. But to read a baby's signals, the caregiver must be paying adequate attention.

Mothers in child welfare cases often use drugs or alcohol, are involved in abusive relationships, rely extensively on other caregivers for the child, or suffer mental problems such as depression. Studies with teenage mothers indicate they are often anxious, particularly when their baby is crying or otherwise indicating some kind of need. In response, the anxious mother withdraws when her child is needy, mainly because she is also feeling distressed and is not always sure how to satisfy her child. In these instances, the child's needs may go unnoticed for long periods of time. The child cries longer or otherwise remains in a condition of stress or discomfort, as he longs for something that isn't being provided.

In cases of abuse or neglect, we place a lot of our emphasis on the physical experience of the child: the pain, the hunger, being cold and other physical conditions. While these effects should never be minimized, the psychological effects of abuse and neglect more often contribute to difficulties as the child grows older. Much of this is because his basic needs were not met within a family where abuse or neglect was permitted to occur, resulting in fear, confusion and anger.

Attachment Patterns Defined

If a mother can identify her child's needs and respond in a timely manner, the child comes to believe that other people can be trusted and relied upon. Over time, the child starts to feel safe in the world and to feel good about himself. Since he is not focused on his basic needs for survival, he is able to explore his environment, play with things, and gradually develop a broader understanding of the world around him. These conditions result in what is called secure attachment. Secure attachment typically results in a child feeling good about himself, trusting of others, and confident about being in the broader world.

For many mothers, their infant's needs, arousal, or distress cause them to experience distress of their own. This is common in situations where the mother lacks confidence in her parenting, is unsure whether she actually wants the child, or is too overwhelmed in her own life. The baby is then left to make sense of this on his own. In some instances, the baby finds that he gets his mother's attention if he doesn't cry or act too fussy. He has likely learned that if he shows too much need, it causes his mother to withdraw. From the child's perspective, the signals he uses to bring his mother closer produce the opposite effect. When he shows distress, his mother physically and/or emotionally pulls away. If this continues, the child is at risk of developing an *avoidant attachment*. What the child finds is that if he "lays low" and doesn't put many demands on his mother, she is less likely to move away from or to reject him. Over time, the infant learns to suppress or minimize his needs, lest they drive his mother away. Thus, when he is anxious, worried, uncomfortable, or scared, he may not readily show this, for fear that it will cause his mother to pull away. He therefore learns to tolerate prolonged periods of discomfort, without "communicating" his needs about this.[†]

[†]A similar experience often occurs for young babies who live in orphanages. Low numbers of staff-child ratios coupled with the fact there are different care providers, means that a child may experience lengthy periods of stress, anxiety, or discomfort before his needs are attended to. To cope with this, the child either has to sublimate his needs or resort to uncontrollable screaming.

In other instances, the child experiences his mother's availability as erratic or unpredictable. Sometimes she appears to know what he needs, while at other times his cries go unheard for long periods of time. This is common in situations where the mother is using drugs, is depressed, or is involved in an abusive relationship. When drugs, her partner, or her emotions compete with the child for attention, the child often loses. Either because she is high, involved in an argument, or in the depths of despair, the mother may not be responsive to her child's cues. Thus, if he is trying to get her eye contact, crying, or reaching for her, the mother may not be aware of this. Yet, at other times she is. These mothers are under-involved with their infants and so they miss many of the attachment signals. Over time, these children hyper-activate their attachment cues. They have learned that subtlety doesn't work. So if they are hungry, wet, or scared, they won't whimper or wiggle. Instead, they will let out a scream and start thrashing, as this behavior is more likely to get the mother's attention. The child learns that over time his mother's attention cannot be relied upon, particularly during moments of distress. In addition, the child never learns what it takes to actually get his mother's attention. These children grow to develop an *ambivalent attachment*. They do whatever they can to elicit the attention of others as they get older, always fearing that people will not have enough interest in them. In school, they are often loud, disruptive, and annoying, as they do whatever they can to keep the focus of attention on them.

Finally, there is the child with *disorganized attachment*. This pattern manifests when the child is either afraid for or afraid of his caregiver. Frightened children naturally want comfort and a reminder they are safe. Thus, the instinctual response is to put forth cues — crying, reaching for, or crawling toward — their main caregiver. But if the caregiver is the one who is scaring the child, he doesn't know what to do. This is common in situations in which children are severely abused or the child is exposed to other forms of violence. Children can develop a disorganized attachment if their primary caregiver hurts them, appears frightened in front of them (because somebody is hurting them), or acts strange or scary due to psychosis or drug use. The child learns he can do nothing to decrease his anxiety or to find comfort. David Howe, et al, in the book "Attachment Theory, Child Maltreatment and Family Support" writes:

> *As infants, the only options appear to be helpless thrashing about, turning around in circles in distress, psychologically opting out (not "being there," becoming trance-like or "freezing"), identifying with the source of the fear (seeing the self as evil, dangerous and bad) or becoming self-absorbed in closed feedback behaviors that at least remain under the control of the self (rhythmic rocking, head-banging, covering the face with the hands or biting the self).*

Collectively, we refer to these last three patterns as disrupted attachment. Children with disrupted attachment can be difficult to parent. These children are often mistrustful, angry, irresponsible, defensive, dishonest, destructive, and rejecting of love and affection. They will challenge adult and parental authority, attempt to take control over the household, and work toward having their parents feel inadequate. I find that many foster and adoptive parents tolerate the manipulative behavior of their child, holding onto the mistaken belief that they will wait out or wear their child down with time. Unfortunately, these parents find that the child's will and determination is often stronger than their own. By the time they contact professionals for services, the parents are exhausted, feeling defeated and feeling out of control of their own lives.

In attachment theory, the direct and indirect messages that a child receives from early caregiving experiences has lifelong consequences. Also, attachment patterns are generally recognized to have an intergenerational quality. Children with ambivalent attachment often grow to give birth to children who develop the same attachment style. This is why early intervention is so important. If we can interrupt a disrupted attachment pattern early in a child's life, we can not only change his life, but that of his offspring as well.

A recent study found that, although foster children have many more attachment-related difficulties than other children, foster parents are not more sensitive or knowledgeable about children's attachment needs than other parents. The authors of the study therefore recommend that foster

DETERMINING YOUR CHILD'S ATTACHMENT PATTERN

Early Caregiving Environment	How Child Deals with Stress	The Child's Relationships
AVOIDANT		
When baby was needy or distressed, primary caregiver withdrew her attention. Baby may have been told nothing is wrong, even if he was tired, hungry, or needed changing. Baby given attention when he wasn't very needy or demanding.	Avoids telling others his feelings or problems. When anxious, withdraws or prefers to be alone. Child tries to please parents, to be good and have few needs. Child prefers to talk about things and objects, not feelings.	Overly compliant. Appears he can take or leave friendships. Relates intellectually, with little emotion. Views others as unavailable or rejecting. Prefers not to depend on others. Not very supportive of others' distress.
AMBIVALENT		
Caregiver underinvolved with infant and missed many of his distress cues. Emotional neglect by caregiver. Child could mostly get caregiver's attention only by being loud or demanding. Child was unable to predict what would work at getting caregiver's attention.	Yells, pleads, demands to get attention. Not readily soothed. Anger if needs not met quickly Will threaten and demand if ignored. Can't self-soothe; must have attention of others. Can act helpless, dependent or manipulative for attention. Child strives to keep environment energetic, active, chaotic.	Poor empathy; unable to take others' perspective. Accepts no responsibility for state of their relationships. Failure always seen as fault of other person. Likely to bully others. Constant demands drive others away. High drama to attract attention to self. Anger and bossiness used to punish unresponsive people. Overly-dependent on others; constantly fears abandonment.
DISORGANIZED		
High rates of alarm by caregivers. Caregiver is scary, threatening, or abusive. Caregiver unresponsive or did not care about child's needs. Child afraid great deal of the time. In infancy, may have thrashed around, self-harm, screaming, not readily soothed.	Sees self as unworthy of care. Uses anger to feel strong or in control. Dislike of being touched. Cruelty to people/animals. Punish people with anger and hostility.	Blames/exploits others. Aggression to others. Avoids any closeness. Rage, violence if provoked. No friends, unless in gang.

parents receive specialized training in childhood attachment. An argument can be made that the same is true for many adoptive parents.

As you read information about attachment, you will hopefully come to a better understanding of your child. Attachment affects us all, not just those in the child welfare system. The faith you have in others, the trust we hold, and expectations we have in our relationships are all affected by our own early attachment experiences.

Identifying Attachment Patterns

When asked to evaluate children for the purpose of determining their attachment pattern, I examine details of their history, behavior, coping and defense mechanisms, and the results from psychological testing. Even then, coming up with the correct classification can be challenging. Part of the difficulty is that many children have features of more than one attachment style, though more often than not one pattern is dominant.

Using the guide on the opposite page should help you to clarify the prominent attachment style of your child.

> *Attachment theory holds that, within close relationships, young children acquire mental representations, or internal working models, of their own worthiness based on other people's availability and their ability and willingness to provide care and protection.*
>
> — Mary Ainsworth,
> "Patterns of Attachment"

Internal Working Models

As children with disrupted attachment grow, each develops characteristic ways of perceiving themselves and relating to others. Often, these children view themselves as unworthy of love and care.

Children with disrupted attachment can develop the following beliefs:

- I am a bad or defective person
- I deserve to be abandoned or abused
- Caregivers can never be trusted
- I must be in control at all times in order to survive
- Never let others know how you really feel
- Other people cannot be trusted
- Be self-sufficient at all costs
- The world is unsafe
- I don't deserve love
- I will be abandoned again
- Love hurts
- Don't let your guard down

The child's belief system, or *internal working model*, then serves as a blueprint for all current and future relationships, making it difficult for the new parents to convince him that things will now be different. Internal working models are fairly entrenched and resistant to change. Even when the message they convey serves to make the child feel bad about himself or others, it is something he has a difficult time letting go of. When we try to tell the child otherwise, he can end up feeling that we don't have a good hold on the ways he feels about himself. In turn, this can increase his feelings of isolation.

The intimate relationships we have with others significantly affect the view we have of subsequent relationships. If your former spouse or partner hit you, cheated on you, or was simply a bad mate, you will likely exercise caution in future relationships. The adult mind can sort out issues such as, "He was simply a bad choice for me," "I was too young to be in a relationship," "I should have taken the time to get to know her," or "All men are alike." Yet, these experiences definitely impact our behavior and expectations in relationships. For children, these dynamics are magnified immensely.

Fortunately, most people receive validation in other ways that they are worthy of love, affection, and a good life. Feelings of low worth quickly dissolve when we accomplish something important, improve another person's life, stop to take stock of what we have been blessed with, or end up in a satisfying relationship.

But, drawing alternative perspectives about the world will be challenging for the child who starts off life forced to absorb physical or emotional assaults. The child may have difficulty believing in his worth, trusting others, or opening his heart to love because his experiences have reinforced that it is not safe or wise to do so. When the child enters our life, we may see a wonderful person with tremendous talent and potential. He may not necessarily see himself in the same way, nor is he apt to come around to our way of viewing him without tremendous resistance.

Use your own life experience as an example. You likely came to believe things about yourself, even if only temporarily, based on what happened to you. For example, an only child may develop the mistaken belief that he is somehow special or entitled; obtaining poor grades can leave a person feeling he is stupid or unintelligent; a failed relationship can leave us questioning our worth as a person or partner; bankruptcy, divorce, or an accident often results in people feeling they deserve to be punished.

Clearly, we all have internal working models about ourselves. If we are to truly bond with the child and expect him to trust us, we must first appreciate what views he holds of himself. Our efforts and interactions with him over time then confirm or modify these beliefs as needed.

ATTACHMENT SYMPTOMS

Later in this book, I make the distinction between Attachment Disorder and Reactive Attachment Disorder. While the symptoms listed below may or may not manifest in Reactive Attachment Disorder, they are commonly cited as indicators of the broader, Attachment Disorder.

- Physical violence to self or others
- Cruelty to animals
- Constant lying
- Stealing
- Preoccupation with fire
- Excessive interest in evil, blood, or gore
- Sleep disturbance
- Hoarding of food or toys
- Poor hygiene
- Difficulty with novelty or change
- Intense rage
- Lack of eye contact
- Difficulty with affection
- Poor social skills
- Blames others for their problems/mistakes
- Mistrustful of others
- Accident prone
- Lack of remorse when they hurt others
- Overly friendly with strangers
- Argumentative for long periods of time
- Tremendous need for control over everything
- Acts amazingly innocent when caught doing something wrong
- Deliberately breaks or ruins things
- No age-appropriate guilt for his actions
- Unable to stop impulsive behavior
- Will demand, instead of asking for things
- Will chatter non-stop

Rarely will one child display all of these symptoms. I find that children's behaviors tend to cluster: One child may be more destructive, while another may be more manipulative. Don't let someone tell you that these behaviors are part of normal child development. Rather, the symptoms I have listed are maladaptive, and they cause many problems for those people in the child's immediate environment.

No variables ... have more far-reaching effects on personality development than have a child's experiences within his family: for, starting during his first months in his relation with both parents, he builds up working models of how attachment figures are likely to behave towards him in any of a variety of situations, and on those models are based all his expectations, and therefore all his plans, for the rest of his life.

— John Bowlby,
"Attachment and Loss"

Disrupted Attachment and Children's Mental Health

Although disrupted attachment is considered a risk factor for pathology, not all, or even most, anxiously attached infants will develop a form of mental illness. Similarly, secure attachment is not a guarantee of mental health but viewed rather as a protective factor. Research has demonstrated that children with secure histories are more resistant to stress and more likely to rebound toward adequate functioning following a period of troubled behavior.

Myths about Attachment

Children adopted at birth don't experience disrupted attachment

This is false. Some of the children I have worked with who have the most severe attachment difficulties were adopted at infancy, right from the hospital. Though adoption in infancy lessens the likelihood of a child developing an attachment disorder, there is no guarantee a child adopted at birth will not become symptomatic. Attachment difficulties can result from biological disturbance, such as prenatal exposure to alcohol or drugs, maternal stress, failure to thrive, nutritional deficiencies, or premature birth.

Adoptive families do not form attachments

This is false. The attachment between a child and his adoptive parents develops under different circumstances than the attachment between a child and his biological parent. Giving birth to a child does not predispose the child to attach only to the biological parent.

All children with disrupted attachment grow up to become criminals

This is false. Many persons with antisocial personalities or behavior do have attachment disturbance. But, there is no guarantee that a child with attachment disturbance will grow to exploit, hurt, or take advantage of others. Many persons with attachment disorder grow up not trusting people, but this does not mean they set out to do other people harm. Studies suggest that risk factors for developing antisocial behavior include: Witness to violence in childhood, parental mental illness, maternal rejection, low I.Q., maltreatment, and re-experiencing traumatic events. Behavioral risk factors include fire play, animal cruelty, violence to self or others, and lack of empathy.

Truths about Attachment

- The earliest attachments are usually formed by the age of seven months.
- Nearly all infants have the potential for becoming attached.
- Attachments are formed to only a few persons.
- These selective attachments appear to be derived from social interactions with the attachment figures.
- Although attachment behavior is seen primarily in children, adults continue to manifest attachment throughout the lifespan.
- Maltreated infants and toddlers are likely to form insecure attachment relationships.

Attachment is Lifelong

Parents often have mixed reactions to hearing that a child's early attachment experiences can affect his mood, behavior, and personality over the course of his life. Many parents fear that this means a child is permanently damaged if his early years were filled with abuse or neglect. Fortunately, we know that children can make sense out of the things that have happened to them. In turn, they can develop skills for interacting with other people in ways that are healthy and functional.

Some researchers have proposed that the parents most at risk for contributing to maladaptive attachment patterns in their children are those who failed to understand and resolve trauma related to their own past. When parents are able to make sense of their own early life experiences, they are in a better position to facilitate a healthy attachment with their child. This is hopeful news for people who work with the parents who have had their children removed due to abuse and neglect. But, facing their own childhood trauma takes a lot of time and work. Some parents simply have too many other barriers in life — substance use, poverty, mental illness, an abusive relationship — that prevents working on these issues. Many of these children will therefore come into foster care or be placed for adoption without having had the opportunity to experience healthy bonding and

---

SIGNS OF SECURE ATTACHMENT

- Explores the environment with feelings of safety and security
- Has the ability to self-regulate, which results in effective management of impulses and emotions
- Has a sense of competency, self-worth, and a balance between dependence and autonomy
- Has a strong moral framework, which includes empathy, compassion, and conscience
- Often resourceful and resilient
- Tends to trust others

attachment with their birth mother. It then becomes our responsibility to provide the child with opportunities for having his emotional and physical needs met. Through our efforts, we can hopefully reverse some of the ill-effects the child suffered in growing up in a chaotic environment.

Defensive Styles

All of us have psychological defenses that we use during times of stress or conflict. This includes defenses such as denial, rationalization, or passive aggression. Defenses help us to cope during difficult times, such as the death of a loved one, relationship problems, or when we just feel too overwhelmed. When someone relies too much on their defenses to cope with — or rather, to avoid — problems, it stands to interfere with their own happiness or satisfaction in relationships. Defenses can also result in immature behavior such as constantly blaming others for what happens, dissociating or "cutting off" any emotional response at all, or acting out in a hostile or aggressive way in order to divert people's attention to something else.

Children with disrupted attachment develop defense mechanisms to help them cope. They use the defense mechanisms to tell themselves:

- I can get through this pain
- This is not really happening
- She is still a good parent anyhow
- All this madness will soon stop
- This is all so-and-so's fault
- Think, don't feel, and you'll get through this
- If I have enough attention I'll feel better

Parents should remain mindful of the part these defensive styles play for the child. The early experiences for a child with avoidant attachment, for example, have taught him that his needs are not important. Since his strong feelings have mostly been ignored, he has learned to minimize or cut off his emotional needs. As he grows older, he relies more on thoughts than feelings to guide his behavior. Since he perceives others as potentially rejecting, the child with an avoidant attachment has little use for others. Instead, he approaches the world in a self-sufficient manner, where little interest or thought is given to others. When confronted with strong emotions — in himself or in others — the child with an avoidant attachment withdraws and "detaches." This behavior makes it difficult to engage them, either as parents, in therapy, or in relationship. If a parent, therapist, or partner places too many emotional demands on them, they will likely become stressed and overwhelmed. Typically, children with avoidant attachment patterns do better in therapy that is more supportive than confrontational. At home, they are also not the kind who will likely act out or aggress. If they are worried, bothered, or under stress, they are more apt to retreat into their room, to read, or to draw.

Children with an ambivalent attachment style, on the other hand, are motivated by the insatiable need to have attention directed toward them. Their defensive style when under stress is to act out, rather than repress their feelings, with the goal of getting others to pay attention. They will do whatever it takes to get this attention. This includes throwing paper in class, hitting other kids, always making noise, and finding other ways of being disruptive. Too often, these children are mistakenly diagnosed with Attention-Deficit/Hyperactivity Disorder (ADHD). This makes sense, as they are often in constant motion, have a difficult time focusing their attention, and do not learn well in the average classroom. Yet, the interventions that work so well with true ADHD children fail miserably with these kids. As the child grows older, he will do what it takes to secure the attention of others, even if it means having to resort to intimidation. Some experts suspect that many male abusers — men who are extremely jealous and do what they can to control their partners — have classic features of an ambivalent attachment style. At home, in school, and in therapy, these children require a great deal of structure, with clear and firm consequences for noncompliance.

More so than with the other attachment styles, children with the disorganized attachment pattern are incredibly angry. Anger helps them feel strong and in control. They have learned that to feel safe, they must take control and dominate others. These children are aggressive and violent. Their defensive style is to act out — but in ways that are more than just annoying or disruptive. This attachment style results in a level of defensive dysregulation, where stress can and often does impact their ability to accurately perceive what others are saying or doing. They often misinterpret the actions of others, responding in a manner as if their very life depended on it. Inevitably, they are assigned diagnoses such as Reactive Attachment Disorder, Oppositional Defiant Disorder, or Conduct Disorder. Their risk for adolescent and adult criminal behavior is high. In placement, these children usually meet the criteria for treatment foster care, while many will require residential treatment. Passive approaches to parenting or therapy will likely fail with these children. Instead, they need to proactively address the anger, rage, and abandonment they experienced. Certainly, many children with this attachment style do manage to make it in adoptive homes and in society. But, at least in my experience, the treatment and support they require must be intensive and offered at an early age.

Interventions

As with any kind of psychological or medical condition or disorder, there is no one-size-fits-all approach to treating disrupted attachment in children. Where a lot of therapeutic intervention falls short, however, is in the beginning phase of the treatment. Without a thorough understanding of the key issues and dynamics at play in a child's life, it is reckless to launch into psychological treatment. Nowhere is this more pronounced than with the treatment of attachment disturbance.

First and foremost, it must be established that the child's behaviors or attitudes stem from impaired attachment. Too many children are being classified, *attachment disordered* without them having had the benefit of an assessment into probable root causes of their actions. Brain impairment, traumatic stress, poor coping skills, and a whole variety of other issues can result in a child appearing to have disrupted attachment. When a thoughtful and comprehensive assessment is made before the therapy starts, other factors that might be causing the behaviors can be ruled out.

The steps to the initial assessment should include:

Meet with parents first. Providers should meet with foster, adoptive, and/or birth parents whenever possible in order to obtain the child's current and historical data. Though the answers to some questions are often not known, I will typically ask: Did the birth mother consume alcohol, drugs, or tobacco; did the child reside in an orphanage and for how long; was the child born premature; what was the nature of the caregiving environment in the first year of life; and what was his behavior like as a toddler? I want to learn as much as possible about the child's current behavior and mood, both at home and in school. I typically ask parents and teachers to complete behavior rating scales to derive some of this.

Review pertinent documents. To the extent these are available, I find it helpful to review social service, mental health, educational, and medical records. This helps me understand the child's history, from the point of view of various professionals who have interacted with him. Even if the child is 12-years-old, it is useful to look at documents from earlier times in his life.

Talk to other providers. If the child has a social worker, a care coordinator, or a prior therapist, I will typically speak with them. These persons have often interacted with the child for quite some time and can therefore provide important information or perspectives. They may also have information about the legal aspects of the case that may be unknown to the foster parents.

Which interventions are required before therapy starts? Based on what I find out from parents, other providers, and the documents, I need to assess if other services should be pursued before I start working with the child or family. For example, does the child first need a psychiatric evaluation or update, to see if medication issues need to be addressed? If the client is a teenager, do they require an assessment for substance abuse or residential treatment? Is a psychological or medical evaluation warranted?

Do the parents fully understand their role? I work on a family/systems model of treatment. This means that parents are intimately involved in the treatment I provide to the child. Other providers choose to only see the child, not the parents. Regardless of the modality used, parents need to know in advance what is required of them during the time the child is in therapy. For example, consider the example of a child with ADHD. Studies have consistently shown that one-to-one therapeutic interventions with a child with ADHD have limited effectiveness. Instead, parents and teachers must also be involved to implement strategies and techniques for managing and modifying behavior. Therefore, if you are the parent of a child with ADHD, are you clear that the therapist may be giving you assignments and duties to use with the child at home?

Has the child been in therapy before? If a child has been in therapy with another provider, I want to know 1) what modality did the therapist use (play, family, one-to-one, group, etc.) with the child; 2) did the child form a meaningful relationship with this provider? If so, why did the therapy end, and how does that relationship potentially affect his involvement with me; 3) what expectations about therapy might the child bring to the work with me? In other words, do I need to educate the child about how therapy with me works, and how it is similar or different from what he is used to?

Are there time constraints? Particularly with children who reside in foster care, the work may be time-limited. Unfortunately, it is not always clear what the time-frame may be. I want to know if the child is likely to return to his birth family or if he will be placed for adoption. In these instances, I must stay aware that sudden changes may occur in the child's life that will be out of my control. Knowing this in advance, I can talk with the child about how to deal with it.

Interview the child. Before I make a final commitment to working with the child and his family, I first want to meet with him. Typically, I do this alone, though sometimes the parents are present. Depending upon his age and maturity level, I might talk or play with the child. I usually administer a few questionnaires (such as the Children's Depression Inventory; the Trauma Symptom Checklist for Children; the Incomplete Sentences Blank), reviewing their responses with them afterward. Again, depending upon the age and maturity of the child, questions I try to get answers to include:

- Tell me your earliest memory
- Tell me the story of your life, including as much detail as you can recall
- Tell me why you believe you no longer live with your birth family
- How often do you think of your birth mother/father/siblings
- What kinds of things make you sad, mad, glad, scared
- Would you say you do or do not trust people
- What do you think your foster/adoptive parent will tell me about you
- Are you willing to commit to working with me to address some of this

Once the assessment is complete, I should be able to answer some or all of the following questions:

- Is it possible that this child's mood or behavior stems from neuro-logical causes, perhaps from prenatal toxin exposure, birth trauma, or severe neglect?
- Is this child reacting to current circumstances or is his behavior in response to events from the distant past?
- Are there indicators of severe mental illness (such as schizo-phrenia or other psychotic disorder)? If so, what type of treatment will serve him best?
- Does this child need to be under psychiatric care before I begin therapy? If he is taking psychotropic medication, do I have reason to believe it is working?
- Does this child have the emotional and cognitive maturity to reflect on their behaviors and feelings? If not, how receptive will he be to non-verbal, nurturing techniques, such being held by his parent during therapy?
- What have I learned about the child's defenses, coping strategies, internal working model, and attachment patterns? How will this affect the way I interact with him?
- Do I feel these parents will be my allies in the treatment? Can I trust they will work with me, shy away from shaming the child, and keep me up-to-date on the child's daily behavior and mood?
- What is a realistic time-frame that I have to work with the child? How does this affect my interventions and goals?

The answers to these questions determine my initial approaches to the treatment. With most children — regardless of their age — it is not realistic to expect them to come to therapy and start talking freely about their lives and feelings. Instead, I prefer to use the early stage of therapy as a time to educate the child about who I am, how I work, what I realistically can and cannot accomplish with him, and what role his parents will play in the therapeutic process.

Equally important, the child needs to be educated about what role he plays in therapy, and why we're even meeting. Too often, children feel like pawns on a chessboard, where others move them around and they have little control. In my orientation to therapy, I remind the child that ours will be a collaborative effort. I let him know I will work hard, and that his parents will also be here. I remind him, however, that he is expected to do some of the work and that we can't effect positive change in his life without his help. I therefore ask him to agree to working with me, in order to address the goals he and I talked about during the first meeting I had with him.

Once therapy begins, the course it takes is so different in each case that there is no way I can outline a standard approach. Each therapist has his or her own style of working, and each identifies their own treatment goals. The important thing is that you, the parent, feel comfortable with the provider who is seeing your child, and that you have faith in his or her ability to help your family. Children differ in how responsive they will be to therapeutic intervention, so it isn't possible to say when you should expect to see change. Overall, though, you should be able to trust that the work being done with your child and family is moving in the right direction.

Regardless of the therapeutic intervention used with a child, its purpose is twofold. First, a primary goal is to help the child to make sense of some of the confusing, painful, or disturbing things that have happened to him over the course of his life. Attachment theory highlights that children need to develop a mental organization and understanding of *why* things happened as they did. Without this, the child is at risk for developing distortions about his history. Given the natural tendency for children to be somewhat self-focused, it is common for them to believe that bad things happen because of them. In fact, a significant number of children in foster care blame themselves for all or most of the circumstances for this placement. Therapeutic intervention with foster or adopted children therefore often focuses on resolving trauma, teaching alternative means of

TEACHING THE APOLOGY

When a child violates a boundary, particularly if it involves another person, I firmly believe he must be required to make amends. It does not matter if his apologies are genuine. For example, I was working with a nine-year-old boy who, over the course of a month, managed to steal something from every child in his class. Even though his parents made him return what items he could, I suggested that he and the other kids sit in a circle in the class. Each child then told him how they felt when they found out he had stolen from them. In another instance, the parents of an 11-year-old girl found out she stole several small items from a store when they were out of state on vacation. Typically, I would ask the parents to phone the police in this kind of situation. But since the crime occurred out of state, the impact or effect on the child would have been minimal. The parents wrote the store manager a letter, explaining what their daughter had done and included the stolen items in a box. The girl, too, wrote a letter to the manager, telling him she was sorry. Her parents and I both know that her words were insincere and that she did not care that she stole the items. Still, it was important for them to model and reinforce that she didn't completely get away with her crime.

In a recent matter, a boy I am seeing cut the seat on the school bus. His parents were required to pay $65 before he could ride the bus again. Even though his mother immediately paid the money, I still recommended that he apologize to the owner of the bus, as well as the driver, and that he find a way to pay his mother back the $65. When he couldn't come up with any ideas of how to raise $65, I suggested he sell his bicycle on eBay. Both he and his mother panicked when I said this, because his bicycle was very special to him. I told them both that it wasn't important how he came up with the money. The important thing was to pay his mother back promptly. When they came to therapy the following week, the boy proudly announced to me that he sold mistletoe in the parking lot of a store earning $83! The remaining $18 was his to spend as he chose.

coping, re-shaping the view they hold of themselves and adults, and helping them to develop a way of thinking about their circumstances that is based in reality.

A second therapeutic goal for children is to teach or remind him about the basic rules of being in a family, being in school, and living in society. The child should learn to be respectful to adults and the other children in the home, even if he does not love them, like them, or want to live with them. The child must learn he is not the only one with needs in school. Instead, school is a setting and opportunity to learn basic knowledge and information, as well as skills such as patience, give-and-take, and cooperation. In broader society, children have to appreciate that there is a common assumption we share that most people are not going to hurt, lie to, or exploit one another.

The disruptions so many of these children have experienced has taken a toll on their understanding of basic social skills. Some of this stems from growing up in a neglectful or chaotic environment, while part can also come from being exposed to so many different family and school environments, with the inconsistent expectations that result from this. Young children in particular are apt to learn behavior that was modeled for them. If they have too many models from which to draw, they will typically go with whatever is easiest or that which most serves their current interests.

THE STEALING LIST

When I am working with a child who steals, I require that he make a "stealing list." He writes down everything he stole and from whom. We then assign a dollar value to it. I've seen some kids do elaborate investigation into the cost of items such as a hairbrush, a trading card, a lighter, or a toy. Once the stealing list is complete, the parents and I require the child to either return the item or find a way of paying the person for the item. Even if the other person doesn't know something was stolen from him, I still ask the child to tell them.

Ultimately, your efforts as a parent should be geared toward helping your child develop the skills needed to do well at home, in school and in society. As I've written elsewhere in this book, our job as parents or helping professionals is to be like a coach, preparing the child for the big game called life!

Guidelines for Parenting a Child with Attachment Disturbance

Don't focus on "fixing" your child. Instead, create a home that supports positive change in behavior. When your child attempts to set a negative emotional tone in the family, counter it with a positive tone. You did not create the original problem, but you can develop a family environment that seeks to find solutions.

Routines must be followed. As annoying as it can sometimes be, it is necessary to establish routines when you have a child with disrupted attachment. Consistent and predictable routines — around mealtimes, bedtime, school, homework — help these children feel safe.

Provide consequences, not punishment. Consequences teach the child a lesson, whereas punishment only inflicts pain and serves as a means for getting even. Also, parents who use punishment as a form of discipline usually do so in anger. Consequences require the child to look at his actions, and to decide if he wants to do different in the future. For example, grounding your child for not doing his homework does nothing to improve his grade. If he has to explain to his teacher why he doesn't have his homework, he assumes ownership for the action.

Establish respect. When you speak to your child, he should make eye contact with you when listening and answering. Your child should speak to you with respect, saying, "Yes, mom," or "I understand, mom." Never allow a child to challenge your rules by asking, "Why." This puts them in control and makes you feel defensive. Your child should practice saying, "Please" and "Thank you." Mealtime should be a time of mutual respect. I'd rather have a child eat their dinner while sitting in an empty bathtub than put up with slurping, gulping, or chewing with their mouth open at the dinner table.

Touch is vital. For many of these children, touch has not felt safe or felt good. But they need to learn that touch is one of the things that remind us we are human. Touch is a form of communication. Slowly introduce different forms of safe touch with your child, even if he is a teenager.

Information on a need-to-know basis. Many children with attachment disturbance will sabotage appointments, family activities, or other obligations. They do this to control the situation and to make their parents angry. One strategy for dealing with this is to only tell the child what they need to know — when they need to know it — about upcoming appointments or events. As an example, if a child isn't told about an appointment until they're in the car and almost there, they have less time to detour the parent from the intended goal.

RESOURCES

ON THE WEB

Association for Treatment and Training in the Attachment of Children www.attach.org
Website: attachmentparenting.org
On-line support group: www.adsg.syix.com

FURTHER READING

Facilitating Developmental Attachment (book)
Daniel Hughes
Attachment, Trauma, and Healing (book)
Terry M. Levy and Michael Orlans
Handbook of Attachment
Terry M. Levy
Parenting the Hurt Child
Gregory C. Keck and Regina Kupecky

The foundation for empathy is laid from the beginning. When the early months of an infant's experience include consistent, sensitive interactions in which the caregiver accurately assesses the child's needs and responds quickly in a soothing manner, and when a child's sadness or joy is mirrored in the face of the parent, the child experiences comfort and trust with the carergiver.

—Robin Karr-Morse and Meredith Wiley
"Ghosts From the Nursery"

Improving the Child's Capacity for Empathy

ABUSE AND NEGLECT TAKES a toll on children's capacity for empathy. Empathy refers to the ability to identify with what another person is feeling. Biologically, we are likely wired to care for other people, given that ours is a social species. Attachment style has also been related to empathy. Children who are securely attached are better able to take the perspective of another person, in essence experiencing that individual's emotions. Yet, in order to help a child fully develop the capacity for empathy, it must be modeled for him. This modeling usually occurs through the process of mirroring, whereby the mother correctly perceives her infant's needs based on his facial expressions, verbalizations, and body movements. Since the infant cannot tell his caregiver when he is hungry, tired, or needing to be held, he signals this in other ways. When the caregiver accurately interprets these signals, it communicates to the child that his needs are understood. Comments that demonstrate empathy are important for infant development: "You must be hungry," "You must be tired," "You're really happy now," or "You don't like that, do you."

Daniel Siegel, M.D., a psychiatrist and researcher on developmental attachment at UCLA, uses the term "mindsight" to refer to the ability to perceive our own minds and the minds of others. In his 2003 book, "Parenting from the Inside Out," Dr. Siegel writes:

> *Mindsight is the ability to perceive the internal experience of another person and make sense of that imagined experience, enabling us to offer compassionate responses that reflect our understanding and concern. Putting ourselves in another person's shoes requires that we are aware of our own internal experience as we allow ourselves to imagine another's internal world. Such a process creates an image of the mind of another inside of our own.*

Dr. Siegel adds:

> *When we can see the mind of another person, we can understand what that person is thinking and feeling and respond with empathy. Mindsight may enable us to have empathic imagination, whereby we consider the meaning of events not only in our own lives but in others' lives as well.*

If a parent is not aware of what her child needs, because she is depressed, on drugs, absent, or indifferent, she misses these signals. Over time, this communicates to the child that his needs are not important. It then becomes difficult for him to recognize or care about how other people feel, simply because he remains confused or ambivalent about his own feelings.

As a child grows older, he should learn that other people also have needs and that he must sometimes defer to them. This is one of the reasons so much emphasis is placed on sharing in the preschool years. By age five, most children fully realize and appreciate that other people have feelings. By this age, the child should be able to readily acknowledge that tears represent sadness, a frown can represent anger, and a smile means happiness.

Karr-Morse and Wiley, in their book, "Ghosts From the Nursery," offer a nice example of budding empathy in a young child:

> *Twenty-three-month-old Jason was strapped into his car seat looking out the window as his mother slowed to a stop light at a traffic signal. As the light turned from yellow to red, an old woman waiting at the corner stepped painfully from the curb and walked across the street directly in front of the car where Jason and his mother waited for the light to change. As the old woman hobbled across the street, bent over with the weight of two bulging shopping bags, Jason began to cry softly. His mother turned to ask him what was wrong. Tears flowing down his cheeks, he pointed at the old woman as she continued slowly toward the opposite curb, "Dat poor old lady," he said.*

Empathy lies at the foundation of our social world. It is one of the main features of being human that helps us feel connected to and understood by others. If a child has not learned to care for the feelings of others by the time he is five- or six-years-old, it is difficult to teach it to him. This is not to say that empathy cannot be taught. Rather, trying to teach someone to genuinely care for another person or what that person might be experiencing is a tremendous task. These children tend to be more self-focused and require a great deal of guidance for recognizing the emotional states of others. As they continue to adulthood, empathy can be a foreign concept to many of them. This is why the lack of empathy has been identified as one of the key risk factors in the development of criminal behavior; if you don't care about the impact of your actions on another person, it makes it easier to harm or exploit them.

Prior to my return to child psychology several years ago, I worked in a maximum security prison. I primarily administered psychological tests to the inmates, but I also maintained a small therapy caseload. For nearly two years, I worked with one individual who was on death row for kidnapping, raping, and murdering a young woman. At times, I had the impression that this individual had developed some capacity for empathy, as he told me, "I feel like I'm married to my victim. I go to bed thinking about her, I dream about her, and I think about her during the day, all the time wondering how the whole ordeal was for her." One day, however, the local newspaper did an article on the case, as his death sentence was up for review. In the article, the reporter quoted an interview with the victim's parents. They expressed the anger they felt toward my client, saying he should definitely be put to death. My client brought that article with him to our next therapy session. He looked sad and he said, "I never thought about how my actions affected the members of her family."

A few years ago there was a fire in one of our local communities that destroyed numerous homes, as well as the adjacent forest. A 10-year-old adopted boy with whom I was working at the time walked in and saw his mother crying as she was watching the news coverage of the fire. The boy asked, "Why are you crying, mom?" She replied, "Look at this, it's horrible. These people are losing their homes, the trees are being burned, pets are lost, and the animals in the forest are losing their home." He looked at her and said, "But why are you crying?"

In order to facilitate empathy in a child, it can be helpful to provide him with the caring and reflective statements he may have missed when he was younger. Parents should therefore constantly strive to communicate to the child an appreciation and awareness of his emotional states. This lets him know you are aware when he is excited, scared, angry, or happy. Too often, we say to children, "What's wrong," or "How do you feel about that?" Usually, the child does not know. Especially with young children, I believe it is better to tell them how they feel rather than ask them how they feel. If I say to a child, "It looks like you're really mad about what just happened," the child will let me know I am right or he will attempt to correct me with a statement such as, "No, I'm really sad. He hurt my feelings."

Parents of foster and adopted children often feel confused about how best — if at all — to validate the trauma or abuse their child experienced before coming to their home. When it comes to offering comments or asking questions, many parents believe this is territory best explored by a mental health professional. Certainly, there are some aspects of the traumatized child's experience which need to be addressed in counseling. I believe it can be tremendously helpful, however, for parents to offer support and acknowledgement for what the child went through.

What makes this difficult is that many of us have trouble comprehending what a child must have experienced, let alone felt. I have heard of abuse so horrific that I've had trouble wrapping my mind around what was going on for the child at the time. To me, however, this is when empathy can be most pronounced. Sympathy entails knowing another's feelings because we went through something similar. Empathy, on the other hand, requires us to intuit or surmise what another individual is experiencing. Fortunately, I did not lose anyone close to me during the attacks of September 11, 2001. With empathy, I can try to piece together in my heart and mind what it must be for those people who did.

In therapy, I use a variety of techniques to strengthen a child's capacity for empathy. For example, I will show them a brief portion of a movie, with the sound off, and ask them to tell me what they think each character is feeling. Since the parents are also in the room with me, I will then have them do the same and then instruct the parents and child to discuss the reasons for their answers. At other times, I will give the child photographs of people with various expressions on their faces, and ask what he thinks the person is feeling. Sometimes, I will show news clips of people who were involved in accidents or who experienced a loss or trauma. Again, I keep the sound off and ask the child to tell me what he thinks each person is feeling. Video clips of interviews with family members of persons killed in the September 11 terrorist attacks are particularly useful in these exercises.

After a child has been in counseling with me for a while, I start to address the issue of empathy in a more personal and direct manner. My goal is to point out the times he likely had certain needs and the ways in which these needs were or were not met by his various caregivers. If I have copies of social service records, I will sometimes use these to help facilitate the discussion. For example, I was working with a nine-year-old girl who was taken into state custody because her parents were using drugs and fighting with one another. I read to her the statement from the record, "When the officer and I entered the bedroom, the child was sitting on her bed, crying. As we started to approach her, she pulled away and started screaming. Officer Jones introduced himself, but she kept crying." At the time of that report, the girl was two-years-old. I read this part to the girl and then asked her to tell me what she thinks a two-year-old girl would be feeling if her parents were arguing and she was alone on her bed and crying. Here, I was not pressing for her memory of what she was feeling, because she was too young to have full memories of that time. By getting her to reflect on the experience in a more general way, it starts to help her appreciate her own feelings, as well as what other children might experience in a similar situation.

With the assistance of the parent, we then offer our own empathic statements to the child, in order to provide her with the feedback and support she likely didn't receive in earlier years. Comments could include: "That must have been so scary for you," "I'll bet you were terrified," "You were so little and unable to care for yourself," or "You must have been so frightened when the two strangers entered the room." This doesn't take away the confusing feelings the child had when she was younger. But it does allow her the opportunity to finally hear someone acknowledge that she was scared, angry, and sad.

RESOURCES

FURTHER READING

Empathy and Moral Development (book)
Martin Hoffman

Between Parent and Child (book)
Haim G. Ginott

TEACHING CHILDREN TO TOLERATE FRUSTRATION

Waiting for Marshmallows

Several years ago, researchers conducted a series of experiments with preschool-age children. The experimenter brought a child into a room where there were three marshmallows on a table. The child was told that the adult would leave the room in a few minutes. The child was told that if he waited until the adult returned, he could have all three of the marshmallows. Otherwise, the child was told he could only have two. The lives of the children who participated in this experiment were tracked for 16 years. The researchers found that those children who waited for the experimenter to return had higher SAT scores, better health, greater income, and more satisfactory relationships than the children who didn't wait. What is the lesson here? There are tremendous benefits to having frustration tolerance. With some children, you may need to start off with something simple, such as, "Wait until I sit down before you start to eat." Gradually, you can increase these requests, giving the child lots of praise when he shows the capacity to wait without having a tantrum or when he exhibits good frustration tolerance.

Emotional Mirroring

Children learn about their physical likeness by seeing their image in a mirror. They learn about their emotional likeness by hearing their feelings reflected to them. The function of a mirror is to reflect an image as it is, without adding flattery or faults. We do not want a mirror to tell us, "You look terrible. Your eyes are bloodshot and your face is puffy. Altogether, you are a mess. You'd better do something about yourself." After a few exposures to such a magic mirror, we would avoid it like the plague. From a mirror, we want an image, not a sermon. We may not like the image we see; still, we would rather decide for ourselves our next cosmetic move. Similarly, the function of an emotional mirror is to reflect feelings as they are, without distortion.

— Haim Ginott,
"Between Parent and Child"

By the age of 10, most children have explored some aspect of sexuality. Because of these experiences, it no longer makes sense to describe puberty as a time of 'sexual awakening' but instead to simply define it as a developmental stage, during which physical maturation results in the ability to reproduce.

— Kathryn Kuehnle,
"Assessing Allegations of Child Sexual Abuse"

Sexual Behavior in Children

S EXUAL BEHAVIOR IN CHILDREN of all ages is normal. In fact, it is expected that upwards of 85 percent of children will engage in at least some sexual behavior before they turn 13. Natural and healthy sexual exploration during childhood is an information-gathering process where children explore their own bodies, show interest in the bodies of others, and play out gender roles and behaviors. Sexual behaviors in children can range from healthy and normal to more disturbing acts. Children involved in natural and expected sex play usually do so with someone of their own age and developmental status. Their participation is also voluntary. For most children, their interest in sex and sexuality is balanced by curiosity about other aspects of their life. Also, while many children will feel some embarrassment about sexual exploration—particularly if a parent finds out about it — these experiences do not usually leave the child with deep feelings of anger, fear, or anxiety.

It is well-established that psychosexual development begins in infancy. Male infants develop erections and boys as young as five months experience orgasmic-like responses. Boys and girls often undress or engage in sexual exploration play by age 4, and both sexes start asking about sex by about age 5.

Genital interest for boys and girls increases between 2 and 5, and genital play at this age is common. As children grow older, the rate of masturbation increases. Studies suggest that 10 percent of 7-year-old boys and girls masturbate, while the rate increases to 80 percent at age 13. Homosexual play also increases in late childhood and early adolescence, with up to 25 percent of 13-year-old boys reporting at least one instance of consensual, same-sex play.

CHILDHOOD SEXUAL BEHAVIORS

PRESCHOOL CHILDREN

Normal Childhood Sexuality	Warning Signs	Professional Help Indicated
Touches and rubs own genitals when going to sleep, when tense, when afraid.	Continues to touch genitals in public even after being told not to many times.	Continues to touch or rub self when diaper changed.
Touches the genitals or breasts of familiar adults or children.	Touches the genitals or breasts of non-family members; asks them to touch him.	Touches genitals or breasts of others in sneaky way; demands others touch him.

AGES 5 THROUGH 9

Normal Childhood Sexuality	Warning Signs	Professional Help Indicated
Asks about the genitals, breasts, intercourse, babies. Plays doctor; inspects bodies of kids/adults.	Shows fear or anxiety about sexual topics. Frequently plays doctor and gets caught again after being told "no" or punished.	Asks endless questions about sex. Sexual knowledge in excess of age. Forces other child to play doctor or take off clothes.
Touches or rubs own genitals when going to sleep, when tense, excited, or afraid.	Continues to touch/rub genitals in public after being told "no." Masturbates on furniture or with objects.	Touches/rubs self in public or in private but to exclusion of normal childhood activities. Masturbates on people.
Playing house; playing mommy or daddy.	Humping other children with clothes on. Imitates sexual behavior with dolls or toys.	Humping children or adults while naked. Intercourse with another child. Forces sex on a child.
Drawing genitals on human figures.	Draws genitals in disproportionate size to body. Genitals stand out as most prominent feature.	Drawings of intercourse or group sex.
Wants to compare genitals with peer-aged friends.	Wants to compare genitals with much younger or much older child or adult.	Demands to see the genitals, breasts, or buttocks of child or adult.
Interest in breeding behavior of animals.	Touches genitals of animal.	Sexual behavior with animals.

Even though sexual behavior in children is normal, it is rare and usually happens without others seeing or being aware of it. If a child's sexual behavior comes to the attention of adults, this could be a cause for concern. Also, if a young child would rather masturbate than engage in normal childhood activities, this should raise questions for parents. With most children, if they are told not to engage in a sexual activity after being caught, they won't do it again. If the child's behavior persists, even after being told "no"` by an adult, this suggests a greater preoccupation with sexual matters and likely needs to be explored.

Many children in the foster care system have been sexually abused or exposed to sexual activity involving adults and/or children. Whether they come into custody or not, it is estimated that upwards of 15 percent of boys and 25 percent of girls experience at least one instance of sexual misuse prior to age 18. For some, they become sexually reactive, where their sexual interests and behaviors are in excess of other kids their age. In many instances, the sexual behavior is not within the full conscious control of the child. Sometimes, they are simply trying to understand something sexual which was done to them by doing it to someone else. Much of the time, the child does not mean to harm or exploit another person. Rather, they simply do not understand their own or others' rights to privacy. Thus, parents should approach the education of appropriate sexual boundaries with children in a matter-of-fact tone.

Most children who were sexually abused do not go on to molest other children, either in childhood or when they become adults. Also, not all sexual contact is perceived by the child as being harmful or traumatic. For many children, there can be a pleasurable aspect to the abuse, which can therefore leave them questioning if it was even wrong or bad. Thus, once it is discovered that a child has been sexually abused, it is important to find out the child's experience and perception of the event, as he or she may need further education about appropriate boundaries and issues of sexuality.

Sexual Behavior Between Siblings

When siblings in foster care are found exhibiting sexual behavior with one another, the unfortunate tendency is to permanently separate them. Too often, I find these decisions are made rather impulsively, sometimes in response to the confusion or anxiety the foster parent experiences when the sexual behavior becomes known. All foster and adoptive parents should be informed during pre-placement training and education that the potential for sexual behavior in this population of children is quite high. Skills for intervening should then be offered.

Approximately 12 to 20 percent of foster children have confirmed cases of sexual abuse. Of these, 63 percent are girls and 37 percent are boys. The number is actually much higher as the sexual abuse may not have been disclosed or substantiated. When doing interviews with foster parents and social workers, many tell me they suspect the child was sexually abused — based on observable behaviors— though the child has not admitted to such.

Even when children are not overtly sexually abused, the dynamics that occur in abusive or chaotic households can be highly sexualized. Keep in mind that many of these children come from families where there are little or no boundaries. Why shouldn't this extend to the area of sexuality? Also, given the elevated rates of substance use in the birth families of foster children — 88 percent of known perpetrators of child sexual abuse have a substance use disorder — inhibitions of all kinds are lowered, thereby increasing the chance that the child was exposed to inappropriate physical contact by adults. It is worth noting that more children are sexually abused by someone within the family (75 percent) than by a neighbor (10 percent) or stranger.

Siblings who exhibit sexualized behavior with one another often do so for a variety of reasons. Particularly with very young children, they may be modeling what they witnessed in the family home, without awareness or

---

**QUESTIONS YOUR CHILD MAY HAVE,
BUT DOESN'T KNOW HOW TO ASK**

- If the sexual abuse felt good, is there something wrong with me?
- If the sexual abuse felt good, was it really wrong?
- If I was abused by someone of the same gender, does that make me gay/lesbian?
- If I was sexually abused, can I get a disease or get pregnant from it?
- Is all sexual activity between adults and children wrong?
- If I have some positive feelings about my abuser, is that okay?
- I don't want to tell all that happened to me. Is that okay?

---

appreciation that they shouldn't be doing this. In some disturbing cases, children were forced or coerced by adults to perpetrate on one another. The act is often videotaped and sold or distributed as child pornography. Situations that are rarer include those in which an older sibling perpetrates on a younger one as a means of aggression or control. Here, the efforts are more deliberate and intentional, and often include overt threats if the abuse is disclosed.

In this last example, it makes sense in most instances to separate the siblings, at least temporarily. The need for separation increases as the age of the perpetrator rises. Thus, if a nine-year-old boy was abusing his five-year-old sister, he may be more amenable to intervention than if he was 12 or 14.

Before siblings are separated because of sexual behavior, it is first necessary to establish whether a lesser course of action can disrupt the activity. This could include having them sleep in separate bedrooms, limiting bathroom time to one person only, forbidding them from playing in the bedroom without an adult present, and/or increasing the amount of adult supervision. Talking with the children about why they shouldn't be doing the behavior together is also important.

If it becomes necessary to separate the siblings — either because adequate supervision can't be provided or the perpetrator is not amenable to changing his behavior — it is necessary to examine the direct and indirect messages given to the children as this occurs. It is acceptable to reinforce for children that some sexual activity, such as masturbation, is something they should do in private. Depending upon the child's age, you can tell her that what she does in private is okay, but she is not to do it with others in the home. This could then lead to a discussion of good and bad touch. Given the high rates of non-abusive sexual play between peers in childhood, I'm reluctant to say that children should be told never to allow another person to touch them. Instead, the message children need to be given is that it is not okay for a much older person to touch them or for someone of any age to force them into doing something they don't feel comfortable doing.

Rather than just moving one sibling to a new placement, it is important to talk with the children about why this change is occurring. This is where the adults involved assume some of the responsibility. For example, the children can be told that the adults in the home are unable to provide them with adequate supervision and from their perspective, it is a safety issue.

Care must be taken to not shame or embarrass the children to excess. If an older child is an aggressive perpetrator, it is doubtful that much of what you say will make him feel bad about his actions. If he does feel bad, that can actually be a healthy sign. With other children, however, the challenge is to point out the unacceptable nature of the *behavior*, without giving the message that something is wrong with *them*.

I believe the children should also be given hope — if this is a genuine possibility— that they can be reunited in the future, once they exhibit better boundaries and self control. Too often, siblings are separated due to sexual behavior and the perpetrator is forever labeled as untrustworthy. Because sexual activity between the siblings took place at one point in time, an assumption develops that the behavior will inevitably occur in the future.

This leaves the children feeling angry, confused and misunderstood. In addition, it stands to "mark" the perpetrator for the rest of his childhood. Often, this labeling means the siblings will never be adopted together.

TOPICS YOU NEED TO BE PREPARED TO ADDRESS

- Menstruation for girls; wet dreams for boys
- Breast development for girls
- The act of sex and where babies come from
- Erections for boys
- Good touch/bad touch: by child to others, by others to child
- Responsible sexual behavior
- Sexual feelings they have toward non-biological family members
- Typical sexual thoughts, feelings, and behaviors

Sex Education with the Sexually Abused Child

Many parents struggle with when and how to talk to their child about male/female anatomy, sexual behavior, reproduction, and puberty. It can feel even more complicated when talking about these topics with a child who has been sexually abused. A child who has been sexually abused may prematurely have knowledge about anatomical differences between children and adults, masturbation, ejaculation, penetration, and the pleasant and not-so-pleasant sensations that can result from sexual activity. But, this doesn't mean that the child has accurate information about sex. Nor does it mean that parents have the luxury of waiting until late childhood or early adolescence before talking with their child about sex.

It is not possible to approach the topic of sex education without acknowledging one's values associated with sex and sexuality. I therefore encourage you to ask yourself what your views are on a variety of issues that may come up with your child. This includes masturbation, premarital sex, and homosexuality. I also encourage you to do a realistic assessment of what you were told about sex and body changes as you were growing up. Then ask yourself if this was helpful and if it adequately prepared you for matters such as masturbation, nocturnal emissions, menstruation, and intercourse.

In cases other than rape, most adults who sexually abuse children engage in a gradual grooming process. Your child may have been told things by his abuser to lessen her resistance or decrease the likelihood he will tell someone what is happening This might include:

- We're not having sex, we're making love.
- This is how I show you how much I love you.
- You're erect or aroused, so you must want to do this with me.
- I didn't want this as much as you did.
- You're the one who came onto me.
- This is how I teach you to be a real man/woman.
- This is our special secret.
- If you tell anyone, I'll say you started it.
- If your mom finds out, it will break her heart.
- If you tell anyone, somebody is going to get hurt/killed.
- There's nothing wrong with what we're doing. It's just playing around.

Generally, you will find it easier to talk with a child about these issues if you and he are the same gender. If this option is not available in your home, consider enlisting the help of an adult the child knows and trusts. This can be a family member, family friend, Big Brother/Sister, or therapist. Also, keep in mind that sex education is a process that occurs over time. You don't need to address all topics in one sitting.

Too often, parents wait to discuss sex with a child until he starts puberty or is exhibiting an interest in the opposite sex. I recommend starting these discussions with children no later than age eight or nine. If the child was sexually abused, you may need to have conversations about the topic even before then. Since sexual abuse can have such a dirty and secretive feel to the child, take the initiative at talking about it and do it in a matter-of-fact way. If the child senses that you are comfortable with the topic, he may be more willing to talk with you about it or at least ask some of the questions he has. Don't make the mistake many adults do, which is to buy a book on the topic and leave it lying around, hoping the child will read and learn from it.

Self-Injurious Behavior in Children and Adolescents

T HERE ARE SOME CHILDREN who purposely hurt themselves by doing things such as:

- Banging their head
- Pulling their hair
- Taking excessive risks
- Hitting themselves with objects
- Slapping their face
- Scratching their skin
- Burning their skin with erasers, matches, or cigarettes
- Biting themselves
- Cutting their skin with sharp objects

When they do this, the intention is not necessarily to commit suicide, but rather to inflict harm, pain, or disfigurement. These behaviors were once thought to be hallmark symptoms of severe identity disturbance or personality disorders. While many people with developing personality disorders do engage in some form of self injury, many children who deliberately hurt themselves do not. Most recently, it has been recognized that self injury is common with children who have experienced severe forms of trauma.

Self injury is not unique to females, as was once thought. When I worked in a maximum-security prison, which housed only adult male inmates, upwards of 80 percent of the men cut or otherwise purposely injured themselves on a regular basis. In my clinical practice, I find that the prevalence of self-harming behavior is nearly equal between boys and girls, with girls doing it in more private or secretive ways than boys. Recently, I evaluated a 10-year-old boy who burns his skin with an eraser, a 13-year-old girl who cuts her inner thigh with a sharpened paper clip, a 14-year-old boy who burns the soles of his feet with a cigarette, and a seven-year-old girl who pulls her hair out, strand by strand.

Self injury is an adaptive and life-preserving coping mechanism. The act helps the child struggling with overwhelming feelings, memories, or emotions to regulate their experiences and stay alive. Whereas suicide is an attempt by the person to harm themselves in such a way as to cause death, self injury is one of the ways the person tries to avoid getting to the point of killing themselves. For the outsider, there is fear, disgust, or shock at the prospect of someone purposely causing themselves pain. Those who engage in these behaviors, on the other hand, report that doing so leaves them feeling in control, relaxed, or even sexually aroused.

Researchers who have studied self-injurious behavior have found high rates of physical or sexual abuse, early loss and abandonment, neglect, intrusive caregiving, significant illness, witnessing family violence, and out-of-home placements in persons who purposely hurt themselves. Foster and adopted children are therefore at high risk for engaging in these behaviors.

Lingering beliefs, attitudes, perceptions, feelings, and sensations continue to operate long after a child experiences trauma or abuse. This is just as true for the infant or toddler as for the older child. A child who experiences trauma typically feels disconnected from those around him. At the same time, the child is flooded with novel sensations or images that he doesn't fully understand. Sensations can include pain, fear, sexual arousal, or illness. For most children, but especially very young ones, these feelings occur in isolation. No one around can help them make sense of what is happening. This proves especially true when the primary caregiver causes the pain or confusion, as when a child is physically abused or sexually molested by a parent or when a child sees their mother being hurt or killed.

Trauma specialist Lenore Terr suggests that children have a more difficult time coping with trauma that is caused by acts of man rather than acts of God. Children can make sense of bad things due to earthquakes, tornadoes, or floods. But when the trauma is deliberate, as in instances of abuse or violence, the child has a difficult time understanding this even as he grows older. For this reason, I believe it best to talk with children about why they believe certain events happened before we press them to acknowledge and express their feelings. In addition, we need to educate children about the natural responses many people have to traumatic events as a way of helping to normalize feelings that are likely confusing for them.

Children who engage in self-injurious behavior report that it helps them to achieve a variety of goals. This can include:

- Releasing built-up tension and stress
- Communicating their feelings
- Soothing one's emotional pain
- Giving them feelings of control
- Help them to avoid the feeling of losing their mind
- Get back at others in an indirect way
- Punish themselves for perceived wrongs

When a child injures himself, he is often trying to communicate his feelings, either to himself or to others. Typically, these feelings include anger, rage, and frustration. Many of these children say they don't want to hurt other people but hurting themselves is acceptable. The behavior may occur when the child is angry at something or someone and this is his way of showing his anger. For others, they injure themselves when they feel shame. The behavior can be a way of punishing themselves when they feel bad, dirty, or unworthy. Some of the prisoners I worked with would cut or burn their skin as a punishment for feeling needy. Given that they are men, let alone in prison where signs of vulnerability are best not shown, they punished themselves for wanting a hug, a touch, or other forms of contact that reminded them they are human. Inevitably, the men were taken to the medical office, where a nurse — often a female — cleaned and covered the wounds, thereby providing them with the only form of safe or gentle touch they may ever receive while locked up.

The child who purposely hurts himself often does so in isolation, cutting or burning parts of the skin that others won't see. Part of this stems from the fact that the trauma survivor feels disconnected from other people. They barely know how to understand the confusing feelings themselves, let alone communicate it to another person. In many cases, children will admit to engaging in self-harm behaviors, often times feeling relieved at being able to tell someone else. The topic is so taboo, however, that most parents and providers aren't asking children these questions.

As parents or providers, we mistakenly believe that our initial efforts should be directed toward stopping the injurious behavior. Since control holds such importance for trauma survivors, our attempts to do this will likely prove unsuccessful. We also take the risk of giving the message to the child that we don't understand what they are trying to communicate. If a young child is doing something that is putting his physical safety at risk, we must immediately step in. But, in instances that are not life-threatening providers should be more accommodating. Therapists will sometimes develop a contract with a client not to hurt themselves. Rarely are such contracts productive and the child or adolescent will often end up feeling even worse about themselves. Until there is resolution of the core reasons for the injurious behavior, it is best to expect that it will continue.

In addressing these issues with your child, try to find a time when he is not particularly agitated. We need to communicate our concern for his physical well-being, while letting him know that we can tolerate what he is doing. Remember, children who self-injure have a very high tolerance for pain. What might be intolerable to us is something they barely flinch at. In therapy, attainable goals should be identified. It may be more realistic for the child to learn why they hurt themselves long before they are ready to stop. If we insist that the child stop hurting himself we risk having a situation in which they still do it, but don't tell us. Some children I evaluate tell me that they've told a parent or therapist that they stopped hurting themselves, when in reality they continue to do it.

With young children, it can be difficult to know what triggered the self-injurious behavior. Parents should write down much of what was said or what occurred around the time of the act. For example, did they just have a visit with someone in their birth family, were they told "no," did someone hurt their feelings, did something scary happen, did someone in the house raise their voice? Teenagers can be taught how to track some of this themselves. Ultimately, we want to know if the injury occurs at certain times, on certain days, after certain events, or in certain rooms. We also want to help the child identify what they felt before, during, and after they injured themselves. In other words, in order to help the child, we have to demonstrate comfort with discussing the nitty-gritty details associated with their actions.

Ultimately, our goal with children who injure themselves is to help them get to the point where they no longer need to use these behaviors to communicate feelings. Parents and the child must therefore work closely with a therapist who has experience treating survivors of childhood trauma. Parents should also be prepared to provide the child with the support he needs and requires. This may mean that the parent has to tolerate the child sometimes doing things to hurt himself.

Throughout this book, I emphasize the importance of providing the child with ample amounts of empathy. In this instance, empathic responses are needed but sometimes hard to generate. If a parent finds that she cannot stomach the fact that her child is purposely hurting herself, this will be communicated to her in direct or indirect ways. In turn, the feelings of isolation the child already struggles with will increase, making it difficult for her to move toward alternative ways of coping.

Eating Disorders

A DIFFERENT FORM OF SELF-INJURIOUS behavior is the eating disorder. While some of the previously discussed dynamics and root causes sometimes apply in these cases, eating disorders occur more often than cutting or burning behavior. Also, eating disorders are subtly more accepted, though equally hard to identify. As noted above, cutting or burning behavior rarely leads to severe injury or death. Upwards of 20 percent of children with eating disorders, on the other hand, die from the related complications.

It is estimated that 8 million or more people in the United States have an eating disorder, with 12 being the average age of onset. Whereas girls and boys engage in self-injurious behaviors at a fairly equal rate, it has been estimated that 90 percent of those with an eating disorder are female. Recent studies, however, have highlighted the growing incidence of these disorders with boys.

As a simple definition, an eating disorder is an obsession with food and weight that harms a person's physical and/or emotional well being. The most common eating disorder is *Anorexia Nervosa*, which causes an overwhelming fear of being overweight and a drive to be thin, leading to a restriction in calories. Anorexics consider themselves to be fat, no matter

---

ANOREXIA: COMMON SIGNS AND SYMPTOMS

- Noticeable weight loss
- Becoming withdrawn
- Excessive exercise
- Always being cold
- Muscle weakness
- Excuses for not eating
- Noticeable discomfort around food
- Guilt or shame about eating
- Depression, irritability, mood swings
- Irregular menstruation
- Frequently checking weight on scale
- Difficulty eating in public
- Pale complexion
- Perfectionistic attitude
- Stomach pains
- Insomnia

---

what their actual weight is. Anorexics close to death will show you on their bodies where they feel they need to lose weight.

Anorexics usually strive for perfection. They set very high standards for themselves and feel they always have to prove their competence. They usually always put the needs of others ahead of their own. A person with anorexia may also feel the only control they have in their lives is in the area of food and weight. From their perspective, if they can't control what is happening around them, they can control their weight. In fact, they feel powerful and in control when they can make themselves lose weight. For many, focusing on calories and losing weight is their way of blocking out feelings and emotions.

The other common eating disorder is *Bulimia Nervosa,* which is characterized by a cycle of binge eating followed by purging to try and rid the
body of unwanted calories. For one person, a binge may range from 1,000
to 10,000 calories. For another, one cookie may be considered a binge.
Purging methods usually involve vomiting and laxative abuse. Other forms
of purging can involve excessive exercise, fasting, use of diuretics, diet pills
and enemas.

BULIMIA: COMMON SIGNS AND SYMPTOMS

- Binge eating
- Secretive eating
- Bathroom visits after eating
- Vomiting
- Weight fluctuations
- Broken blood vessels
- Harsh exercise regimens
- Fasting
- Mood swings
- Severe self-criticism
- Fatigue
- Complaints of sore throat
- Need for approval from others
- Headaches
- Dehydration
- Hair loss
- Depression

The popular press likes to highlight the pressures young girls experience
to be thin as the root cause of anorexia or bulimia. Typically, these
articles implicate models and female performers who are incredibly thin,
suggesting that girls strive to attain this look. While the pressure to
appear a certain way is something adolescent girls and boys must
confront in our society, it is naïve to attribute eating disorders solely to
this phenomenon.

In light of their elevated rates of trauma and abuse, foster and adopted
children are at a statistically higher risk of developing an eating disorder
than other subgroups of children. When faced with physical or sexual
abuse, a child may turn to an eating disorder to gain a sense of control. If
they can't control what is happening to their bodies during the abuse, they
feel they can at least control their food intake and weight. Self-imposed

starvation may also be their way of trying to disappear so they no longer have to suffer through the abuse.

Children may also develop eating disorders as a way of dealing with the many emotions that they feel, especially if they are raised in a home that does not allow feelings to be expressed. Children who are compulsive eaters are usually using food to help them deal with feelings of anger, sadness, hurt, loneliness, abandonment, fear and pain. If children are not allowed to express their emotions, they may become emotional eaters. Also, if parents are too involved in their own problems, the child may turn to food for comfort.

If the child was in a family where emotional, physical, or sexual abuse was taking place, they may have developed an eating disorder to gain a sense of control, to block out painful feelings and emotions, or as a way to punish themselves, especially if they blame themselves for the abuse.

Screening teenage girls for eating disorders should be part of every psychological and medical evaluation. Unfortunately, most girls will not admit to it. With anorexia, it's pretty obvious, though the baggy clothes kids wear today help camouflage the weight loss. With bulimia, many of the girls are quite secretive. In advance of taking your child for an evaluation or assessment, don't hesitate to ask the provider to screen for an eating disorder.

If you suspect your child has an eating disorder, you have an obligation to explore the issues and to get them help. That is easier said than done, given the pervasive denial of those afflicted. Your child might even get mad at you, which can leave some parents feeling reluctant to address the topic. Still, the child will not stop the behavior on their own; you must take steps toward opening the door. Doing so may not change your child's attitude or stop the behavior, but it starts a discourse on crucial areas of concerns you have.

When talking with your child about eating, dieting, and weight, consider the following tips:

- Convey concern for her health, while still respecting their privacy. Eating disorders are often a cry for help, and the individual will appreciate knowing that someone is concerned.
- Avoid commenting on appearance; the child is already focused on this. Comments on weight or appearance, even if the intent is complimentary, will only perpetuate the obsession with body image.
- Demanding change or berating the child for her eating habits will not work. Avoid power struggles around eating. Eating disorders are often expressions of a need for control, a substitution for lack of control that the person feels in other areas of her life.
- Seeing someone you love struggling with an eating disorder might make you feel very scared, angry, frustrated, and helpless. However, be careful not to blame them for their struggle. Try to understand eating problems as a problematic coping strategy for dealing with painful emotions or experiences. Despite the grief the eating disorder causes the child and those around her, it may be hard to let it go.
- Finally, do not take on the role of a therapist. Do only what you feel capable of.

RESOURCES

ON THE WEB
National Eating Disorders Association
www.nationaleatingdisorders.org
Eating Disorders Association
www.edauk.com
National Eating Disorders Information Center
www.nedic.ca

> *Ironically, violence in boys also sometimes represents a vain attempt
> on their part to reconnect with others, to make and keep friends.
> Whether it's winning a fight and thus impressing one's peers, helping
> other boys to beat up another kid, or actually joining a gang, violence
> may give some boys a false impression that they're somehow growing
> closer to one another, bonding, in effect, through their individual and
> collective acts of aggression and malevolence.*
>
> — William Pollack
> "Real Boys"

If Your Child Needs to be Hospitalized

I F YOUR CHILD IS ON PSYCHIATRIC medication, has received inpatient treatment in the past, or suffers from chronic mental illness, there is a risk that he will require psychiatric hospitalization in the future. If you are raising a child whom you adopted, you will need to be prepared to deal with this mostly on your own. If you are a foster parent, the agency that placed the child in your care will likely play a part in assisting you, though you must also be ready in case the child needs to be hospitalized.

Children and adolescents are hospitalized usually because they pose a threat to themselves or to others. At times, their mental condition may be deteriorating and hospitalization is needed to stabilize their medications and behaviors. A psychiatrist may request that a child be hospitalized to help with an assessment, such as determining if a child is having seizures.

Depending on where you live, there may be a hospital for children and adolescents nearby. Otherwise, your child will have to be transferred to the nearest city where appropriate services can be provided. Except for emergency situations, such as efforts to prevent a child from hurting himself, many hospitals are not equipped to meet the psychiatric needs of children.

You should have a game plan in place long before your child requires hospitalization. This includes having ready access to phone numbers for the police, the local ambulance service, the hospital intake desk, the child's psychiatrist, the child's care coordinator, and the insurance company. If your child suddenly becomes violent, you will probably need to call the police rather than taking him to the hospital yourself. You should have a written summary of important information pertaining to your child, including a current list of the medications and dosages. The name and phone number of the psychiatrist who prescribes your child's medication should be included, as the hospital will require this information at admission. Finally, write down the things you think your child would want to have with him if he is hospitalized. This includes any clothes, books, toys, or hygiene items the hospital will permit him to have.

If you are providing foster care services, find out what your agency expects of you when a child needs to be hospitalized. For example, do you have the authority to call the police and request that the child be admitted on your own, or do you first need to consult with a staff member at the agency? Regardless, keep a copy of the document that grants you the right to make decisions pertaining to the child nearby. Many agencies give foster parents badges or letters that acknowledge the right to advocate on behalf of the child. With the concerns about malpractice and liability that many healthcare providers have, the hospital may require that someone with more "official" status sign the admission papers. They should at least keep the child under safe watch, however, while the legal custody arrangements are sorted out.

In the event your child is hospitalized, it may be necessary for you to notify his therapist and psychiatrist. In most cases, the hospital staff will not do this on their own. You may need to tell the hospital staff that your child's therapist has your permission to speak or visit with him while he is hospitalized. Some hospitals may offer some form of individual or group counseling for the patients. I believe the child's therapist should play a part in deciding if your child — her client — should participate in this. Finally, if your child is in foster care, alert the medical staff that a variety of people may likely come to visit him, such as a social worker, attorney, or court-appointed advocate.

In today's healthcare environment, your child may not be hospitalized for the length of time you believe is required. I have seen situations where children who were aggressive and in a psychotic state were admitted and discharged on the same day. In one instance, a client of mine, in a state of extreme rage, physically attacked his adoptive mother during the therapy session. His father and I had to literally pin him down until the police arrived. He was transported to the hospital by ambulance and was back home the next morning. Granted, he was somewhat calmer than the previous day. The root cause of his aggression was never addressed, however, and he attempted to assault his mother three days later.

You should have an aftercare plan in place for your child before he is released. The aftercare plan should address matters such as:

- Who will watch the child when he returns home?
- Will he immediately return to school? Should the teaching staff be informed that the child was hospitalized?
- If the child's medications were changed, what are they and what are the potential side effects?
- If the child will not be returning to your home, how will you ensure that he gets his belongings?
- If the child moves to a new placement, what mechanism is in place for you to have contact with him?

- Will your family require debriefing in order to help cope with the stress associated with putting a child in the hospital? If so, who will provide this?
- What follow-up plans are in place to reduce the risk of your child needing future inpatient treatment?

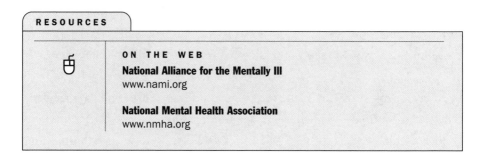

RESOURCES

ON THE WEB
National Alliance for the Mentally Ill
www.nami.org

National Mental Health Association
www.nmha.org

When You've Become the Child's Therapist

S OME CHILDREN FEEL A STRONGER personal connection to a foster or adoptive parent than with the therapist they see for mental health counseling. In some instances, the child feels comfortable sharing details about his life or feelings about the past that they may have no intention of sharing in therapy. This happens frequently with children who have had numerous therapists. For others, they just don't have positive feelings about therapy or feel comfortable making use of it. For some children, the relationship between them and a parent simply feels more natural and the parent communicates to the child that he can be talked to and trusted.

When this happens, it can put the parent in a difficult position. On the one hand, they appreciate that the child trusts them enough to open up and confide in them. On the other hand, the information the child shares may include content that is best handled by a trained professional. For example, one foster parent told me that her child was telling her that she was secretly cutting herself in places on her body where no one would notice. In another instance, a foster son admitted to his parent that he was smoking marijuana. Another foster parent said her child told her he was seeing his birth mother on the weekends when he visited with his aunt, even though the court had said the child and his mother should have no unsupervised contact.

If you work for a foster or treatment foster care agency, it is important to clarify in advance the expectations the agency holds regarding the things told to you by a child. The obvious example is instances of physical or sexual abuse. If the child shares details of previously undisclosed sexual abuse, are you required to notify the agency or Children's Protective Services first? What about other kind of disclosures? For example, are you required to tell someone if the child admits to drug use, is engaging in sexual activity, is skipping classes at school, has stolen, or is smoking cigarettes?

Because trust is a central issue in the lives of many foster and adopted children, it is important for you to be candid and honest with the child about what you will do with the information they share with you. In therapy, the counselor usually says something to the effect of: "Much of what we discuss in here stays between you and I. But, if I find out that you're going to hurt someone or that someone is hurting you, I will have to tell your parent or social worker." You will find your own style for cautioning the child about what you can and cannot keep between the two of you, but it's important to let him know you cannot assure full secrecy if he opens up to you. Much of the time, this requires a judgment call on your part. If you have doubts, consult with another parent or the child's treatment coordinator.

I am not one who believes that a child must share all the details of their life with a therapist. If they are disclosing information to you, they are likely deriving some benefit by being able to talk about it. Your job isn't to try to force the child into telling their therapist all that they've told you. You should explore your child's reasons for not telling the therapist and validate the comfort level they share with you. If you are an adoptive parent, you have more choice in determining whether your child continues to meet with their current therapist. You probably won't have this option if you are providing foster care. You can tell the treatment coordinator or social worker that the child doesn't feel comfortable talking with their therapist. But, this doesn't mean that the child will be given a new therapist. You may want to tell the therapist that your child is reluctant to open up in therapy. Without sharing all of the details of what the child has told you, consider telling the therapist why you think the child feels more comfortable with you. Is there something the therapist can learn from you about helping to make the child view therapy as a place to share more of his thoughts and feelings?

Keep in mind that a central role you have is to model and enforce appropriate boundaries for the child in your home. You therefore need to make sure you are listening to what the child shares as a trusted adult. Try not to let the relationship develop into one of being like a peer, where the child starts to perceive you as an equal. Be especially careful about sharing details of your own past with the child. While you may want to talk about traumatic or abusive experiences you've experienced as a way of normalizing the child's feelings, stay sensitive to how this can affect your relationship with the child. At times, it is appropriate to talk with your children about struggles you've had, especially when you were younger. But the reality is that you are still in a position of authority and you don't want to overwhelm the child or put yourself in the position of having a child know too much about your private life. If you do choose to disclose details about your past, make sure that your motive is to empower the child. For example, it may be helpful to tell the child how you coped with pressure to use drugs or to engage in sexual activity in your teenage years. Even though the demands put on teenagers today are different that they were in the past, your comments may provide the child with support and validation for their own struggles.

If the child shares information with you that you are obligated to report to an agency or the police, try talking to the child about this first. Yes, they will be angry, but it is better if they find out about this from you than from a social worker, therapist, or police officer. Explain the rules or laws you are bound by and let the child know that you have no choice. If you know what will happen next for the child — such as having to go through a more detailed interview with someone — tell them what to expect. You don't have to tell them how to approach the investigation, but remind them that you care about them. You can also consider saying things such as, "I know you don't want anyone to know what happened between you and your Uncle Joe. But the law says I have to report what you told me. Also, your uncle still has young children in his home. Perhaps by talking about this, you can help make sure that those kids don't have to go through what you did."

Mental Health Conditions You Need to Know About

T HERE ARE SEVERAL GOOD books and resources that outline the features and causes of a variety of childhood psychiatric disorders. My goal here isn't to cover all that is known about these disorders. Rather, I will review basic information about a few of the diagnoses foster and adopted children are often assigned.

> *ADHD probably is not primarily a disorder of paying attention but one of self-regulation: how the self comes to manage itself within the larger realm of social behavior...What is not developing properly in your child is the capacity to shift from focusing on the here and now to focusing on the future. That capacity is crucial to our ability to be organized, planful, and goal-directed, and it is directly dependent on how much control we have over our impulses.*
>
> — Russell A. Barkley,
> "Taking Charge of ADHD"

Attention-Deficit/Hyperactivity Disorder

Of all the psychiatric diagnoses, Attention-Deficit/Hyperactivity Disorder is the one most commonly given to children. Unfortunately, many children are given this diagnosis without having had a thorough evaluation. I find that some of the behaviors and attitudes common to foster and adopted children — such as reactions to trauma or disruption — are misunderstood by clinicians unfamiliar with this population. The child is then diagnosed with ADHD, when in reality something else may be occurring. Certainly, a child who experiences the changes and chaos common to the lives of many foster and adopted children will have a difficult time concentrating, paying attention, and staying calm.

A comprehensive evaluation for ADHD should include:

- Questions for the parents and teacher about the child's behaviors at home and at school
- Attempts at discovering whether there is a family history of psychiatric disorders in the child's birth family
- Checklists for parents and teachers to complete
- An interview with the child, alone and with the parents
- A thorough understanding of the child's physical development
- An exploration of the techniques and approaches used by the parents to manage the child's behavior, with emphasis placed on what does and does not seem to work
- Standardized psychological testing, to include measures of attention, behavior, and activity levels

What is ADHD?

Attention-Deficit/Hyperactivity Disorder refers to a constellation of behaviors. The central feature of these behaviors is a pattern of inattention that may or may not include hyperactivity. ADHD is characterized by developmentally inappropriate levels of inattention, distractibility, and/or hyperactivity. This means the behaviors must be out of line with children of the same age. Onset usually begins in late infancy or early childhood, and the symptoms may be mild, moderate, or severe. It is estimated that the prevalence of ADHD is between 3 and 5 percent of the general population. In order to qualify for the diagnosis, some hyperactive-impulsive or inattentive symptoms that cause impairment must have been present before age 7.

A small percentage of babies display ADHD symptoms. These infants are not easy babies to care for. They often have sleeping and eating problems and they often wake up during the night every hour or two. These infants can display sharp mood swings and an intense response to stimuli. They may spend many of their waking hours crying or fussing, and efforts to calm them are mostly ineffective. In addition, the baby with ADHD resists holding and cuddling. Clearly, this puts these children at risk for later attachment disturbance, as parents are faced with the option of persevering in the face of stressful interactions or emotionally backing away altogether.

ADHD manifests in a variety of situations. In order to meet the criteria for ADHD, the symptoms must be present in at least two settings. ADHD may not be the correct diagnosis if a child is inattentive and hyperactive only at home or school but not in other places. This can be tricky for the diagnostician. If a child resides in a home or school setting where there are firm rules, boundaries and lots of structure, the symptoms of ADHD may not be too pronounced. I therefore ask parents to provide me with detailed descriptions of the child's behavior across several settings: home, school, stores, church, parks, and family gatherings.

Experts believe ADHD is generated by a biochemical imbalance in the brain that is either inherited or caused by head injury or trauma, perinatal insult, or toxic agents. Studies suggest that infants with small birth weight have a 40 to 50 percent chance of developing ADHD. For about 50 to 60 percent of the children, ADHD symptoms will continue into adulthood. Although not related to IQ, ADHD impairs a child's ability to learn, behave, and socialize. Children with ADHD are considered less motivated to learn than their peers leading to a prevalence of learning disorders.

Though not a criteria for diagnosis, children with ADHD often have poor social skills and a very hard time relating to other kids in appropriate ways. For many of these children, they act younger than their chronological age. They are usually immature and, as a result, tend to play better with younger children because they cannot successfully do what their peers do. Even if they are able to make friends, they often have a difficult time keeping them, due to the problems with picking up on social cues and engaging in cooperative play. Sadly, many of these children do not make the connection between their actions and how others treat them. Therefore, they have no idea why other children ostracize them.

The symptoms of ADHD vary from situation to situation. In novel situations, these kids can do quite well. Thus, untrained evaluators often miss the diagnosis in children. Most children with ADHD can start to focus on something, but retaining the focus proves difficult. For some children with the disorder, they can maintain focus until what is being said is simply too challenging. Therefore, the disorder may not fully manifest until third or fourth grade when schoolwork gets more complex.

Children with ADHD cannot pace themselves when they're under pressure. This stems from the difficulty with self-regulation common to these children. Most children with ADHD know what is expected of them, but they just can't get motivated. Having insight into what needs to happen is not enough to motivate people to change. Many of us know that we need to exercise more, eat better, or lose weight. But, to do that we need a coach. The same is true of children with ADHD. They require the adults in their lives to coach them in the right direction.

Those with ADHD often have difficulty following through on instructions and adhering to rules. The child therefore ends up being "off task" or engaging in activities unrelated to what he has been told to do. The result of this inattentiveness is that others frequently have to remind those with ADHD of what they should be doing. Those who supervise the child with ADHD end up frustrated and angry. Ultimately the ADHD child may fail in school, be retained a grade, and eventually drop out. The general impression left with others is that the individual is less mature and lacks discipline and organization. At worst, it implies that the person with ADHD is intentionally lazy, unmotivated, and doesn't care or is actively trying to avoid his responsibilities.

As if parenting wasn't challenge enough, when you are caring for or raising a child with ADHD, you will find yourself having to supervise, monitor, teach, organize, plan, structure, reward, punish, guide, buffer, protect, and nurture the child in ways that can be demanding and trying. You will also need to meet more often with the other adults involved in the child's daily life — such as school staff, pediatricians, and mental health professionals. More than anyone, you probably have a good idea of what to expect from your child across situations or time of day. You know which interventions work and which don't. You know what frustrates and what motivates him. You therefore need to educate those who interact with your child about what works best, how to intervene or redirect, and which battles to fight.

Medication Interventions

Medication is probably the most widely publicized, hotly debated treatment for ADHD. Medication interventions for ADHD began in the 1950s. Psychiatric medication is useful at doing some things, but it can't make up for all of an ADHD child's deficits. For example, the medications used to treat ADHD are great for helping the child pay attention, improving mood, increasing overall compliance, and reducing negative social interactions. But, medication can't make a person more organized, improve social skills, take away anger, or improve memory. These children must, therefore, take advantage of other avenues for learning new skills. Unfortunately, many children with ADHD don't have subjective distress — that is, they don't believe their behavior is out of the ordinary — and are not motivated to take their medication as prescribed.

More than three thousand scientific articles have examined the subject of stimulant medication and ADHD. These studies consistently show that 60 to 70 percent of children with ADHD show improvement in behavior, attention, and/or learning when taking stimulant medication, although these positive effects do not continue once the medication is stopped. The studies also substantiate improvement in peer interactions and more compliance at school.

Studies indicate that fathers are more reluctant than mothers to let a provider prescribe medication to their child for ADHD. Part of this may be that the fathers spend less time with the children than mothers often do. Typically, by the time medication is presented as an option, the mothers are at the end of their ropes with the child and are willing to try anything that sounds promising.

If your child is prescribed medication for ADHD, it is important for you to learn what the medication can and cannot do. The child's psychiatrist should be able to clarify this for you, though you can also do reviews on the medication online or by reading over-the-counter books on prescription medication. The questions you should have answers to include:

- How is this medication supposed to work? Will my child be less hyperactive, less inattentive, or both?
- What are the possible side effects and which should be reported immediately to the doctor?
- What time of day should the medication be given? What happens if I forget to give it to my child? Should my child take the medication on weekends or school holidays?
- What impact could this medication have on my child's ability or willingness to learn?
- What should I tell my child's teacher or school nurse about this medication?
- How often should my child be re-evaluated? At that time, what information will you want to hear from me?
- How will this medication interact with other medications my child is taking?

THE MILWAUKEE STUDY OF ADHD

The longest running study on the effects of ADHD is taking place in Wisconsin. The researchers have studied children who were diagnosed with ADHD at around age five. The observations and findings from this study are compared with an equal number of individuals who do not have ADHD. The study has been ongoing for two decades and the sample group is now in their late 20s. The findings of the study have confirmed much of what we know about ADHD. It has also uncovered some additional risk factors that other researchers had not identified. These include:

- **Increased risk of medical conditions.** Those with ADHD exhibit a greater lack of concern for diet and exercise. They smoke more than the control group and they engage in more risk-taking behaviors. This means the incidence of accidents and speeding tickets is higher with the ADHD group than with the control group.
- **Heedless sexual conduct.** The ADHD group has more sexual partners than the control group. They are also less likely to have protected sexual intercourse. Because of this, 25 to 30% already have at least one sexually transmitted disease.
- **Children at an early age.** In the study, 42 subjects in both the control and ADHD group had children. 41 of these children were born to persons with ADHD.
- **Child custody.** Of those persons with ADHD who have children, 54% do not have custody. In most instances, custody was denied by the courts.
- **Driving behavior.** Those with ADHD speed more and obey driving laws less. The researchers have found that the persons with ADHD know how to drive and they can accurately state driving rules and laws. In contrast to the control group, they simply do not apply the rules.
- **Sense of time.** Those with ADHD over-estimate time intervals. They perceive that time is moving more slowly than it really is. This is why those with ADHD are often late; they think they have more time than they really do.

WHEN TO CONSIDER A PROFESSIONAL EVALUATION

A professional assessment for ADHD may be in order when any of the following conditions exist:

- For at least 6 months, the child has displayed activity, inattentiveness, and impulsive behavior far greater than in other children of the same age.
- For at least a few months other parents have been telling you that your child has much poorer self-control or is far more active, impulsive, and inattentive when with other children than is normal.
- Far more of your time and energy is required to manage and keep the child safe than other parents invest.
- Other children do not like to play with your child and avoid him because of the child's excessively active, emotional, or aggressive behavior.
- A daycare staff member or school teacher has informed you that your child has been having significant behavior problems for several months.
- You frequently lose your temper with your child, feel as if you are on the verge of excessive physical discipline or might even harm the child.

Morning Routines

Perhaps the biggest complaint I hear from parents with children who have ADHD is that morning routines are a big struggle. Particularly for children with symptoms of irritability, mornings can be an unpleasant time for all the family members. Maintaining morning routines for all members of the family proves extremely important. The child will not always be compliant. But it helps bring order to a household that often feels out of control when one or more members have ADHD.

You and your family will probably find it easiest if routines are slowly integrated into day to day life. Routines you can implement include:

- Giving baths at the same time each day
- Feed the baby and children at the same time each day
- Follow the same schedule on school days
- Family quiet time
- Do your bills/paperwork while your child does homework

Making Morning Routines Manageable

- Lay out clothes and other morning items the night before. This way, the child knows what he will wear, what he will pack for lunch, and what items need to be taken to school.
- Use an alarm clock, placed well out of arm's reach, to wake your child. This helps prevent a struggle between parent and child, as the child fights to stay in bed.
- Use timers. Put them in the bedroom, in the bathroom, and in the kitchen. The child must finish each task (e.g., dressing, cleaning up, eating) before each timer runs its course. If your child completes each task in the allotted time, permit them to choose one special snack to put in their lunchbox.
- Use meaningful consequences. For example, if a child cannot get out of bed responsibly, when the alarm goes off, the next night they must sleep on the living room floor or in their sibling's bedroom. List several chores on pieces of paper and put them in a box. If your child does not finish a morning routine on time, they must take one of the cards, doing the chore when they get home from school.
- Reward positive behaviors with greater frequency than you punish negative behaviors. Catch your child being good and behaving responsibly. At these times, give them a hug, offer a special treat or reward, and tell them how proud you are of them.

- Think of the things your child is most apt to argue about in the morning. Find ways of eliminating these as sources of conflict. For example, if you can't get him to stop watching TV in time for breakfast, make it a rule that no one watches TV in the morning.

Making Evening Routines Manageable

- Use a timer as a warning, to alert the child that he should get ready to do homework, take a bath, do the dishes, walk the dog, or go to bed. Let them know when you have set the timer, and tell them they must begin their chore before the timer goes off.
- Make sure your child has a designated homework table or area, complete with pens, pencils, a dictionary, an encyclopedia, and other essentials. Find ways of minimizing visual or auditory distractions near this area. In other words, it is best if your child can't see the TV, hear the radio, or turn on a video game when in their homework spot.
- When your child is working on homework, use it as a time to do your own paperwork or pay bills. This models that the time is devoted by both of you to your respective obligations. If he needs your assistance, ask him to raise his hand or alert you in a respectful manner.
- Keep your child's bathroom fully equipped. This helps minimize excuses and slow-and-pokey behaviors at bath time. The bathroom should have their toothbrush and toothpaste, shampoo, soap, bath toys for younger kids, bubble bath, towels and washcloths, and a comb.
- Let your child know you will sit with and/or read to him once he is dressed for and in bed. Sit or lay with him, talking about his day, practicing meditation or relaxation techniques, reading together, or listening to a soothing audiotape.

BASIC STRATEGIES IN PARENTING A CHILD WITH ADHD

- Get your child's attention before giving directions. This means face to face and direct eye contact (not just calling out what you expect your child to do).
- You may need to walk over to touch or physically cue your child prior to giving directions.
- Don't attempt to give directions or instructions if you are competing with the distraction of TV, music, or video games. First turn off distractions to gain their attention and focus.
- Show your child what you want him to do. Model and walk through the steps.
- Depending on the developmental skill of your child, one direction at a time is often all they are capable of remembering and following through on.
- A helpful technique for young children is to draw or cut out pictures on a chart hanging in the room that shows the sequence of morning activities or evening activities.
- Always check for understanding of directions. Have your child repeat or rephrase what you ask him to do.
- Keep directions clear, brief, and to the point.
- Reward your child for following directions as appropriate.
- Try not to lose your temper when your child fails to follow directions.
- Remember that it is characteristic of ADHD to have difficulty:
    - Disengaging from activities, especially fun ones that they have not finished
    - Responding and following through without structuring, adult prompting and cueing
    - With recall/memory
- Break down tasks into smaller steps that you want to get done. Give one step at a time.
- Your job is to provide choices and opportunities for your child. Their job is to accept these choices and to make decisions that are in their best interests.
- Ignore annoying behavior. Don't convey to your child that you can be manipulated by rude comments, obnoxious faces, or disgusting behavior.
- Use positive reinforcement. Many children with ADHD feel bad about themselves, and much of their daily life can be quite a struggle. Tell them how good they are when they are sitting quietly, remind them that you appreciate their help around the house, and be creative when giving compliments.

Children don't outgrow ADHD, but their symptoms may vary from one day to the next. By establishing clear routines, relying upon natural consequences, and encouraging your child to take responsibility, you start to tackle some of the biggest hurdles associated with raising these children.

Get the Child's Teacher on Board

If your child has ADHD, the teacher can be your greatest ally. The relationship between you and the teacher should be collaborative. Ultimately, you both have similar goals. She wants a class with a stimulating environment and minimal distraction, while you want your child to have a good learning environment. When parents and teachers work together, these goals can be achieved.

- Meet with your child's teacher before school starts or as soon as your child will be enrolled in her class. A face-to-face meeting with the teacher communicates your intent on working together as a team.
- Be prepared to educate the child's teacher about ADHD. Each teacher will have her own knowledge about ADHD. Bring along a few articles on ADHD and offer to give them to the teacher.
- Offer empathy and support. You know how challenging it can be to raise your kid at home. Communicate to the teacher your awareness that your child can be disruptive, draining, or needy.
- Tell the teacher what works. If you have found ways of gaining your child's attention, getting him to focus, or encouraging him to do his work, share this with the teacher.
- Identify the feedback you want from the teacher. Tell the teacher what kind of information you want about your child. For example, will you need a daily or weekly summary of behaviors?

- Ask the teacher about how she handles homework. Children with ADHD are often very frustrated with homework. Ask the teacher how long it takes most of the other students to complete the homework assignment. If your child is taking almost twice as long to finish his, it may be necessary to eliminate or reduce the amount of homework your child is given.

RESOURCES

ON THE WEB

Children and Adults with ADHD
www.chadd.org

Attention Deficit Disorder Association
www.add.org

Posttraumatic Stress Disorder

P OSTTRAUMATIC STRESS DISORDER (PTSD) is often assigned to foster and adopted children particularly if they experienced physical or sexual trauma. PTSD refers to a variety of symptoms that develop following exposure to an extreme traumatic stressor. Events that can trigger PTSD include: personal experience that involved actual or threatened death or serious injury; a threat to physical integrity; witnessing an event that involves death, injury, or a threat to the physical integrity of another person; and learning about unexpected or violent death, serious harm, or threat of death or injury experienced by a family member or close associate. This can include:

- Being physically harmed
- Being taken hostage
- Natural or man-made disasters
- Witnessing abuse of parent, sibling, animal, or another person
- Hearing of death of family member, friend or animal
- Fearing for one's safety, as in auto accident, fire, gun activity, domestic violence, physical abuse

In order to meet the criteria for PTSD, the child's response to the event must involve intense fear, helplessness, horror, disorganized or agitated behavior. The symptoms resulting from the exposure to the extreme trauma include persistent re-experiencing of the traumatic event, persistent avoidance of stimuli associated with the trauma, and numbing of general responsiveness. Your child may have difficulty going to or staying asleep, nightmares, night sweats, and/or high motor activity as he sleeps. Sudden or loud noises may cause him great alarm and he may be mistrustful of new people or places. The symptoms of PTSD may be especially severe or longstanding when the stressor is of human design.

As a result of the above, the child develops a variety of symptoms that may include:

- Acting or feeling as if the traumatic event were still occurring
- Intense psychological distress at exposure to cues associated with the event
- Inability to recall important aspects of the trauma
- Feeling of detachment or estrangement from others
- Sense of foreshortened future
- Difficulty falling or staying asleep
- Irritability or outbursts of anger
- Difficulty concentrating

Some children will likely remain haunted by images or thoughts of trauma from the past. It is quite difficult for a child to lose or stop the memory of seeing their mother being beat, watching their pet get killed, or of having someone hurt them physically or sexually. Still, the symptoms associated with these events should subside with time, a safe placement, and effective therapy. In too many cases, children present reactive symptoms long after the trauma occurred. Trauma does not get better by itself. Yet, the symptoms of trauma are highly responsive to effective mental health treatment. Typically, therapy for traumatized children includes:

- Reinforcing to the child that he is safe
- Teaching practical steps for protecting the self
- Relaxation training
- Thought-stopping techniques
- Visualization exercises

RESOURCES

FURTHER READING
Healing Trauma: Attachment, Mind, Body, and Brain (book)
Marion Fried Soloman

Young Children and Trauma (book)
Joy Osofsky

Reactive Attachment Disorder

A TTACHMENT REFERS TO THE AFFECTIONATE and emotional tie that develops between the infant and his primary caregiver, usually the mother. In developing an attachment relationship with the mother, the infant forms mental representations for all other subsequent relationships in life. If the infant learns, through attachment with the mother, that his needs can be met, he grows up learning to trust other people and to develop what is called, *secure attachment.* On the other hand, if the infant experiences fear, pain, discomfort, or sadness on a regular basis, he learns that other people cannot always take care of his needs, which places him at risk for *disrupted* or *impaired attachment.* You will often hear this referred to as *attachment disorder.*

The only generally accepted definition of attachment disorder is the DSM classification, *Reactive Attachment Disorder of Infancy or Early Childhood.* While the DSM acknowledges that this condition may result from pathological care in the first five years of life, the symptom profile described in DSM relates primarily to the child's social relatedness.

DSM indicates that Reactive Attachment Disorder manifests in one of two ways:

- A persistent failure on the part of the child to initiate and respond to most social interactions in a developmentally appropriate way, or
- Indiscriminate sociability or a lack of selectivity in the choice of attachment figures.

Missing from these descriptions is any reference to the child's maladaptive behaviors beyond those that deal with social relatedness. In clinical practice, however, there is a trend for some practitioners to assign a diagnosis of Reactive Attachment Disorder to children who exhibit behavior problems above and beyond the DSM definition. Many practitioners modify or disagree with the DSM definition of Reactive Attachment Disorder and reference many attributes when talking about children with the disorder that DSM does not intend. What we now have is a blend of terms: *Reactive Attachment Disorder*, which is an official classification within the field of mental health, and *attachment disorder*, which is a term with no mutually agreed upon definition or meaning. Curiously, this is one of the few areas of diagnostic classification in which this schism occurs. For the most part, it does not happen with other diagnoses such as Conduct Disorder, Oppositional Defiant Disorder, or Attention-Deficit/ Hyperactivity Disorder.

One of the root causes of this schism is that many practitioners are aware that children with disrupted bonding and attachment histories often present symptoms that exceed difficulties with social relatedness. Instead, "reactive" behaviors that include conduct and/or mood disturbance are common. If you read books or articles on *attachment disorder*, you will often see descriptions and definitions that go far beyond what the DSM intended. Instead, you will see reference to behaviors that are aggressive, controlling, and attention seeking. This sometimes includes lying, stealing, animal cruelty, self-destructive behaviors, and refusal to accept responsibility for consequences or actions.

A major concern I have is that parents sometimes see the diagnosis of Reactive Attachment Disorder assigned to a child they are interested in adopting and they run the other way. I recently consulted on a case in which two prospective parents refused to adopt an eight-year-old girl, solely because she carried the Reactive Attachment Disorder diagnosis. In her case, the diagnosis was applicable, as she had difficulties in social relatedness. But, these parents feared she would be a highly disturbed child who would be unmanageable, aggressive, and a threat to their safety. Yet nothing in her history suggested these concerns were realistic.

Parents should be aware that neglect, abuse, and trauma can affect the child's ability or willingness to bond with other people. Yet, we cannot predict with any certainty which children will simply have a difficult time trusting other people, versus those who will behave in destructive or manipulative ways. Ideally, you should do what you can to find out why your child was given the diagnosis of Reactive Attachment Disorder and explore the reasoning behind it.

From a diagnostic standpoint, it is common for some clinicians to assign the diagnosis, Reactive Attachment Disorder, without listing the other classifications which capture and therefore describe the full range of the child's behaviors. For example, if a child lies, steals, and hurts animals, the appropriate diagnosis would be *Conduct Disorder*. If social relatedness with others is disturbed or inappropriate, Reactive Attachment Disorder could also be assigned.

This is important for a couple of reasons. If I know that a child has been assigned the diagnosis, Reactive Attachment Disorder, it tells me he likely experienced inadequate or pathological care as an infant. If I see a diagnosis of Conduct Disorder, on the other hand, it tells me the child has been acting out his anger in ways that are aggressive or exploitative of others.

The current research on effective interventions for Reactive Attachment Disorder is limited. But experts believe for the therapy to be effective, it has to be long-term and directed at changing the child's internal working models — the way he perceives himself and the world around him. Since so many of these children live with feelings of anger, fear, and ambivalence about other people, the therapy is often directed toward helping the child release his rage, accept love, let others take care of him, and start to trust others. Traditional psychological treatment, with its emphasis on support, reflection, or play, is often considered ineffective with children diagnosed with Reactive Attachment Disorder.

Bipolar Disorder

ONE OF THE MORE CONTROVERSIAL diagnoses assigned to children is Bipolar Disorder. Even in the professional medical press, debate persists over whether Bipolar Disorder manifests in young children or whether the mood swings and behavior problems some children have aren't features of some other condition. Coming to an accurate diagnosis therefore has tremendous implications for a child's placement and treatment. If your child has been assigned a diagnosis of Bipolar Disorder, you will first want to clarify the best you can that this diagnosis is correct. If it is, this is a diagnosis you need to take very seriously, given the high rates of alcohol abuse and suicide in persons with the condition.

Until very recently, bipolar disorders were almost never diagnosed in children and only rarely in adolescents. Yet, of the two million adults who are assigned the diagnosis, upwards of 40 percent indicate that their first symptoms appeared in teens or earlier. In one study, 60 percent of the respondents reported onset of the disorder's symptoms before the age of 19.

Even though Bipolar Disorder often causes more problems for children than for adults, it is less recognizable in youngsters. Most adults with typical Bipolar Disorder have episodes of mania or depression that last a few months with relatively normal functioning in between. Many children with Bipolar Disorder will be both manic and depressed at the same time and will often have a more chronic course of illness without intervening well periods. Pediatric Bipolar Disorder is difficult to recognize because children are not capable of many of the telltale signs of bipolar symptoms in adults, such as charging too much on a credit card or having sexual sprees. Also, children are happy and expansive by nature, so it often doesn't occur to others that the behavior is pathological.

Symptoms of childhood Bipolar Disorder wax and wane, sometimes very rapidly. Hallmark symptoms include disruptive behavior that gets worse, extreme moodiness and irritability, insomnia and sleep problems, angry or aggressive episodes followed by periods of remorse and guilt, declining academic performance, increasing impulsiveness and hyperactivity, decreasing ability to concentrate and pay attention, and a decreasing ability to handle frustration. In these children, strange behaviors and moods occur out of nowhere. While a child with ADHD will be hyperactive most of the time, a child with Bipolar Disorder will swing from happiness to aggression to irritation to excitement. In childhood, daredevil and reckless behaviors are common in the child with Bipolar Disorder. This can include jumping off roofs, chasing moving vehicles, approaching vicious dogs or juggling sharp objects.

Bipolar Disorder manifests in two forms, Bipolar I and Bipolar II. With Bipolar I Disorder, the person experiences one or more manic episodes that may or may not include episodes of major depression. A manic episode occurs when the person presents an elevated, expansive, or irritable mood for at least one week, as well as with symptoms such as inflated self-esteem, decreased need for sleep, pressured or talkative speech, racing thoughts, distractibility, and/or excessive involvement in pleasurable activities that have a high potential for painful consequences (e.g., unrestrained buying sprees or random sexual behavior).

Bipolar II Disorder is characterized by the occurrence of one or more major depressive episodes, as well as hypomania, a condition similar to mania but that interferes less with daily functioning. During a major depressive episode, the person has several symptoms over a two-week period that may include a depressed or irritable mood, diminished interest in pleasure, failure to make expected weight gains, insomnia or hypersomnia (the inability to stay awake), psychomotor agitation or retardation, fatigue, loss of energy, feelings of worth-lessness, diminished ability to think or concentrate, and/or thoughts of death.

One of the things that make a diagnosis of Bipolar Disorder in children so alarming is its implications for long-term functioning. Bipolar Disorder is

DEPRESSION MAY BE EQUAL IN BOYS AND GIRLS

In one of the largest studies of depression in children, a survey in 1982 of 2,790 children in rural Pennsylvania, found that there were no differences in the numbers of boys and girls who were depressed, nor in the severity of their depression. In another poll of 1,000 teenagers conducted for Ms. Magazine in 1997, 28 percent of young women aged 15 to 21 stated they feel depressed daily or several times a week. 20 percent of young men in the same group reported to the magazine that they feel depressed just as frequently.

not conceptualized as a single event. Rather, its course tends to be chronic, with high risk of future symptoms. For those persons with Bipolar Disorder, the majority experience severe consequences socially, at school, or at work. For some, their manic symptoms may include psychotic symptoms. Obviously, most people diagnosed with Bipolar Disorder need to take prescription medication, often for a good portion of their childhood and adult years.

Bipolar Disorder is tied to a genetic component. It manifests in both males and females, though females tend to have more depressive episodes and males have more manic episodes. If it is unknown whether a child's birth parents had Bipolar Disorder, the possibility is increased if there is a history of substance abuse, early sexual activity, or a pattern of risk-taking behaviors.

The children I have counseled with Bipolar Disorder experience mood and behavior fluctuations that are random and not usually in response to a trigger such as limit-setting by the parents, a change in homes, or the holidays. The most prominent features I have observed in these children are: extreme irritability upon wakening and chronic sleep disturbance.

If your child has been diagnosed with Bipolar Disorder, it is important that you have faith in the provider who assigned the diagnosis. If in doubt, obtain a second opinion. Since your child will likely be prescribed psychotropic medication, do what you can to learn about the benefits and risks of the medication, as well as the common side effects. Anticipate that you will need to stay in close contact with your child's psychiatrist. Finally, as the parent of a child with Bipolar Disorder, you need to be prepared for added levels of stress. The symptoms of Bipolar Disorder can be intense, bizarre, or threatening. You will need to have a safety plan in place for dealing with sudden changes in your child's behavior, particularly if he becomes violent to himself or others.

At all times, make sure you have:

- The psychiatrists' pager and emergency contact number
- A written list of the child's medications and dosages
- The phone number for the hospital emergency room
- Numbers for friends or family members who you can call upon in an emergency

Many children diagnosed with Bipolar Disorder are also diagnosed with Attention-Deficit/Hyperactivity Disorder. While the two conditions can occur simultaneously, some of the distinguishing characteristics include:

- Elated mood, grandiosity, racing thoughts, or decreased need for sleep is not common to children with ADHD
- Children with ADHD don't usually exhibit hypersexuality or uninhibited people seeking
- Children with both conditions can experience irritable mood, distractibility, and increased energy
- Children with Bipolar Disorder might engage in angry destructiveness, while the child with ADHD will engage in careless destructiveness

- If a child with ADHD has a temper tantrum, it is usually for minutes at a time. When a child with Bipolar Disorder has a tantrum, it can last an hour or longer
- Children with ADHD often have learning disorders. Children with Bipolar Disorder, on the other hand, can sometimes be early talkers and readers
- At night, a child with ADHD may have a difficult time relaxing and falling asleep. Children with Bipolar Disorder often complain of disturbing dreams, with violent and gory content
- Children with ADHD experience most of their problems at school, where inattention and hyperactivity is difficult to manage. Children with Bipolar Disorder have difficulties is any situation involving strong relationships, so their behavior can be worse at home than at school

---

RESOURCES

ON THE WEB
Child and Adolescent Bipolar Foundation
www.bpkids.org

> *I believe that one of the main reasons child therapists often hesitate to allow parents to observe them is that they are basically ashamed of what they are doing.*
>
> — Richard A. Gardner,
> "Psychotherapy with Children"

Counseling Issues for Foster and Adopted Children

MANY PARENTS ARE MYSTIFIED by counseling and therapy. While they may believe it holds the promise of helping their child, they often find themselves confused about what it takes to change troubling attitudes or behaviors. For a lot of parents, taking their child to see a counselor triggers tremendous feelings of frustration, shame, and inadequacy. I have had parents tell me, for example, that they feel like a failure because they are not able to manage or control their child's behavior on their own. By the time a parent brings a child to therapy, they have likely tried many ways to deal with his behaviors. More often than not, it is a crisis time for the child and family when they first come for treatment.

I find that parents vary with respect to their knowledge about the process and goals of counseling. Some may have had treatment of their own and are therefore intimately aware of how therapy works. Others know very little and may only be taking the child for counseling because somebody tells them they have to.

If you have been in counseling, you know the process typically involves sitting down with a trusted professional, sharing your thoughts, feelings, fears, and confusions about life and relationships. For her part, the therapist listens to these concerns, offering validation and perhaps suggestions along the way. With children, the treatment looks quite different. Most children are not able to reflect on their life experience and articulate the thoughts and feelings they have about it. The therapist therefore needs to find more direct or creative ways for engaging the child and getting her to talk about things she has seen, thought about, or heard. Therapists do this in a variety of ways, depending upon the age, maturity, verbal skills, and cognitive functioning of the client. While their techniques may differ, most therapists are of the opinion that it is better for a child to release their feelings—through words, actions, or play — rather than hold on to or act out in ways that can be maladaptive.

One of the realities about the mental health field is that a good number of clinicians who work with children never received formal training and supervision in this practice. Most graduate programs in psychology, counseling, or social work require students to take a course or two on human development or family dynamics. Yet, more detailed aspects of doing therapy with children are not typically included. I also find that a large number of clinicians who supervise other staff or interns in family service agencies were not trained as child therapists. They therefore do not always ensure the therapist adequately takes into account what role the parents will play in the therapeutic process.

Too often when providing consultation or supervision, I find that the providers do not have adequate knowledge about child development, let alone how foster care and adoption issues play out in a child's life. The therapy therefore becomes a frustrating process for the provider, child, and family. What sometimes ends up happening is that I have to do a crash course on child psychology for these clinicians before we can even address specific issues affecting the child and her family. Part of the problem stems from the fact that therapeutic work with foster and adopted children is a highly specialized area. It can be difficult to take general principles of child therapy and apply them across the board to this population of children. Yet, therapists rarely get opportunities to receive hands-on training in working with this group of kids. So they fall back on techniques that are familiar to them.

QUALITIES OF A GOOD THERAPIST

- Thorough understanding of child development
- Solid training in childhood psychological disorders
- Familiar with common psychiatric medications prescribed to children, as well as typical side-effects
- Able to set firm limits and boundaries with children and adults
- Skilled in educating parents about child behaviors
- Able to confront a child, without shaming
- Have a sense of humor
- Willing to talk about and explore painful and sensitive topics
- Able to come across as caring, competent, and effective
- Willing to try new approaches when old one's don't work
- Willing to function as part of a team, which includes parents, teachers, social workers, psychiatrists, and others
- First-hand knowledge about their regional adoption and foster care systems
- Willing to seek professional consultation and supervision
- Must not believe they have all the answers

Parents typically seek out mental health services for their child because his behavior is impacting the home and school environment. As observers to this process, parents naturally view themselves as the one who can best communicate to others what it is like to live with the child. Parents may not necessarily think in terms of family-based approaches to treatment, but they clearly expect to be involved in work that stands to affect their child and family. Many are surprised, however, when the therapist tells the parent that the treatment will only involve the provider and the child. Too often, parents become frustrated with the therapeutic experience when they feel excluded from what is happening between the counselor and their child.

An unfortunate trend in the treatment of foster and adopted children is to assume that all of their behavior or emotional disturbance stems from disrupted attachment. As I emphasize throughout this book, issues of attachment and bonding are paramount for this population of children. But to assume the child's presentation resulted solely from attachment problems is irresponsible. A child's behavior can be motivated by a variety of factors. This includes features that are common to all children, such as temperament. Other factors include the more unique issues that many foster and adopted children are at high risk for, such as prenatal exposure to toxins, a family history of mental illness, abuse and neglect, or exposure to other forms of traumatic stress.

Prior to developing a treatment plan, it is important to understand all we can about the child's history, behavior, and mental status. Too often, children are referred to me for an evaluation because the therapy they are receiving is not working and the provider wants input about what may be helpful. I believe that the child's needs are best served if the evaluation occurs before therapy is implemented. This evaluation can help determine whether issues such as untreated mental illness, attention problems, neurological damage, or mood disturbance require intervention before therapy begins.

As stated above, I believe that therapeutic intervention with foster and adopted children requires specialized training and experience. I am concerned when therapists who have no direct experience with this population of children provide counseling to them. I frequently find that therapists who lack the proper training do not adequately address issues of relinquishment, grief, anger, fear, and the attachment issues so common with these children. Nor do they fully comprehend the complexity of the child welfare or adoption systems and how this affects the child and the family. In many instances, parental concerns go unaddressed or ignored when the therapist chooses to only work with the child. In situations where the child has severe attachment disturbance, my experience is that the child — not the therapist — is typically in control in the therapy due to unfamiliarity on the therapist's part of effective interventions with these children.

As a parent, you should feel comfortable interviewing prospective therapists in order to learn about their experience in working with foster or adopted children. You will also want to find out how they will communicate the key issues of the treatment to you and how they identify treatment goals. If you are unaware of therapists in your area who specialize in treating foster or adopted children, check with various placement agencies in your region. Many adoption and attachment websites also have resource lists of therapists throughout the country.

When interviewing therapists, find out how they will educate the child about what will be happening in counseling. When providing counseling for a child, I believe it is important for therapists to explain to the child the rules, parameters, and expectations. It is unrealistic to expect a child to come to therapy each time and talk about feelings or life experiences. More often, children need to be guided toward this goal. They also must understand, at their developmental level, the importance of talking about these issues. When providing therapy to a child and his family, I spend a good portion of our initial time together providing an introduction to therapy, explaining how I work and why I explore the feelings and topics that I do.

**QUESTIONS PARENTS NEED TO ASK
ABOUT THEIR CHILD'S THERAPY**

- Have my child's problem behaviors decreased since starting therapy?
- Does the therapist involve me in the work being done to help my child?
- Has the therapist provided me with useful skills to use outside of therapy?
- Do I have a clear sense of the treatment goals pertaining to my child?
- Is the therapist willing to use a team approach, to include contact with the teacher, psychiatrist, or others if needed?

Play Therapy

Therapists who have received training or education in working with children typically get exposed to what is called the play therapy model. This model highlights that play is the natural mode of communication for children and encourages interacting with the child in a playful manner during therapy. This might include playing board games, permitting the child to draw or build scenes in a tray of sand, or making a project together. In this approach, the therapist provides the child with many avenues for play — toys, clay, dolls, puppets, paint — and the child is usually free to use these things as he sees fit.

The basic premise of play therapy is twofold. On the one hand, it is believed children will exhibit the dominant themes of their inner life — anger, sadness, abandonment, abuse — through their play, thereby permitting the therapist to identify the child's significant issues. The therapy becomes an avenue for symbolically expressing what the child feels. On the other hand, play therapy assumes that a trusting relationship may develop between the therapist and child, thus making him feel he can eventually share his feelings with the therapist. Play therapy often provides children with feelings of mastery, as they have the freedom to create and express themselves in many ways.

Play therapy can be an effective technique for many children, but I generally do not support or recommend it for foster or adopted children, particularly in cases where the child is having extreme behavior problems, adjustment reactions, or difficulty bonding to the parents. Rarely do I employ a play therapy model unless I am evaluating a young child or providing therapy to someone four years of age or younger. By the time many foster or adopted children are referred for counseling we often have a good idea about some of the major issues they are dealing with. This could include issues of abuse, neglect, abandonment, parental loss, betrayal, attachment, or changing homes.

While foster and adopted children should have ample opportunity for play, I don't believe that therapy is the time for it. By the time a child is five or older, he has some capacity for using his words and turning his attention toward his behavior and relationships with others. Rather than have a child play with me for an hour, I would rather address key issues affecting his identity, behavior, and his peer and family relations. This doesn't mean that the interactions between the child, parent, and me are not fun and playful at times. Yet, the child and parents are given the message that therapy is a time to take a close look at significant matters of the child's life. This entails going after these issues in a more direct manner.

I will sometimes engage the family in an activity such as throwing and catching a ball, role-playing, or doing a group drawing. But, I do not find this should be a prominent part of the treatment. Certainly, playtime allows me the opportunity to obtain information about how the child does with competition, cooperation, spontaneity, and limit setting, and occasionally proves useful to take a break from the intensive work of therapy. I remind the children with whom I work, however, that therapy is mostly a time to address the important issues in their life. If they are coming to me for treatment, there are usually legitimate concerns about how the child is feeling or behaving. The therapy must work toward understanding and modifying these as needed.

An exception occurs when there is not a clear idea about what feelings or issues a child is dealing with. If the parents are not sure what their child is experiencing inside or if the child is not verbally expressive, play techniques can help the therapist gain some perspective on the child's needs. Play therapy, therefore, has more value as a diagnostic tool than for treatment. Once the child's issues are made clearer to the therapist, I still believe it best to move toward more proactive efforts in the treatment.

Many children are not motivated to participate in therapy, mainly because they are more focused on the present than on the past. Rather than look inward, most children will act out their feelings. While much of this will show in play therapy, rarely do I find that this results in significant changes in attitude or behavior. If therapy is to succeed with a child who is not motivated, then other techniques have to be used to engage them.

Parental Involvement

A man told me this recently regarding the 15-year-old girl he and his wife are raising and preparing to adopt:

> *She's been in therapy with the same therapist for close to two years. But this therapist isn't giving us what we feel we need in order to work with our daughter. We went through the education classes offered by the adoption agency, but they haven't prepared us for what we're experiencing at home. We desperately need some guidance if this adoption is going to work out for all of us.*

Since a primary goal in treating foster or adopted children is to address issues of their behavior, emotions, bonding and attachment, my view is that parents should be involved in the treatment. The therapist and child should meet alone at times, but by and large, I advocate parental involvement. I tell parents that their job is to work as my co-therapist, both in and out of therapy, as we address the important issues affecting their child's life. The parents and I work as a team, trying to explore the child's thoughts, beliefs, and actions. Also, the parents and I mutually address the problematic behaviors of the child, effectively communicating our interest in seeing him "make it." I rely upon the parents to clarify any lies or omissions the child tells me about his life, as parents quite often have a better grasp on the full story. I consistently find that parents view the therapy as a worthwhile and more productive endeavor when they are included in the process.

As I stated in the Introduction, parents are the front line of defense to help the child. Even if the child works with an excellent therapist, he won't likely make many changes or gains if his efforts aren't encouraged and supported in the home. When parents are included in the therapy, they have clearer ideas about the therapist's goals. Parents are also in a better position to take what was practiced or discussed in therapy and use it at home.

When actively involved in the treatment, parents come to recognize and appreciate that growth and healing is not a linear process. It is well-established in the counseling field that children and adults will make strides in therapy but also experience relapses or dips. This doesn't mean the therapy isn't working or that the client is not motivated to attain their goals. My experience shows that parental involvement in the treatment helps them understand this reality, without getting angry at the therapist or losing faith in their child. Instead, the parents and I can talk about this fact while the child is present, assessing why this is occurring. For example, by brainstorming on the issue, we can become more sensitized to the hard work the child has been doing, the stress he may be experiencing, or to other issues currently affecting the child's life.

I know from my own experience that I can do little to modify a child's attitude or behavior without significant parental involvement. This is especially true with children who are assigned diagnoses such as Oppositional Defiant, Conduct, Reactive Attachment, Bipolar, or Attention-Deficit/Hyperactivity Disorders. Many children can focus their attention or contain their erratic behaviors when in a therapist's office. Doing so at home and at school may prove more difficult. Talking with a child about behavior I have not observed has a vague and abstract quality to it. A parent who lives with these behaviors on a daily basis, on the other hand, can introduce a more realistic aspect to the discussion. I am then in a better position to help the child examine his behavior, while also offering practical strategies and interventions to the parent.

I do not believe that every foster or adopted child will develop or struggle with significant attachment issues. As highlighted elsewhere in this book, however, this population of children does carry a greater risk for attachment disturbance, which is one of the reasons their referral rates for mental health services are quite high. The research is fairly consistent in identifying greater rates of attachment issues among children who experienced abuse, neglect, or trauma at a very young age. By gaining an understanding of the dynamics between the parent and child, I am better able to determine to what extent the child's behaviors are attachment-based, since disrupted attachment directly affects all of the child's relationships, especially with his primary parent. This may not be as evident if I am just meeting with the child alone.

As psychologist Daniel Hughes writes, maintaining an emotional engagement with the child, regardless of the behaviors manifested during treatment, is the foundation of all therapeutic interventions with the poorly attached child. Each session models ways to maintain a connection with the child in spite of the various misbehaviors in the home. Parents should see and participate in these models, particularly if they are feeling frustrated and angered by their child. By participating in the child's therapy, parents learn techniques for engaging him in ways that don't result in a power struggle. Parents also learn strategies for looking beyond the child's behavior in order to empathize with what it is he is truly feeling. When observing a parent and child, I can see how they play off one another or how the child responds to what the parent says or does. I can then direct the interactions between them in a manner that strives to strengthen the parent-child bond.

If your child is seeing a therapist who does not include you in the process, you should still have a good idea about what is and is not happening in therapy. Parents frequently sit in the waiting room while their child is in therapy and receive little information about the therapeutic goals or processes affecting their child. Unless you are seeing significant behavioral changes in your child at home and at school, I encourage considering alternatives to this approach. Therapists, too, will find that parents are more receptive to their recommendations if they are included in the process. Many foster parents tell me that they do not believe their role is to be involved with the child's treatment. With few exceptions, I beg to differ. Even if the child is only living with a family for a short period of time, his actions still impact the others in the household. While I may not be able to address all of the root causes of the behavior — given the limited amount of time I have to work with the family — I can still use interventions that help the child to examine how his actions affect those around him.

I do not believe that confidentiality should play a major part in the psychological treatment of children. If a therapist tells you that what he and the child discuss is confidential, I encourage you to exercise caution in working with that provider. Confidentiality is fine in the treatment of a 16-year-old, but not in therapy with a nine-year-old. As child psychiatrist Richard Gardner says, telling a child there will be confidentiality creates a structure of "we" (the therapist and the child) and "they" (the parents). "We" and "they" can easily become "we" versus "they," which can create further conflict for the family. In order for child therapy to be useful and effective, parents should know about and appreciate the issues affecting their child. Most children do not have a great many secrets they wish to keep secret from parents. Therapists who permit children to confide their stories often do so under the guise of building a trusting relationship with the child. I contend that this is counterproductive and ends up doing little to help the child or his family.

Parent-child interventions are also more likely to yield greater information about the child's Internal Working Model, a concept introduced in the section on attachment. As Terry Levy and Michael Orlans note, the child's internal working model includes core beliefs about self, caregivers, and life in general. This internal working model serves as a blueprint for all current and future relationships. Parents should attempt to understand the internal working model of the child they are raising, as the thoughts he has about himself influence all aspects of his life. Modifying negative internal working models of foster and adoptive children is a large part of the therapy but it requires the active efforts of the therapist and the parents.

Many of these children grow up believing that adults cannot protect them, that parents cannot be trusted, that they are destined to be "given away," and that the world is unsafe. What is the theme here? Parents! In fact, when we talk about the role of bonding and attachment in children's lives, we're primarily talking about the parents who are raising the child. Therapeutic efforts must be directed at challenging, confronting, and attempting to re-work these beliefs, while focusing on the relationship the child has with the primary adults in his life. Otherwise, most of the other interventions used with these children miss the key aspects of why they feel and behave they way they do.

Does My Child Have to be in Counseling?

Particularly with placements arranged through state social service agencies, parents are sometimes told that their child must be in counseling. In some situations, the child may have been in counseling while in one placement and the former therapist recommends continued treatment once the child is in a new placement. My opinion is that the decision to start a child in therapy should be a thoughtful one. Not every child needs counseling, even if they have a challenging past. Therapy can be helpful for children, but parents need to carefully consider when and if to start this process.

Within their new families, children should experience the rituals, behaviors, and routines that facilitate a respectful, loving, and trusting relationship. The initial weeks and months of a new placement can be fragile, as the parents and child get to know one another, and as the child struggles with feelings that may include excitement, fear, anger, sadness, and confusion. When children are brought to therapy during the early stage of the placement, I sometimes find that it can interfere with the bond that needs to develop between the parent and child, particularly in cases of adoption. As with parenting, therapy is a highly intimate and personal encounter. In order for counseling to be effective, the therapist must establish that his office is a safe environment for the expression of all kinds of emotions. The therapist needs to communicate that therapy is not a place for keeping secrets and that most aspects of the child's current and past experience will be explored in depth. Therapy with most foster or adopted children is not a short-term proposition, unless forced so by nature of the fact that the child's placement changes. In therapy, it can be expected that the provider and child will develop a unique relationship, where boundaries, emotions, and trust are constantly challenged.

In order to deal effectively with these dynamics, it is best if aspects of an intact relationship between the parent and child are already in place. Allow me to use couples counseling as an example. While many couples could benefit from guidance and advice at the onset of their relationship, it is difficult to do actual therapy with a couple until they have been together for a while. Only when problematic themes and patterns of behavior have been identified can alternatives be explored. This analogy holds true in the treatment of children. Also, if a parent takes her child to therapy immediately after he arrives in the home, it sends the message that the parent does not have the knowledge or ability to tackle matters on her own. This can diminish the positive views the child needs to have of his parent.

In my experience, the intensity of the therapeutic relationship can make the child feel confused, as he develops a relationship with the therapist while also building on the one he has with his parents. In these instances, the child often strengthens ties to the therapist. For one thing, the therapist places less demand and expectation on him than do the parents. Many parents also communicate to him their desire to have the child love them unconditionally. A therapist does not impose this on the child, thus becoming less of a threat to his psychological defenses.

Attachment Therapy

Within the fields of counseling and psychology, there are mixed definitions about what constitutes attachment therapy. If your child is seeing a therapist who tells you they work on an attachment model, you should fully understand what they mean by this.

In a general sense, attachment-based approaches assume that the relationship a child has with others is influenced by his history of trauma, abuse, or neglect. Attachment disturbance in children, therefore, is sometimes referred to as a *relationship disorder*. In light of this, the bulk of therapeutic interventions deemed attachment-based are directed toward strengthening the relationship the child has with others, especially his parents.

In most attachment-based therapies, children are encouraged to express the full range of feelings, to include the sad, the mad, the scared, and the glad. Parents, too, are supported in expressing the feelings they have about the child. To reduce feelings of vulnerability that can come with the expression of raw or intense emotions, therapists who work on an attachment model will periodically offer the child supportive touch, hugs, or holding and will encourage the parents to do the same. For example, as we're talking about a particularly difficult time in the child's life, I may place my hand on his shoulder or ask that he cuddle up with his mother as we talk about the issues. Touch is a powerful form of communication, yet for too many children touch has been hurtful or exploitative. Various forms of touch are often integrated into attachment therapies, something that has its advocates as well as its critics. In some instances, touch has been forced on children in therapy, making them feel further victimized or afraid. I always point out to the child in advance that I will sometimes touch him, yet I emphasize that his parents will be in the room when I do, that he can tell me "no," tell me to stop, and that I will not hurt him.

As mentioned earlier, many children will regress in therapy as they explore feelings related to their past and present. The child will use words or actions that are common to much younger children, such as curling up in a fetal position, thumb-sucking, having a tantrum, using self-soothing behaviors such as stroking his hair, holding a small toy, or talking like a baby. In attachment therapy, these behaviors are supported and sometimes encouraged. During a child's regression, I will ask the parents, "What age does this behavior look like to you?" Their responses are usually correct and it helps us both understand the emotional age their child reverts to when he is feeling afraid, sad, or stressed.

In many respects, attachment-based therapy is a re-parenting process for the child. In treatment and at home, he is offered the nurturing responses and interactions he may have missed out on in earlier years of his life. While not done in an offensive or belittling way, the parent and therapist relate to the child — regardless of his age — as parents often do with infants. This includes tolerating a broad range of behaviors and emotions, permitting the child to safely act out his fears or frustrations, using lots of playful touch and physical interaction, and assuring the child of his safety every step of the way. If you watch a parent interacting with her infant, it is usually more playful and hands-on than with her older child. Attachment therapy takes the meaning this mode of interacting has for the child and brings it into the treatment.

Medication probably serves its most beneficial purpose when used in combination with supportive services and appropriate therapy. There is no medication alone that can restructure the personality and further its development.

— Gregory Keck and Regina Kupecky,
"Adopting the Hurt Child"

Children and Psychiatric Medication

THE USE OF PSYCHOTROPIC MEDICATION in children is not without controversy. In some instances, the decision to use medication with children is a confusing one. In my opinion, the choice to use medication with children often comes down to this: use the medication and be prepared to deal with any side effects which result, or don't use the medication and accept the side effects that result from that choice. In other words, there is not always a perfect answer when it comes to this topic. In many cases, there is a poor outcome associated with doing nothing.

Current estimates are that 12 to 22 percent of American kids — that's upwards of 14 million — suffer from psychiatric disorders. Whether a particular child requires psychotropic medication, though, can be a difficult decision. Some mental and emotional disorders are treated successfully with psychotherapy alone. Others are treated with a combination of psychotherapy and pharmacology. Often, a medication offers the straight-forward solution to the child's problem because some agent specifically targets the medical cause of the disorder. In ADHD, for example, medicines bring improvement in a way that no other form of treatment alone has been able to do.

A stigma still surrounds using medication with children. Whereas we rarely question the use of medication for conditions such as diabetes or seizures, some people have a difficult time appreciating that many behavioral and emotional disorders can result from conditions in the child's brain. As an example, ADHD results from structural changes in the neurons of the brain. The medications used to treat ADHD are highly effective at reversing some of these effects. Because some parents do not want their child to take medication, they seek out alternative treatments that have virtually no impact on the root cause of their child's symptoms. Yet, emerging findings consistently suggest that the bulk of emotional, cognitive, and behavioral disorders are caused by subtle chemical differences in the brains of children. The medications that are prescribed normalize the transmission of these chemical signals and thus reduce the child's symptoms.

Some medications such as Prozac and Ritalin have the backing of hundreds of clinical trials that indicate their use with children is safe and effective. For other medications, several clinical trials show effectiveness with adults but not necessarily with children. The usefulness of medication with children represents a tremendous advance in science. It wasn't too long ago that children with emotional or behavioral problems were institutionalized.

Recently, much controversy has arisen around the use of certain antidepressant medications with children. A report out of Columbia University demonstrated an increase in suicidal thoughts or behaviors in children who were taking certain antidepressants. The Columbia experts were asked to determine whether instances of self-harm that occurred during clinical trials were truly suicide attempts. No child actually killed himself during the trials but there were incidents ranging in seriousness from a hanging attempt to a girl who slapped herself in the face. Still, in the 15 clinical trials of depression, youngsters on certain medications were no more likely to experience what the researchers termed, "emergence of suicidality" than those on placebo.

What the Columbia report did find was that youngsters on medications for other conditions — such as anxiety or Obsessive-Compulsive Disorder — as well as for depression, were 1.78 times as likely as those on placebo to exhibit "definitive suicidal behavior/ideation." It was this finding that sparked the media attention.

Whether your child needs medication depends on the problem, its causes, and its effect on the child's life. Some symptoms simply do not respond to talk or play therapy. In my experience, I have seen children who are prescribed medications that have little or no impact on their mood or behavior. On the other hand, I have seen many children who would not be able to function in society without the help the medication provides. Realistically, the use of psychotropic medication with children has prevented more suicides than it has caused. Also, as long as your child takes the medication as prescribed, psychotropic medications are very safe.

As a foster or adoptive parent, you are a key player in your child's mental health care, particularly if he is taking prescribed medication. As you probably know from your own experience, medications of any kind can cause a variety of effects on the mind or body. Effects may include sleepiness, dry mouth, difficulty urinating, difficulty sleeping, upset stomach, light-headedness, mental confusion, hyperactivity, increased appetite, motor agitation, or restlessness. Young children particularly may not be able to recognize or communicate that any of these symptoms are occurring.

It therefore becomes necessary for you:

- To find out from the psychiatrist the common side effects of the medications.
- To observe your child for signs of side effects.
- To ask your child if he is experiencing symptoms such as those listed above.

It usually takes at least one month to determine if a medication is working. Parents should note that kids can develop tolerance to medication over time. Tolerances can develop because the child's brain has adapted to the medication, the amount of medication needed to achieve desired effects has increased, or another disorder may have emerged in the child.

If you are working with a psychiatrist who specializes in treating children, you can have greater confidence that the practitioner has knowledge and experience on his side. But, if your child's provider doesn't specialize in childhood conditions, he may not be fully aware of the risks and benefits of using certain medication with children. This leaves you the choice of getting a second opinion from another provider or asking your child's current provider to consider consultation with a more experienced professional.

I believe parents should play an active role in the basic monitoring of their child's medications. This should include making sure the child takes the medication as prescribed, asking the child about side effects, and understanding what medications can and cannot realistically do. Medications given to children are typically reviewed in books written about drugs for the lay public. These can be found in the medical section of bookstores. Internet sites such as www.webmd.com or www.apa.org (the American Academy of Pediatrics) may also prove useful. It is perfectly acceptable to share the information you find on websites with the child's psychiatrist and obtain his opinion about the material. Web sites that are targeted to parents whose children carry certain diagnoses (Obsessive-Compulsive Disorder, for example) also offer good information about medications and their effects.

If your child experiences a symptom you believe is a side effect of the medication, consult with the doctor or even the pharmacist. Most of the major side effects are listed in the handout given to you with the prescription. Any severe side effects such as shortness of breath, chest discomfort, severe agitation, fainting, or disorientation call for immediate contact with your child's doctor even if they are occurring infrequently.

Finally, make sure your child's medications are prescribed and monitored by a psychiatrist, not a pediatrician. A child who is prescribed psychiatric medication should be seen by their psychiatrist at least once every 30 to 60 days. Medication effects vary with each child, modifications in dosage may be required, and some medications require that the child's blood levels be checked periodically. These procedures are not outside the realm of most physicians. But, parents should work closely with someone who specializes in prescribing medications for children.

Unfortunately, many psychiatrists only allot 15 to 30 minutes per follow-up appointment, leaving little time for parents to fully communicate questions, observations, and concerns. Parents should therefore bring written notes to the appointment, as well as a symptom/side effect log such as the ones that follow:

SAMPLE MEDICATION LOG

Child's Name:_____   Date of Birth: _____

Medications	Prescribing MD	Last Appointment	Next Appointment
Prozac, 10 mg, 1x/day	Anderson	08/15/05	09/23/05
Ritalin, 5 mg, 1x/day	Anderson	08/23/05	09/17/05

Date	Medication	Time Given	Response	+/- Effects
08/15/05	Ritalin, 5 mg.	8:00 AM	Good	Teacher said he was alert in class. Fewer verbal outbursts today. Ate all of his lunch.
08/15/05	Prozac, 10 mg.	8:00 AM	Good	No irritability upon wakening. Energy level and appetite is good.
08/16/05	Ritalin, 5 mg.			I forgot to give him the pill today and his teacher said his behavior was horrible. He pulled a girl's hair. Teacher said he hardly ate any of his lunch. Was very tired after school.
08/17/05	Ritalin, 5 mg.	8:00 AM	Good	He was more settled today, but teacher said he looked a bit spacey. No remorse for pulling the girl's hair. Slept all through the night.

SIDE EFFECTS RATING SCALE

Medication: _____   Doctor: _____

Start Date: _____

Child: _____   DOB: _____

Person completing this form: _____

Instructions: Please rate each behavior from 0 (absent) to 9 (serious). Circle only one number beside each item. A 0 means that you have not seen the behavior in this child during the past week, and a 9 means that you have noticed it and believe it to be either very serious or occur very frequently.

Behavior	*Absent*									*Serious*
Insomnia or trouble sleeping	0	1	2	3	4	5	6	7	8	9
Nightmares	0	1	2	3	4	5	6	7	8	9
Stares a lot or daydreams	0	1	2	3	4	5	6	7	8	9
Talks less with others	0	1	2	3	4	5	6	7	8	9
Uninterested in others	0	1	2	3	4	5	6	7	8	9
Decreased appetite	0	1	2	3	4	5	6	7	8	9
Irritable	0	1	2	3	4	5	6	7	8	9
Stomachaches	0	1	2	3	4	5	6	7	8	9
Headaches	0	1	2	3	4	5	6	7	8	9
Drowsiness	0	1	2	3	4	5	6	7	8	9
Sad/Unhappy	0	1	2	3	4	5	6	7	8	9
Prone to crying	0	1	2	3	4	5	6	7	8	9
Anxious	0	1	2	3	4	5	6	7	8	9
Euphoric/unusually happy	0	1	2	3	4	5	6	7	8	9
Dizziness	0	1	2	3	4	5	6	7	8	9
Tics or nervous movements	0	1	2	3	4	5	6	7	8	9
Delusional thoughts/words	0	1	2	3	4	5	6	7	8	9
Inattentive at home/school	0	1	2	3	4	5	6	7	8	9

A significant number of children suffer some sort of brain damage that causes emotional or behavioral disorders. These are common in foster and adopted populations because of higher rates of poor prenatal care, in-utero exposure to toxins, premature birth, or head trauma (such as in cases of severe child abuse). Symptoms can include acting out of control, prolonged temper tantrums, rage attacks, aggression, panic reactions, or isolation.

The diagnosis of a neurological disorder can be made through a physician, who may order an EEG, MRI, CT or similar tests, or through a psychologist, who can administer neuropsychological testing. If it is suspected or known that a child's behavior is likely caused by brain damage, medication may be prescribed. The medication used will depend on the type and severity of symptoms displayed by the child. Typically, psychiatrists opt to use mood stabilizers, antihypertensives, or antipsychotics for these conditions.

What's Inside the Child's Placement File?

WHEN A CHILD IS PLACED in your home, or prior to the finalization of an adoption, you will likely be provided with varying amounts of information about his background. In some instances, parents are actually provided with significant portions of the child's medical, mental health, and social services file. In other circumstances — particularly with international adoptions — the parents know very little about the child's history. My personal belief is that parent's should be provided with as much information about their child as possible.

If you are providing foster care, it is doubtful you will be given any written material about the child, unless she is in treatment foster care. You may then be provided with a copy of the treatment plan, which outlines the child's background, diagnoses, and goals. Even if the agency you work for does not provide you with many details about the child, you should identify in advance which questions you need to have answers for. This will vary, based on how your home, family, and life are structured.

These questions could include:

- Will the child need to be enrolled in my local school?
- Does he have any significant behavior problems I should know of?
- Is he taking any medication? If so, does he have enough and how do I get more?
- What is the name of his social worker, guardian, and therapist?
- What appointments does he have each week?
- What is a realistic time line for him remaining in my home?

When provided with records and documents about a child's history, you can anticipate that much of the information will be confusing and overwhelming. At times, the information contained in these documents may even be contradictory. I saw a set of reports recently where one diagnostician coded Attention-Deficit/Hyperactivity Disorder, but no one else did. Naturally, I was left wondering if the child was misdiagnosed, if his ADHD symptoms were under control, or if the other evaluators missed key aspects of the child's behaviors. It is also possible that the evaluator who coded ADHD for the child either did or did not have access to persons who could round out the clinical picture.

Keep in mind that documentation regarding a child is a snapshot, offering information about the child at a given point in time. At one point in time, the child's behavior may be totally out of control. The same may not be true when he is ready for an adoptive home. Similarly, a child may appear healthy one day, but require extensive medical tests on another. If possible, ask the placement agency if you can discuss the contents of the file with an outside therapist, doctor, or educator. This person becomes your consultant, helping you to know which details of the child's life require close examination versus which are less important.

When you meet with a social worker or director of a placement agency, you may find a variety of documents in the child's file. The following sections provide information on those documents.

Psychological Evaluations

A licensed psychologist typically conducts a psychological evaluation. The evaluation determines a child's psychiatric diagnosis and offers recommendations regarding placement or treatment. Most psychological evaluations start off with a brief history of the child, followed by a list of tests administered. Some evaluations, known as neuropsychological evaluations, focus on the overall brain function of the child. Neuropsychological evaluations are administered to determine whether the child has a neurological disorder as a result of poor prenatal care, premature birth, head injury, exposure to toxins (e.g., alcohol, tobacco, or drugs), neglect, or physical trauma. They are also frequently conducted to determine whether a child has Attention-Deficit/Hyperactivity Disorder.

You cannot assume that a particular psychological evaluation was comprehensive. The cornerstone of the psychological evaluation is the referral question — the manner in which the referral source communicates the main questions they want answered by the evaluation. Children are only referred for a psychological evaluation because someone has questions they need answered. In some instances, the person requesting the evaluation just has one question she wants addressed (e.g., Is the child performing at grade level?) The report may therefore only focus on this issue, without attention paid to the broader aspects of the child's behavior or mood.

Common referral questions include:

- What are the child's educational needs?
- Is a referral to a psychiatrist for a medication assessment in order?
- What kind of therapy would be most effective for this child?
- What level of placement does the child require?
- What are the child's psychiatric diagnoses?
- Should the child be placed with his siblings or not?
- Is the child ready for discharge from the program he is in?

In reviewing the psychological evaluation, pay attention to whether the evaluator reviewed relevant documents and spoke with key persons in the child's life. Without this information, it is not always easy to make sense of the data obtained during the evaluation. For example, I can meet with a child and quantify the extent of his mood, learning, or behavior disturbance. Without details of his behavior at home and school, though, I can't really state why these symptoms are present or which interventions are likely to be effective. By nature of their age, children are part of broader systems and rarely can they articulate the extent of their actions or struggles. This is why collateral contact with parents, teachers, therapists, social workers, or others is so important when evaluating a child. As I noted in my earlier discussion of ADHD, I firmly believe that in order to confirm the diagnosis, the evaluator must speak with parents and the teacher, and preferably have the teacher complete a rating scale.

In reviewing the psychological evaluation, you should pay attention to where the evaluation was performed. For example, was the evaluation completed in an outpatient office, a psychiatric hospital, a residential treatment facility, or at the child's school? The location of the evaluation can help cue you into some of the concerns other people had about the child at the time.

Most psychological evaluations will include a diagnosis. The diagnosis is the "language" of the mental health field, communicating important information about the child's current level of functioning. Written diagnoses are also required for third-party reimbursement.

All diagnostic classifications for children must be in accordance with the Diagnostic and Statistical Manual of Mental Disorders (DSM). A DSM diagnosis is usually assigned to the individual's current presentation and is not typically used to denote previous diagnoses from which the individual has recovered. Many diagnoses can be classified: Mild, Moderate, Severe, In Partial Remission, and In Full Remission. DSM is updated periodically. The most recent version is DSM-IV-TR (DSM, Fourth Edition, Text Revision, 2000.)

The DSM classifies a person's diagnosis on five axes, each of which refers to a different domain of information that may help the clinician plan treatment and predict outcome. These include:

Axis I:	Clinical Disorders
	Other Conditions That May Be a Focus of Clinical Attention
Axis II:	Personality Disorders
	Mental Retardation
Axis III:	General Medical Conditions
Axis IV:	Psychosocial and Environmental Problems
Axis V:	Global Assessment of Functioning

It is common for many foster and adopted children meet criteria for at least one Axis I diagnosis. A typical one is *Adjustment Disorder*, which means the individual is having difficulty adjusting to changes or stressors in their lives. Given the amount of stress this population of children confronts, you can see why this diagnosis is coded often.

There is a myth that Axis I diagnoses are the most serious. This is not true. The five Axis system is not based on severity of the illness; it is merely a classification system. Therefore, an Axis I diagnosis is not necessarily more severe than an Axis II diagnosis.

Just because a child meets the diagnostic criteria for an Axis I condition at one point in time does not mean he will always meet the criteria. Axis I diagnoses are assigned based on symptoms, not life events. For example, if a child was physically abused, but does not manifest with sadness, feelings of worthlessness, recurrent and distressing recollections of the event, or bad dreams of the event, he does not meet the criteria for Major Depressive or Posttraumatic Stress Disorder. But, he may have in the past.

Unless a child has Mental Retardation, he probably will not have a diagnosis listed on Axis II. Axis II is for reporting Personality Disorders, Mental Retardation, and may be used for noting prominent maladaptive personality features and defense mechanisms. Personality Disorders are usually not assigned to children or adolescents except in relatively unusual instances in which the individual's particular maladaptive personality traits appear to be pervasive, persistent, and unlikely to be limited to a particular developmental stage.

There are 10 specific personality disorders: Paranoid, Schizoid, Schizotypal, Antisocial, Borderline, Histrionic, Narcissistic, Avoidant, Dependent, and Obsessive-Compulsive.

The DSM has a separate section, titled "Disorders Usually First Diagnosed in Infancy, Childhood, or Adolescence." These diagnoses are assigned only for convenience and are not meant to suggest any distinction between childhood and adult disorders. This section of diagnoses includes:

- Mental Retardation
- Learning Disorders (e.g., Reading Disorder, Mathematics Disorder)
- Motor Skills Disorder
- Communication Disorders
- Pervasive Developmental Disorders (e.g., Autistic Disorder, Asperger's Disorder)

- Attention-Deficit and Disruptive Behavior Disorders (e.g., ADHD, Conduct Disorder)
- Feeding and Eating Disorders of Infancy or Early Childhood
- Tic Disorders
- Elimination Disorders (e.g., Eneuresis, Encopresis)
- Other Disorders of Infancy, Childhood, or Adolescence (e.g., Separation Anxiety Disorder, Reactive Attachment Disorder)

Psychiatric Evaluations

Unlike the psychological evaluation, a psychiatric evaluation relies less on testing of the child, and more on interview and observation. The psychiatric evaluation is symptom-based, designed to determine whether a child has symptoms of such severity to require medication. Psychiatrists, like psychologists, can determine if a DSM diagnosis applies to a particular child.

Since a psychiatrist will possibly prescribe medication for the child, the child will likely need to have monthly or periodic visits with the provider. In contrast, the child will typically only see a psychologist for an evaluation one or two times.

A psychiatric evaluation is usually requested when any of the following symptoms are present:

- Suicidal thoughts or behaviors
- Homicidal threats
- Severe anger or rage
- Auditory or visual hallucinations
- Sudden withdrawal or isolation
- Rapid weight loss

For a child who will be taking medication for the first time, the psychiatrist will need to have information about his medical and family history. The child may even need to go through a physical examination or receive laboratory tests. If you have ever taken a child for a psychiatric evaluation, you know that the psychiatrist will want to know if the child has had all his vaccinations, ever had surgery, is allergic to medication, or experienced other adverse effects from medication in the past.

A psychiatrist may decide that medication is warranted at the time of his assessment. At other times, he may want to wait until the results from a psychological or neurological examination are in before he prescribes medication. Regardless of his decision, it should be written down in a report or summary letter. Therefore, if you see in the report that the psychiatrist made a recommendation for further psychological or medical procedures, look through the documents you have in order to see if this was ever done.

Symptoms that require medication may include:

- Seizures
- Depressed mood
- Anxious mood
- Sleep difficulty
- Inattentiveness
- Hyperactivity
- Hallucinations
- Eneuresis
- Severe behavior problems

If your child was prescribed medication in the past, look to see if it is the same as his current medication. If the answer is "yes," what steps were taken to confirm that the medication was effective? If the answer is "no," how was the decision made to change or stop the use of certain medications with the child? The answers to these questions are not always easy to find.

Individualized Education Plans

I F A CHILD EXHIBITS BEHAVIOR or learning problems in school, federal law requires in-class interventions to see if the disturbance can be managed. If it cannot, the child is then eligible to receive an Individualized Education Plan (IEP). The IEP is a summary document, based on the verbal input of the teachers, school counselor or social worker, school nurse, and parents. It identifies the child's strengths and weaknesses, pointing to "target areas" that require improvement. The IEP becomes a blueprint, instructing school staff as to which interventions or services the child will require in order to attain these goals. Typical IEP goals or services include:

- Place child in a class with no more than 10 other students
- Child will have two teachers in his class at all times
- Child will be placed in a full-time special education classroom
- Child will receive one-to-one counseling, once a week
- Child will be seated next to the teacher
- If child becomes aggressive, he will be retained in the nurses office until the parents arrive
- Child is permitted 10 extra minutes to complete tests
- Child will receive speech therapy, occupational therapy, etc.

The IEP is not a contract. It is a guideline for individualized instruction. While the school maintains responsibility for providing the instructional services listed in the IEP, it is not the school's obligation to ensure that your child reaches any or all of the goals.

If an IEP is included in the child's placement file, you will want to find out who served as his representative at the meeting. In most cases, this is the child's parents. Because of his status as a foster or adopted child, you should look to see if his representative was a birth parent, foster parent, prior adoptive parent, social worker, attorney, or court-appointed advocate. By law, the child's representative is afforded the right to participate fully in the educational decision-making process. The question for you to ask, however, is whether the individual who served in this capacity truly understood the child's needs. Often, I come across instances where the child's representative barely knows the child, let alone what it will take to increase chances of school success.

Foster and adopted children sometimes move a great deal. Unfortunately, the written IEP does not always follow them. I am frequently asked to evaluate children in order to determine whether an IEP should be held. The referral sources may believe that the child was in special education in the past, but no records are available to substantiate this. The teacher at the child's new school may report he is having behavior or academic struggles, but without a current IEP, they are under no obligation to implement special services. Depending on the community in which the child lives, just getting to the initial evaluation phase can take months.

Therefore, as you review the placement file and conduct your investigation into the child's past, you will want to know if an IEP was developed and if it was reviewed and updated each year. If not, this could suggest that you need to take steps to quantify what your child's educational needs are.

RESOURCES

FOR MORE INFORMATION

The Council for Exceptional Children
Association Drive
Reston VA 22091
www.cec.sped.org

Learning Disability Association of America
4156 Library Road
Pittsburgh PA 15234
www.ldanatl.org

Treatment Plans

Before a parent's rights are terminated, they were likely given a chance to improve the condition of their life. They may have been ordered to go to counseling, seek substance abuse treatment, take parenting classes, or leave an abusive relationship. The living conditions of the family were also investigated, to determine whether the environment was fit for a child. This information is typically summarized in the birth parent's treatment plan.

Often, foster or adoptive parents may not be provided with this documentation. In my opinion, you should ask whether this information is available for you to review. In the event that your child requires medical or mental health care, information about the child's birth family will be helpful. If the child's biological mother had a mental disorder or substance addiction, the child may be at risk for developing these conditions, and the behaviors the provider is concerned about may therefore be precursors to similar disorders.

While the actual treatment plan developed for birth parents is only a page or two long, the information that will be of most use for you are the related documents. If you see that the parent was required to attend a substance abuse assessment, all you know is that there were concerns about her use of alcohol or drugs. Ultimately, though, you will want to know if she attended the assessment, followed through on the recommendations, and/or attained a period of recovery. Similarly, if the parent was required to attend parenting classes, written feedback of the providers who observed the mother and/or child should be available. By reviewing this, you will be able to read about the parent's strengths and weaknesses with respect to her child. This will cue you into what the child experienced with his mother.

By reviewing documents pertaining to the birth parents, you will have more information about your child's story. That is, you will learn how and why she came into custody, why the parental rights were terminated, what contact — if any — the child had with a birth parent, and what level of abuse or neglect the child experienced.

As you read through these documents, I believe your emphasis should be directed toward understanding as much as you can about the birth parent's history and background. While post-birth factors have a tremendous influence over a child's attachment and behavior, genetics also plays a huge part in a child's development. The child is not destined to manifest the features and symptoms of the birth parent, but genetic science tells us the risks are elevated.

Therefore, it will be helpful if you can find out the following information about the child's birth parents:

- Medical history
- Mental health history
- Educational history
- Substance use history
- Abuse/Neglect history
- Age when her child was born

Bonding Assessments

In some instances, a child and his birth parent may have participated in a bonding assessment. The bonding assessment is usually done with young children, under the age of five. In a bonding assessment, the evaluator will observe the parent and his or her child, paying particular attention to whether there appears to be an intact bond or relationship. A bonding assessment is a highly specialized type of assessment whose goal is to determine the nature and quality of the child's attachment to birth parents and sometimes foster parents, especially to address the question of who occupies the position of greatest centrality in the child's emotional life. One of the goals of this kind of assessment is to establish what the bond between the parent and child is, as well as the likelihood that this can be strengthened. If the assessment establishes that there is the chance the parent can build on the relationship she has with her child, the court will want to know how to facilitate this. The court will also want to know what a realistic timeline for increasing the bond is. If it appears that a bond is not present and will likely be hard to establish, the court may then move toward terminating the parent's legal rights and the child is placed for adoption.

In the bonding assessment, the objective is to see if the caregivers can identify and respond to the subtle and obvious cues put forth by the child. Particular focus is paid to the child's relation to the caregivers, to see if the child appears bonded to these persons. We expect children to behave differently with their primary parent figure(s) than with a therapist, social worker, other family member, or stranger.

A primary area of focus in the bonding assessment is to evaluate the ways in which the child gets his attachment needs met by the parent. Children use a variety of signal behaviors — such as smiling, reaching, facial expression, crawling, walking, and crying — to let the parent know they need warmth, love, feeding, comfort, or attention. Based on the manner in which the parent responds to the child's attachment behaviors, theory and clinical experience is used to anticipate how the child will attempt to get his basic needs met in subsequent relationships, through the course of their development.

Unlike a standard psychological evaluation, the evaluator in a bonding assessment assumes a more neutral role. In a bonding assessment, emphasis is placed on parent-child interactions. Thus, with infants and toddlers, the evaluator does not typically take part in the play, conversation, or activities of the parent and child, unless safety or logistics require otherwise. The evaluator may, however, instruct the parent on what to do during the assessment. As an example, I typically tell the parent in advance that I want them to leave the room in the middle of the observation. I ask them to casually get up, approximately 20 minutes after the child arrives, and simply leave the room. I ask them not to give the child any cues they are leaving and for them not to say goodbye to the child or to inform the child they will be returning. The parent is instructed to stay outside the room for at least 10 minutes, while the child remains in the room, under my supervision.

Some of the most powerful data I obtain about the parent-child bond comes when I do this exercise. If an infant has a strong bond with a primary parent, her sudden departure from the room is going to cause the child distress. Depending upon her age and abilities, the child will look around the room, cry, crawl or walk toward the door, reach for a security object such as a bottle or blanket, or urinate/defecate in her diaper. These are interpreted as stress responses on the part of the child. At times, the child may look at me, the evaluator, and smile, hoping I will come soothe her. When the child discovers that none of this is successful in bringing the parent back or reducing her distress, she will sometimes enter an agitated and disorganized state, whereby she will start to scream or rage. If this still doesn't bring the return of the mother, the child will eventually withdraw, shut down, and look incredibly stressed. When the parent finally returns, it can take the child quite a while to rebound from this traumatized state.

If, on the other hand, there is not a strong bond between the parent and child, the level of responses noted above may not occur. Instead, the child may not respond when the mother leaves, simply because she does not perceive her mother to be a source of comfort during times of stress. In fact, the mother's absence may not even represent stress for the child, mainly because she is used to being neglected, left alone, or abandoned. Thus, when the parent leaves the room, the child may not notice or care.

The value for you in reading the bonding assessment is to find out what the quality of interaction between the parent and child was prior to termination of parental rights. This can provide you with clues about how the child will react to you if you become his primary caregiver. It is important to note that a young child will not treat all caregivers the same. In many instances, I observe infants or toddlers who are rejecting of their birth mothers, avoidant of her attention, or anxious in her presence. Yet, when the birth mother leaves the room and the foster parent enters, the child becomes more relaxed, spontaneous, and comfortable. Certainly, it took a lot of work and effort on the part of the foster parent in order for the child to feel comfortable in her presence. But it shows that with the same amount of dedication, you can likely achieve the same.

When It's Time to Say Goodbye to Your Child

IF YOU ARE PROVIDING FOSTER CARE for a child, the time will likely come when either he goes to an adoptive placement, moves on to a new foster home, enters adulthood, or perhaps returns to his birth family. If you have adopted a child, there is always the possibility that the placement may not work out. In short, with foster and adopted children, the prospect of having to say goodbye persists either in the short or long term.

Leaving one's home to move to another represents additional grief and loss for these children. Even if their new home represents permanency and high hopes for a good future, having to say goodbye to familiar persons, animals, and places is really difficult for children. Foster children, in particular, tell me of times they had to leave a foster home with little notice and few opportunities for saying goodbye to those with whom they developed relationships.

ASSISTING YOUR CHILD WITH A MOVE TO A NEW HOME

- Remind your child why the move is taking place. It is important to state and re-state the reasons for the pending move. Reinforce that the move is designed to provide him with new opportunities, not to punish him.

- Talk with your child about the good times you shared. Even if the placement was challenging at times, let him know he has many qualities you will miss.

- Give your child a transitional object or two, something that represents the time he spent in your home. This can be a special photograph, a piece of jewelry, a book, or anything else he can easily transport to his new home.

- Identify your child's strengths. Tell him how resilient and brave he is, and acknowledge your belief in his ability to do well in his new placement. Let him know you have faith in him.

- If you are relinquishing an adopted child, speak to him about the ways in which the placement was a mismatch. Even though you will be angry and hurt at having to make such a decision, be careful not to convey that he's a bad child.

- If you have concerns about the family or environment your child will be going to, never express this directly to the child. He needs to believe that you and others are hopeful about the changes he will experience.

- It will be helpful if you can actually talk to the next family with whom the child will reside. Unfortunately, this sometimes isn't permitted or encouraged. As an alternative, you can write a brief summary about the child, outlining important things you believe the next family should know. This can be placed in the child's Life Book or given to the social worker, with the request that she give it to the next family.

Kids Do Get Better!

W HEN PARENTS READ THE VARIOUS written reports pertaining to a child they are about to foster or adopt, they can often feel intimidated and overwhelmed by what they see included about the child's history, behaviors, or diagnoses. Naturally, parents want to be able to predict what the child's behavior will be like in the future. When reports contain references to animal cruelty, stealing, fire starting, drug exposure, poverty, or violence, it can leave parents wondering if the child is destined for a life of unhappiness or even crime.

As I was writing this very page, the adoptive mother of a boy I once counseled phoned to let me know how well he is doing. He is now 14-years-old, getting good grades in school, earning money, and starting to identify long-term goals. She stated how proud she is of her son, while acknowledging what a struggle it has been raising him. At times, she questioned if she could continue raising him and at one point she and I had even talked about alternative placement options.

As parents or providers, we must believe it is possible for children to heal from trauma. We need to trust that the child is not necessarily destined to live an unhappy life or to grow up to take advantage of others. This is one of the reasons we provide children with lots of structure, firm limits, and opportunities for healing. True, some children don't seem to be able or willing to move beyond the anger or terror they feel. Others are held hostage to symptoms or conditions that limit their ability to exercise adequate impulse control or use good judgment.

Most adults are able to look back and appreciate the efforts other people made on their behalf. Even those kids who later end up incarcerated can acknowledge the important role a grandparent, aunt, or neighbor played in trying to set them on a good course. It is hard to know which children will ultimately respond to our efforts and which ones will not. Still, we should do what we can to instill hope in the children we encounter, knowing that in the long run, most of them will probably have good lives.

Copies available at a discounted rate.

Normally, this book sells for $16.95. When ordering copies with this form, pay only $12.95. This includes the cost of the book plus shipping.

Order now. We accept Checks, Money Orders, Visa, Master Card, and Discover Card.

NAME: _____

ADDRESS: _____

CITY:_____ STATE: _____ ZIP: _____

PHONE: _____

CARD #: _____

Visa ___ MC ___ Discover ___ Expires: _____

SIGNATURE: _____

MAIL TO: Mountain West Publishing
           3615 New Mexico 528 NW, Suite 200
           Albuquerque, New Mexico 87114

FAX TO: 505-890-5414

PHONE: 505-898-1117

E-MAIL: alexanderphd@msn.com

WEBSITE: alexanderphd.com

Visit our website for information about seminars, workshops, reproducible articles, contact information and other resources.

About the Author

Christopher J. Alexander, Ph.D. is a child psychologist who specializes in the assessment, diagnosis, and treatment of foster and adopted children. Dr. Alexander is a recognized expert on bonding and attachment, frequently speaking at conferences and testifying on these issues in court. In his practice, Dr. Alexander consults with foster and adoptive parents, offering practical strategies for assuring a good placement for their child. In addition, Dr. Alexander offers clinical supervision and workshops for mental health professionals. Dr. Alexander is on the Board of Namaste Child and Family Development Center, a non-profit treatment foster care agency in New Mexico. He maintains the website, alexanderphd.com, which offers a variety of useful information and resources for foster and adoptive parents, as well as the providers who work with them.